PRECISION, LANGUAGE AND LOGIC

PRECISION, LANGUAGE AND LOGIC

by

F. H. GEORGE

Brunel University
and
The Bureau of Information Science

PERGAMON PRESS

OXFORD · NEW YORK · TORONTO · SYDNEY · PARIS · FRANKFURT

U.K.	Pergamon Press Ltd., Headington Hill Hall, Oxford OX3 0BW, England
U.S.A.	Pergamon Press Inc., Maxwell House, Fairview Park, Elmsford, New York 10523, U.S.A.
CANADA	Pergamon of Canada Ltd., 75 The East Mall, Toronto, Ontario, Canada
AUSTRALIA	Pergamon Press (Aust.) Pty. Ltd., 19a Boundary Street, Rushcutters Bay, N.S.W. 2011, Australia
FRANCE	Pergamon Press SARL, 24 rue des Ecoles, 75240 Paris, Cedex 05, France
WEST GERMANY	Pergamon Press GmbH, 6242 Kronberg-Taunus, Pferdstrasse 1, Frankfurt-am-Main, West Germany

First edition 1977

Library of Congress Cataloging in Publication Data
George, Frank Honywill.
Precision, language and logic.

Bibliography: p.
Includes indexes.
1. Logic. 2. Languages—Philosophy. 3. Thought
and thinking. 1. Title.
BC108.G36 1977 160 76-54986
ISBN 0-08-019650-0

*In order to make this volume available as economically and rapidly as possible the author's type-
script has been reproduced in its original form. This method unfortunately has its typographical
limitations but it is hoped that they in no way distract the reader.*

Printed in Great Britain by A. Wheaton & Co., Exeter

DEDICATION

I would like to dedicate this book to the Beaconsfield Golf Club, not only because I spent so many pleasant hours writing the notes for this book and the book itself there, but also because a large part of the original impetus for writing the book sprang from discussions with some of the other members which made me realise - and I mean this in the nicest and most humble way - the need for such a book.

F.H. George

Beaconsfield,

1976

CONTENTS

FOREWORD

This book is intended to provide a text to guide people in the main ingredients of clear thinking and logical discussion. It emphasises logic itself, both informal and formal, including a certain amount of symbolic logic. There is enough of the latter (with the references) to guide the reader as to its further development. The book though is intended for the undergraduate and the graduate student as well as the layman. To this end the book can be approached from more than one point of view.

The reader who is interested in everyday debate and discussion only, and not concerned with the formal technical details of logistic systems can "skip over" (preferably glancing through the pages and getting the gist of the contents) Chapters 4, 5 and 6 of Part I, and possibly the first few pages of Chapter 9 of Part II, but the rest is essential reading - even the section on Bayes Rule should be reasonably easy to follow and certainly relevant to his needs. In fact even Chapter 4 (and as a result Chapter 5) should be attempted seriously by almost everyone. Only the first part of Chapter 6 (up to the section on Predicate Calculus) can reasonably be skipped over by the person who is definitely disinterested in the technical development of logic.

If on the other hand the reader is interested in the technicalities of logic and clear thinking, which are kept at a fairly simple level, he should read everything. Those interested primarily in logic concentrating on the first and second parts, while those with philosophical or psychological interests might concentrate on the second and third parts.

In a sense the book has two roles to play. One is to show how a knowledge of logic coupled to a knowledge of semantics, philosophy and pragmatics can clarify one's thinking and the second is to show how such logical and semantics considerations lead to the process of formalisation (or making precise) which takes you from a theory to its underlying (logical) model.

In taking pragmatics (or behaviour) for our theory, we have, as it were, tried to indicate the way we formalise our own use of language and logic. We have in a sense gone full circle, if only in outline, to try to show how scientific method, explanation and the like are closely akin to common sense and ordinary sensible behaviour and also to precise logic.

In fact we should guess that those readers interested in science as such would find Part III of more interest and Part II of slightly less interest; those readers primarily interested in clear thinking would probably find the opposite. We would however like both to read both, as we believe both are relevant.

Some mention should be made of summaries, exercises and references. Summaries have been supplied in those chapters which are, as it were, "broad brush" chapters which lend themselves best to summarisation. In the latter part of the book these have been dropped because the text did not seem to be suitable for summaries. The exercises were maintained throughout (should the reader wish to try his hand at them) but they become rather more abstract as the text changes especially on moving into Book III. Finally, references presented some difficulty. In the early chapters these were clearly intended as "further reading" and no references were made in the text. In the later chapters, a compromise was made between "further reading" references which were not referred to (by date) and others which were. But still the references at the end of the chapter were chosen on a "further reading" basis and the remainder not already referred to at the end of chapters are collected together at the end of the book under the heading "additional references". Thus if a reference is made in the text to some author, and his work is not quoted at the end of the chapter, the reader should look in the "Additional References" list at the end of the book.

Finally we should say that this book deals with its subject at more than one level. In ending the book on the subject of neural nets and automata it is completing a sort of circle, which has been traversed in rather general terms. We have moved from logic and clear thinking to philosophy, which enriches the backcloth to both, and then on, more speculatively and more controversially, to abstract models of the brain and nervous system. This work is one aspect of the suggested link between language and logic, brains and nervous systems and the world around us. It has been suggested that language, brains and the physical world are all in some way structurally similar to each other, and we have taken the implications of this view seriously. But it should again be emphasised that this book could simply be read as a treatise on logic and clear thinking.

PART I

SOME BASIC LOGIC

This first part of the book is mainly concerned with introducing ideas in basic logic and clear thinking in order to prepare the reader for the second part of the book which is concerned with the application of logic and other methods of precision to everyday discourse and also to the sciences and other disciplines such as law and economics. The third part of the book discusses a formalisation of the sciences.

CHAPTER 1

A BACKGROUND TO LOGIC

This book is intended to describe logical, or what is sometimes called clear, thinking. The word 'logic' is often used rather broadly to cover a wide field of activities including semantics, scientific method, probabilities and statistics, and even human behaviour. We shall certainly be thinking of logic in this broad sense, although we shall also be thinking of it in the more precise and narrow sense of classical logic, of both an informal and a formal variety. We shall try to emphasize the complex relationship that exists between all these aspects of the problem of thinking and talking in a clear and logical manner.

The basic ideas of logic go back a very long time indeed over a period of two thousand years; such basic ideas are concerned with the ability to carry out a rational discourse when something, such as a statement or set of statements, is proposed; that is when something is set out in terms of propositions using terms or classes. All these central concepts such as <u>rational discourse</u>, <u>terms</u> and <u>classes</u> will be explained.

The purpose of logic is to apply correct reasoning to certain assumptions, and the purpose of rational discourse is to derive certain valid consequences from those assumptions which are themselves true, or at least highly confirmed. It should be made absolutely clear that valid consequences, that is the result of applying logical principles to assumptions, do not necessarily lead to <u>true</u> statements. By 'truth' we mean something like the ability to accurately describe, in the form of a statement or proposition, a state of affairs. A true statement is a statement which represents affairs accurately, and we shall not primarily concern ourselves with various notions of truth in this book, because we are mainly concerned with logical validity and ability to carry out rational discussion and debate. A valid argument is one that follows logically from its assumptions and is independent of the truth of the propositions (or statements) involved.

Although we shall not make concepts like "truth" and "meaning" a main concern of our discussion, we should try to indicate our attitude to such matters as they are important to the broader contexts of logic.

'Truth' will be used to designate true propositions on one hand and reality on the other. Thus we shall say that propositions (or statements) are true if they correctly describe reality. This is, in essence, what is called the Correspondence Theory of truth. It also embodies the Semantic Theory in that it refers to the statements insofar as, for example, the statement "It is raining" is true if and only if it is raining. That we can specify the place and time and other details can, of course, be assumed.

There is also a theory of truth known as the Coherence Theory which asserts that true statements are consistent with - or cohere with - statements we already believe to be true. We shall think of such coherence as applying to the extent to which statements are confirmed by evidence rather than as to whether or not they are true.

The distinction between confirmation and truth is of some importance. Empirical statements are true or false, assuming them to be meaningful or testable, but we never <u>certainly</u> know whether empirical statements are true or false. All we can ever know of empirical statements is the extent to which they are confirmed. The actual process of confirmation (or the opposite process of infirmation) is certainly something which is susceptible to coherence, since the extent to which a statement coheres with statements already accepted is most certainly a part of the measure of the extent to which we believe in a statement, or a measure of the extent to which it is confirmed.

At the same time as we have expressed our attitude to the concept of truth, we should perhaps also express our attitude to the related problem of meaning. We are not expecting this to be universally acceptable, but it at least indicates our way of thinking. A statement or proposition is meaningful we shall say if it is capable of being tested for its truth. We reserve the right to accept 'testable' as meaning directly testable, or "testable in principle" or to imply (as we shall generally expect it to mean) "capable at least in principle of being confirmed or infirmed".

Meaning, like explanation, is a matter of degree of precision, and the meaning of statements can be tackled at various degrees of precise definition as accords with the precision of the discourse in which the statements arise.

We should make clear that we shall think of both meaning and explanation as contextual in the sense that words and propositions (expressed in sentences for example) depend for their effectiveness on the nature of the context in which they occur. Words can change their meaning (by qualification, for example) according to the context, and explanations need only to be as detailed as their use requires. Finally, on this point, we should add that any statement needs a degree of precision that (like explanations) is as precise as the discourse requires.

There is something to be said for the view that meaningfulness refers to complete propositions and not to isolated terms, except insofar as those terms are interpreted as shorthand for a complete proposition. Much of what is meaningful in language can be <u>formalised</u>. This means it can be subject to formation rules which eliminate meaningless combinations of words and hopefully leave only meaningful ones.

"The the the the the"

is clearly meaningless, whereas

"The man sat on the sofa"

is clearly meaningful, whether or not it is true.

We shall sharply distinguish between meaning and truth, since a statement can be meaningful and either true or false, but if it is meaningless it can be neither true nor false. This is what creates the notion of testability, since we argue that if an empirical statement cannot be said, even in principle, to be true or false then it is meaningless. We should note the following meaningful statements:-

"Get off the field immediately"

or matters of opinion such as

"Beethoven is the greatest composer".

We have here a criterion of meaning for statements which may be neither true nor false.

We are very much concerned with formal logic, since this is the background subject which eventually led to symbolic logic, which will represent a part of our study of logic. By formal logic we mean to assert that an argument is formal if it is independent of the factual content of the assertions it makes. In a sense this is much the same as saying that a formal argument is independent of the truth or falsehood of the assertions it makes. In a sense this is much the same as saying that a formal argument is independent of the meaning the assertions involved may contain by virtue of the interpretation placed upon them. In other words, if we make statements such as:-

"Charles is the father of Jack"

or

"Harry is the brother of Camille"

then the relationship of "being a father to" or "being a brother of" is independent of the people actually mentioned, or the names actually used in the propositions. "Being a brother of" or "being a father to" or any other sort of relationship which might be stated in words, may be independent of the people actually involved in that relationship. What is entailed by the relationship is independent of the people so named. This is the study of form, or formal logic, as it is sometimes called.

We have to be fairly careful in making this distinction between formal and what is sometimes called "factual" information, because in many arguments the factual features, sometimes said to be governed by the semantic rules which are involved in the interpretation of the formal words used, are so closely associated with those formal words that they affect the logical inference.

To see one aspect of the difficulty of separating the factual from the formal, we only have to remind ourselves of the implications of the above example. "If X is the father of Y and Y is the father of Z" it does not follow that "X is the father of Z"; he is, of course, the grandfather. If on the other hand we had "If X is the brother of Y and Y is the brother of Z" it does follow that "X is the brother of Z". In other words, we can only use our formal logical structures to describe those occurrences or events which have the same logical structure.

A further example may help to clarify the point. If we say Euclidean
Geometry in three-dimensions is a formal system we may or may not be able
to use it to describe the physical world around us. Whether we can or not
depends upon the nature of the physical world. We know such a Euclidean
Geometry fits much of our immediate experience very well, but we also know
that for astronomical distances forms of Non-Euclidean Geometry are
required. Let us now look at another more obviously logical sort of
example.

If I say that there are 366 people in a particular room, then it
follows, by logical argument (Leap Year excepted) that at least two people
in that room have the same birthday. This is logically true and is entailed
by the meanings of the terms actually used. This can easily be seen to be
so if we say that the word 'birthday' does not mean the day you were born
but the hour you were born. If we accepted this new meaning of the word
'birthday', then the logical entailment fails.

The haziness of the distinction between factual and formal arguments
comes about because so much of logic is couched in ordinary English, or
some other natural language, and as a result cannot be independent of the
semantic rules or meanings we ascribe to the terms used. Therefore we will
not wish to press too strongly that formal logic is independent of facts
when logic is phrased in ordinary language. This in part is what leads us
to symbolic logic, where arbitrary symbols are used to replace ordinary
English words. This highlights the nature of the formal relationships
between the symbols which represent terms or classes or whatever, and thus
places greater emphasis on the formal nature, and the relative semantic
independence, of the argument.

We have already used a number of new key words such as 'proposition'
and 'statement', and also 'terms' and 'classes', which we promised to
explain, so we ought now to explain what these mean in the logical context.
By 'proposition' we mean something which is exemplified by a statement,
whether written or spoken, or a sentence which is the most usual form of
statement because of the syntactical form that Indo-European languages take.
The proposition is in some sense what is proposed by the utterer of the
proposition, something which is a belief or something which can be
exemplified in the statement and is thus susceptible of various tests of
logical validity and semantic truth. A proposition, therefore, is
something prior to its exemplification as a sentence, but it will not lead
us too far astray if we think of a sentence or statement as exemplifying a
proposition.

Within the proposition, which is expressed in the Indo-European
languages as sentences in subject-predicate form, we have the notion of a
'term'. A 'term' is a word or collection of words that makes up a subject
or predicate, and most often refers to a 'class'. The word 'class'
usually refers to a collection of objects or events. "All red objects",
"all tall objects", "all circular objects" are classes of objects which
may be referred to by class names such as 'red', 'long' or 'circular'. A
class is a combination or collection of objects which is relatively well
defined. In most of logic, although we shall explain later in our
discussion that there are exceptions, we mean by a 'class' something which
is complete and well-defined. We should bear in mind that in symbolic
logic we expect these classes to be independent of their meaning, though
there is an intended meaning in mind in most cases. We can then assume

that by using letters such as a, b, ..., n, we are referring to classes of
things which are always precisely defined. Indeed if we have classes of
things which are not wholly precise, it may be said that they are not
appropriate to the interpretation that will be placed upon them by a
precisely defined class logic.

Thus it is that combinations of propositions are put together, such
as in our example of "if there are 366 people in this room..." which allow
valid or invalid arguments, fallacies and the like, to emerge. Logic
is the study of these relationships with a view to trying to show that
certain combinations are valid, and if possible, to characterize sets of
such valid combinations by some sort of general formula.

Rational discourse is our main aim, and this requires the ability to
be precise - by definition and by use of explanation - in one's
statements and descriptions. This involves logic, but also involves, as
we shall see, a great deal more besides.

It is not easy, because of the shadowy distinction between factual
and formal logic, to distinguish logic as a study independent of science,
from science and scientific methods. Thus it is important to realize that
scientific method involves deductive argument, where by 'deductive
argument' we mean the ability to draw inferences, and this means deductive
inferences from assumptions, in order to derive their logical entailments
or consequences. Scientific method, of course, involves more than this;
it also involves inductive arguments which proceed from the particular to
the general and is necessarily probabilistic in form. Such inductive
arguments too are necessarily descriptive and refer to the empirical
world in which they occur.

Insofar as we are concerned with the factual features of the world,
then of course we are also involved in the definition of terms and the
explanation of certain - often causal - features of the environment.
These two concepts of definition and explanation are fairly closely
related. We can mean many different things by the word 'definition', but
more often than not we mean something like a synonym for a term used. This
is very much a lexicographer's type of definition and is exemplified by
dictionaries and thesaura which say roughly what a word means by telling
us its synonyms. A rather more precise form of definition is a
substitutional definition where we substitute one word for a complete
phrase, where the phrase is more descriptive of the word than the word
alone, which is in a sense symbolic of the class of objects to which the
phrase refers; the phrase is therefore the definition of the word. The
substitutional type of definition is a sort of shorthand; so rather than
say "people who are related to other people by such and such a
relationship", we can in shorthand simply say 'brother'.

There are other forms of definition besides the lexicographers'
definition and the substitutional form of definition, as exemplified by
ostensive definitions where we point to things and say "by X I mean that"
and point at a particular feature which we are concerned with defining,
whether it be a colour like red or whether it be a shape like circular.
Another form of definition is an operational definition whereby we try to
describe a feature of our environment or our experience in terms of how it
actually affects us. We can describe an electric current in terms of the
effect it has up to certain terminal points, for example, and indeed it

has sometimes been argued that words like 'intelligence' could be defined
by that which is tested by intelligence tests. One can see the danger of
circularity here, sometimes such circularity is wholly unhelpful, but
sometimes it supplies a useful operational definition of the concept
underlying the term which is being defined.

Explanations are somewhat similar to definitions but they are usually
in the form of statements or propositions which characterize a process
rather than a single concept. Thus we try to explain a concept by saying
what it does under a whole set of circumstances. We try to explain the
behaviour of people in terms of their experience and their relationships
to other people in a particular social context. Explanatory statements
are propositions of a factual kind which are related to each other
causally in order to provide an historical picture of how such activities
come about.

In general, in our discussion of logic in this book, definitions play
an important part, particularly formal definitions, relating classes of
objects to each other or defining new operators in terms of their effect
on classes of objects, whereas factual definitions or explanations tend to
play a slightly less central role. It is, however, important to realize
that logic and scientific method certainly have a considerable degree of
overlap.

Two other terms which we should mention here are 'symbols' and 'signs'.
By the word 'symbol' we mean any mark on paper or any sound which is used
to stand for, in any sense, something other than itself, although one can
also have self-referring symbols. Words are most often used in ordinary
language to stand for objects, and therefore there is a sense in which the
word 'Chicago' refers to Chicago, the city in America, and the word 'pencil'
refers to a class of objects called pencils which are made of wood, lead,
etc., and there is also a sense in which the words are symbols. They are
symbols in the sense that they are arbitrarily chosen, even if they have
grown up over a period of time there is a sense in which they are arbitrary,
since we could quite easily decree at any time that the word 'pen' would
stand for what we have normally called a pencil and the word 'pencil'
would stand for pen. They are, however, also signs in that they represent
things and they refer to things, and the actual letters which make up the
words are manifestly symbols; they have no "meaning" as they stand. Signs
tend to be of two kinds in general. They are either linguistic signs in
the form of words or they are natural signs in the form of such things as
clouds which signify the possibility of rain. The overlap of symbols and
signs occurs in linguistic signs where the linguistic sign is in a sense
being used as a symbol and is certainly made up of individual letters which
are symbols, and yet has some of the properties of being a sign by virtue
of referring to, or signifying, a class of objects or even a single
particular individual.

We shall now draw attention to a convention which we have already
introduced and that is the use of quotation marks. We shall use single
quotation marks to indicate the word rather than the thing signified or
referred to by the word, we shall use double quotation marks for phrases
or sentences or actual quotations, and we shall also use double quotation
marks to draw attention to the fact that a term may be vague or ambiguous
in some sense. It is important to recognize this distinction between

single and double quotation marks since it is the intention to use this convention consistently throughout the book. It becomes especially important when we discuss semantics and pragmatics as opposed to syntax and formal logic, as we shall see.

One other fairly traditional convention we shall adopt is to underline (i.e. put into italics) words that we want especially emphasized.

One further point we should mention by way of warning. Logical discourse does not depend upon the use of true assumptions. We can start with false assumptions and apply logical inferences and draw the valid conclusions. This is standard practise among scientists who, by such means, discover the likely truth of the assumptions. For example, it is quite usual to consider alternative hypotheses in situations where we know _both_ cannot be true and deduce the (logical) consequences of both in order to examine, in effect, the plausibility of the assumptions.

We are embarking on a fairly complex field of thinking, reasoning and talking, which is intended to produce a degree of precision into our thinking reasoning and talking. It is particularly intended to sharpen our capacity for rational discourse or logical argument. Not that we expect or wish to encourage tedious pedantry or needless precision. What is required is the ability to recognize the degree of detail or precision of definition which is required in any particular debate.

SUMMARY

This chapter attempts to set the scene for our whole analysis of what should be the rational man's equipment.

We need to use language - both so-called "natural languages" such as English and French, and we need as a result to define the terms involved in our linguistic discourse. This in turn involves us in problems of meaning, truth and logic. It also involves us in the relationship between formal and factual statements, as well as other sorts of statements involving, for example, opinions.

EXERCISES

1. What are the essential ingredients of a valid argument? What in an argument (or even a dispute) depends upon "fact" and what on "reasoning"? Provide a check list.

2. To what extent can we separate "factual" from "formal" features in a carefully argued discourse? Give some examples of both, and if possible, a "borderline" case.

3. Definitions are obviously important to precise discussion. Explain what the concept of a "definition" entails. Write down some examples.

4. The notion of _context_ is going to be important to us in rational discourse. What do we mean by a "contextual definition" or a

"contextual explanation"?

5. What thoughts do you have on "meaning" and "truth": you ought to be
    prepared to say what they mean for you since they are basic to our ways
    of describing "things".

6. The two basic questions which arise in most debates are:-

        i) What do you mean?

        ii) How do you know?

    Do you regularly use these two questions as a guide to sensible
    discussion (as well as to destroy an opponent)? If not, why not?

REFERENCES

BARKER, S.F.   The Elements of Logic. McGraw-Hill, 1965

COHEN, M. & NAGEL, E.   An Introduction to Logic. Routledge, 1963

KLEEN, G.B.   Language and Reasoning. Van Nostrand, 1961

LUCE, A.A.   Teach Yourself Logic. English Universities
                                                 Press, 1958

STRAWSON, P.F.   Introduction to Logical Theory. Methuen, 1953

CHAPTER 2

PROPOSITIONS AND THE SYLLOGISM

Propositions and the relation of implication between them are the main subject matter of logic. By a proposition we mean anything, such as a belief held by a human being that may be true or false. Propositions are not the same as written or spoken sentences or statements. This can be seen easily from the fact that the same proposition can be expressed in various languages. "The world is round", "der monde ist runde" and "le monde est ronde" are all different sentences, although equivalent in the sense of expressing the same proposition.

Symbols are used to convey propositions and of course the symbols used should not be confused with the proposition it expresses anymore than a word should be confused with the object or whatever it is that the word refers to. The word 'leaf' is clearly not the same as a leaf anymore than a statement is the same as the proposition it expresses.

We say of terms that they have extension, denotion or reference which determines the class of objects the term refers to. Terms also have intension (or connotation) which is roughly speaking the same as the "meaning" of the term. "The present King of France" referred to in 1976 has intension but no extension. If, however, we used terms to refer to the concept the term refers to (compare concept and proposition) then we could say that the extension and the intension were the same.

We might also want to distinguish propositions from the act of mind or brain which thinks it. Although there are also arguments for saying that propositions are beliefs and these are "mental", or even "physiological" activities taking place within our nervous systems (some of these features are discussed in more detail in Part III).

The above difficulties of sometimes distinguishing between different aspects of a problem and sometimes intentionally confounding them is typical of the vitally important analytic process of looking for similarities among differences and differences among similarities.

We can now go through the process of classifying propositions as simple or compound, they can be general, two propositions can be independent, or two propositions can be equivalent. Let us look briefly at these distinctions. A simple proposition is of a form such as:-

"The king is tall"

whereas a compound proposition could be of such a form as:-

'The king is taller than his brother and also taller than the Queen."

9

In other words, compound propositions contain other propositions as their components. Propositions which deal with the relationships between total classes are called general. They can take four forms which can be exemplified as:-

"All kings are tall"
"No king is tall"
"Some kings are tall"
"Some kings are not tall"

The first two of these examples are said to be universal and the last two are said to be particular. We shall be using such examples shortly in our discussion of the Syllogism.

Two propositions which are irrelevant to each other are also said to be independent of each other. Thus:-

"The king is tall"

is apparently independent of the proposition expressed in the form:-

"Sugar is sweet"

It is not always quite so easy as it might appear to decide on whether propositions are independent or not, and we shall return to this matter in our later discussion of induction or inductive logic.

Equivalent propositions represent, in essence, the fact that there are different ways of saying the same thing. Thus:-

"The King is dead"

and

"The King is no longer alive"

are, in an obvious sense, equivalent propositions, or more correctly, different ways of expressing the same proposition and are equivalent statements. We have already discussed a similar case in the example of the use of different languages to express the fact that "the world is round".

One point of importance should be noticed here, and it is a point we shall return to in our discussion of pragmatics, and it is that different statements expressing the same proposition may nevertheless produce different responses from a listener. This is part of the process that depends on inflection and emphasis in language, which in turn can depend upon the turn of phrase used. Hints and innuendo are certainly a part of meaning and logic in the wide sense of human communication, even if not in the narrower sense of logic or semantics.

We shall be saying a great deal more about propositions in this chapter and later chapters, but now we shall concentrate on that branch of formal logic known as the Syllogism.

Before going into some detail on syllogistic forms let us distinguish between <u>categorical</u> and <u>hypothetical</u> propositions. Categorical propositions assert a fact or belief, such as "All men are mad" or "All Kings are tall", whereas a hypothetical proposition is compound and of the form:- "<u>If</u> all Kings are tall <u>then</u> King Richard is tall".

In exactly the same way we distinguish between categorical and hypothetical syllogisms. The first represents an argument that asserts a fact or facts, the latter draws the consequences of assumptions and therefore does not assert the antecedent or assumptions underlying the argument. Let us though now look at syllogistic forms of reasoning.

THE SYLLOGISM

Much of logic goes back, we have said, over two thousand years, and owes its origins to the work of Aristotle and Plato, particularly the former. Aristotle developed a form of logical reasoning which held sway for the better part of two thousand years and it is only relatively recently that significant improvement has been made on Aristotle's work, and it is only very recently indeed that we have developed a form of symbolic logic which has emerged from the formal logic of Aristotle.

The development of symbolic logic, or mathematical logic as it is sometimes called, is closely associated with the development of mathematics itself, but also is representative of an attempt to make formal logic even further removed from factual statements which refer to the empirical world. At the same time mathematical logic has primarily been developed (although this will not play a major part in our own exposition) in terms of providing an appropriate logical analysis of the foundations of mathematical thinking.

There are large tracts of logic which were directly developed by Aristotle and we shall not attempt to give an exhaustive description of these tracts here, rather we shall merely illustrate the form that they take by referring to the syllogism and one or two other similiar logical forms. The syllogism, in fact, is the best known part of formal logic, which is not essentially symbolic in form, and which was directly dependent on Aristotelian thinking.

The syllogism is a formal argument which is concerned with the relationship between three propositions. The propositions are all of the form which we have described as general universal or general particular, i.e. "All S is P" (A) or "No S is P" (E) or "Some S is P" (I) or "Some S is not P" (O) and the sort of statement we have in mind here is

"All men are kind" (A)
"No man is kind" (E)
"Some men are kind" (I)
"Some men are not kind" (O)

All of these statements can be related three at a time and be tested for their validity although the syllogism is restricted in what are accepted as valid syllogisms. A valid (hypothetical) syllogism is in fact a relationship between three propositions for which we can use the letters p, q and r, where we say

"If p and q, then r"

so we can easily think of a number of examples such as "If all men are kind and Charles is a man, then Charles is kind". This is a (hypothetical) syllogistic form of argument which allows the deduction of a conclusion from a major and a minor premise. The major premise is the first statement, the minor premise is the second statement and the conclusion is the third statement, the three statements or propositions making up the syllogistic argument.

We shall not concern ourselves overmuch with the detailed technicalities of syllogistic arguments, but we must say that there are various restrictive rules we must place on syllogisms to try to establish their validity. One rather awkward concept which has to be understood is that of distribution of the terms in a syllogism.

We say, for example, that if a subject is <u>distributed</u>, it refers to all the possible members of some class of objects or people. If we say "all Scottish people", Scottish people is distributed because it says "<u>all</u> Scottish people". If we said "some Scottish people", on the other hand, it would not be distributed because there are some Scottish people to whom we are not referring. Similarly we say that a predicate is distributed if it refers to a class of which there are no members such as in the proposition "No S is P" and similarly if it refers to a proposition such as "Some S is not P". In both these cases the predicate is distributed. The significance of the distribution of the predicate is mostly to be seen in the cases where the predicates are undistributed. If we said "all men are wise", the predicate 'wise' is obviously undistributed since many people can be wise other than men, in fact it could apply to all women or even possibly animals. So there is a sense in which the distribution of the predicate is subject to the same sort of restrictions as the distribution of the subject of a proposition.

We will anticipate now in part the so-called Euler-Venn type diagram which we will be discussing in the next chapter which deals with formal logics in general and Boolean Algebra in particular. Let circles represent classes and let the rectangle represent the total universe of discourse and then we can represent "All men are wise" as

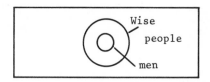

where we say the subject "all men" is distributed, and the predicate "wise people" is undistributed. If we similarly represent "Some men are wise" in diagram form we get:-

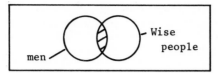

and say the subject "some men" is undistributed as of course is the
predicate "wise people". The shaded area represents the conjoint class
of "those men that are wise".

The statement "No man is wise" is represented:-

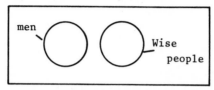

where the subject "all men" remains distributed and the predicate "wise
people" is also now distributed. Finally, the statement "some men are
not wise" can be represented:-

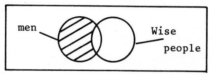

where the shaded area depicts the class of "the men who are not wise" and
here the subject is again undistributed, while the predicate is distributed.
Note that the shaded area in this figure falls wholly outside the circle
for "wise people".

We should repeat here that reference to the <u>complete</u> class of the
subject makes it, the subject, distributed, otherwise not, while the
predicate is distributed if it has no overlap with the subject. If it
overlaps or includes the subject it is undistributed.

. We append a table which shows the forms of proposition acceptable to
the syllogism and the distribution of the subject and predicate.

Proposition	Subject	Predicate
All S is P	Distributed	Undistributed
No S is P	Distributed	Distributed
Some S is P	Undistributed	Undistributed
Some S is not P	Undistributed	Distributed

We can easily remember this by saying that <u>some</u> is always undistributed
in the subject and when the proposition is <u>positive</u> it is always
undistributed in the predicate.

It is important to have the concept of distribution absolutely clear in order to understand the rules which make for valid syllogisms, which are as follows:-

(1)   That every term must be distributed once at least in the syllogism.

(2)   No term must be distributed in the conclusion which was not distributed in one of the premises.

(3)   You can make no inference from two negative premises or two particular premises.

(4)   If one premise is negative (or particular) the conclusion must be negative (or particular) and vice-versa.

In the above, by the middle term we mean the term that is involved in all syllogisms which occurs in both the major and minor premise but does not occur in the conclusion. So for example "If Taunton is in Somerset, and if I am in Taunton, then I am in Somerset". 'Taunton' is clearly the middle term as it occurs in both the major and minor premises, but does not occur in the conclusion.

We have referred to our four types of proposition in the syllogism by the letters A, E, I and O. They stand for universal affirmative, universal negative, particular affirmative and particular negative.

Since the syllogism contains three propositions and each of these may occur in any of four forms, there are 4 X 4 X 4 i.e. 64 moods (as they are called) which syllogisms might take. They can clearly be written out in the form AAA, AAE, AAI, AAO, AEA, AEE, ... etc.

Many of these 64 moods are clearly not valid syllogisms. AIA, for example, is invalid, since the minor premise is in this case particular and a syllogism with either premise particular must have a particular conclusion. So:-

"All men are enemies"
"Some men are wise"

cannot lead to a conclustion about "all enemies" or about "all wise people".

We can by analysis of the rest of the moods in relation to the rules easily show that EEI, IEA, IOI and many other moods are also invalid.

Thus to take EEI:-

"Some men are enemies"
"Some men are wise"

tells us nothing about "some enemies" or "some wise people" which is not already stated in the premises. It should be noted in both the above examples 'men' is the middle term and cannot occur in the conclusion.

We can thus reduce the number of valid moods to 11. These moods
themselves are subject to a further analysis in terms of what are called
figures.

The three terms of the syllogism can be represented by X, Y and Z
and then the allowable figures are as follows:-

	I	II	III	IV
Major premise	YX	XY	YX	XY
Minor premise	ZY	ZY	**YZ**	YZ
Conclusion	ZX	ZX	ZX	ZX

The application of both moods and figures reduces the number of valid
syllogisms to only 24 and 5 of these are "weak", that is of the form

"All material substances gravitate;
all metals are material substances;
therefore some metals gravitate"

the conclusion could clearly have been

"All metals gravitate"

and this leaves only 19 useful and valid syllogistic forms.

More often than not, a valid syllogism can be derived by a commonsense
understanding of what is being asserted in the propositions and to this
extent, of course, it is semantically orientated. We are not going to
investigate in great detail (we are merely pointing out) the fact that
there are forms of logical argument which are formal and which have been
developed long before symbolic logic was ever seriously thought of and
one of such forms is called the syllogistic logical form of argument, or
the syllogism.

The syllogism is a particular case of a more general process of
drawing inferences by elimination of one or more terms contained in the
premises. One example of an argument which looks syllogistic is the
following:-

"Charlie is taller than Bill"
"Bill is taller than Harold"

therefore

"Charlie is taller than Harold"

This form has 'Bill' as the only possible middle term and if the
form of each statement, all of which are clearly the same, is A, then the
mood is AAA. So 'Charlie' and 'Bill' are distributed in the premises but

Harold is not. In fact, although the argument is not syllogistic it is still valid. Many other such valid non-syllogistic arguments between three propositions also exist which makes clear that the syllogism is indeed a particular case of a more general process of inference making.

We shall next look at a logical form which is very closely related to the syllogism, and is called the Antilogism.

THE ANTILOGISM

Let us look now at an extension of the syllogism. Consider the syllogism:-

"All men are wise"
"All Irish people are men"

therefore

"All Irish people are wise"

The terms 'Irish people', 'men' and 'wise people' are the subject, middle term and predicate respectively. If the two premises imply that "All Irish people are wise" this implies that these premises are incompatible with the contradictory of this conclusion, and therefore

"All men are wise"
"All Irish people are men"
"Some Irish people are not wise"

are incompatible. This is easily seen from a diagram:-

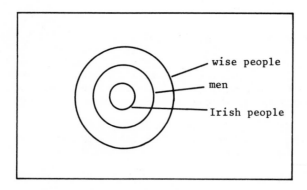

Clearly there are no Irish people who can get outside the class of being wise. More generally the antilogism shows that <u>any</u> two of its propositions imply the contradictory of the third. Thus

"All men are wise"
"All Irish people are men"

therefore

"All Irish people are wise"

and then

"All men are wise"
"Some Irish people are not wise"

therefore

"Some Irish people are not men"

and then again

"All Irishmen are men"
"Some Irishmen are not wise"

therefore

"Some men are not wise"

It is possible to take any valid syllogism and obtain from it the antilogism and then the other two valid syllogisms to which it is equivalent.

An antilogism always contains two universal and one particular proposition, such that the universal propositions have a common term which is once distributed and once not, while the particular proposition contains the other two terms.

We can use such conditions on the antilogism to test the validity of any syllogism.

Consider the valid syllogism

"All men are wise"
"Some men are tall"

therefore

"Some tall men are wise"

This has the figure III which is of the kind:-

YX
YZ
ZX

The equivalent antilogism is

"All men are wise"
"Some men are tall"
"No tall person is wise"

and this cannot be represented by a valid diagram.

We can now derive the equivalent syllogisms, but we shall derive only one of them. It is:-

"Some men are tall"
"No tall person is wise"

therefore

"No man is wise"

which is represented by the diagram

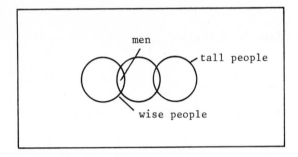

THE SORITES

We will now look very briefly at the Sorites, which is another set of logical forms which has been worked out in some detail. An example will show the form:-

"All men are tall"
"All tall men are fat"
"All fat men are stupid"
"All stupid people are cruel"

can be taken as premises for the conclusion

"All men are cruel"

This is really a chain of syllogisms in which the conclusion of one becomes the premise of another. If all the conclusions except the last one are unexpressed and in which the premises are so arranged that any two successive ones contain a common term, then the result is a Sorites.

The Aristotelian Sorites has special rules:-

1. No more than one premise may be negative
2. If a premise is negative it must be the last
3. No more than one premise may be particular
4. If a premise is particular it must be the first.

At this point we shall end this chapter, which has been concerned with a brief exposition of formal inference making of an Aristotelian kind and has been closely concerned with propositions. We shall turn in the next chapter to consider the representation of logic by symbolic means.

SUMMARY

In this chapter we have developed the first stages of formal logic. The syllogism is the main example. The antilogism and the sorites are two further examples which are mentioned much more briefly.

As far as the syllogism is concerned we distinguish between the categorical and hypothetical forms. The categorical form asserts such antecedent statements as "all women are wise" whereas the hypothetical form asserts a form such as "if all women are wise". The rules of the syllogism represent the beginnings of the sort of formal logistic systems which we discuss in the next chapter.

EXERCISES

1. Try to write down a careful description of the following features of the syllogism:-

    i)   Moods

    ii) Figures

    iii) Subject

    iv) Predicate

    v)   Distribution

2. Write down some examples of valid syllogistic arguments and identify their mood and figure.

3. What is a "weak" syllogistic argument?

REFERENCES

BOCHENSKI, I.M.   Ancient Formal Logic. North Holland, 1963

LUCE, A.A.   Teach Yourself Logic. English Universities
                                              Press, 1958

LUKASIEWICZ, J.   Aristotle's Syllogistic from the Standard of
                       Modern Formal Logic. Oxford University Press,
                       1951

CHAPTER 3

FIRST STEPS IN SYMBOLIC LOGIC

SYMBOLIC LOGIC

What is sometimes called symbolic logic, or mathematical logic, depends on the use of symbols in place of terms, and the development of axiomatic systems based upon these symbols which are used to examine logical arguments, the foundation of mathematics, and can also be used as empirically descriptive languages. Thus they can be made into formal systems in a much stronger sense than could be constructed by the mere replacing of ordinary English terms by symbols. As a result, such axiomatic systems have complex properties which we shall want to examine.

Leibniz was one of the people who helped to set symbolic logic on its way when he devised the notion of an ideogram which was an attempt to improve on Aristotelian logic and release it in some measure from the factual overlap which clearly occurred. But it was not until the work of George Boole, and also to a lesser extent the work of de Morgan in the nineteenth century, two hundred years after Leibniz, that the first serious steps were taken in symbolic logic.

Later in this chapter we shall be explicitly discussing Boolean algebra, therefore we shall say very little about it at this stage, but we shall concentrate on setting the scene from which Boolean algebra, and subsequently other more complex symbolic axiomatic systems, were developed.

In setting the scene for symbolic logic we should say that to formalise is to be seen as an essential procedure. If we formalise something, we try to make it precise. Therefore if we try to formalise a term such as 'true', or 'meaning', then we try to say precisely what it means in every conceivable context. To do this we have to restrict its meaning in ordinary language, where terms are necessarily kept vague so that they can be contextually defined. We cannot accept the usual vagueness and ambiguity of ordinary language with its contextual form of precision, if we are going through the process of formalising.

Formalisation requires rules and the rules which formalise or make a system precise are themselves relatively informal, therefore we have to think in terms of a hierarchy of languages in which we say the language in which the rules of precision for some other language are couched in what is called a meta-language.

The idea can be illustrated here if we think of trying to teach French to an Englishman; French would be the so-called object language, and we should talk about it in terms of English, where English would be the meta-language. Our attempt, if we were trying to formalise French,

would be to be completely precise about the syntactical and semantic rules
of French and the rules which made for this precision would be couched in
the meta-language. We can have a meta-meta-language to then formalise the
rules for the meta-language and a meta-meta-meta-language to formalise the
rules for the meta-meta-language and so on. What it is important to
realize is that precision can only be gained at the expense of having a
hierarchy of languages, since every language presupposes some undefined
terms. You cannot define every term precisely without having either
undefined terms or circularity. The reader can convince himself of this
by thinking of dictionary definitions and trying to write out the dictionary
definitions for a whole set of terms; he finds himself in the end either
going around in a circle or taking a sub-set of terms which he either
assumes or takes as given; this sub-set of terms is rather like a set of
assumptions or a set of axioms, in terms of which the other parts of the
system are defined.

This imprecision that we have in our formalisation is always pushed
into the meta-language "above" the language we are making precise. It is
rather like a clearing in a wood; the wood is infinite and all we can do
is to clear the wood and if we want to clear more wood, we clear more wood
and so on - there are always more trees left to be cleared. This is
because the whole process of communication and understanding etc. is
ultimately lodged within the people who are using the language in talking
to each other. In symbolic logic we tend to talk of the lowest language
as the object language, as we have mentioned already, and we talk usually
in terms of one level of meta-language which in this content is often
called the syntax language. Therefore the syntax language, which we can
make as precise as we please, although it may involve the use of a higher
level language, refers to the object language which is intended to be
wholly precise. In the case of such logical systems as the propositional
calculus - which we shall be looking at later - the object language will
be devoid of meaning.

It goes without saying that we shall not develop any precise systems
which are devoid of meaning without having some intended interpretation
in mind. Thus it is we want to make a distinction between models and
theories, or models and their interpretation. We can take a map and it
can be an abstract map, but it happens to be of the same shape and of the
same dimensions as, say, Great Britain or North America and then we shall
say that the interpretation we intend to place on the map is that of Great
Britain or North America. The details of the maps and the interpretation
placed on them will depend on the purpose for which the map is going to
be used. If we are constructing a map for aerial use we shall emphasize
different features of Great Britain or North America than if we are
providing a map for road or railway use.

The important thing to appreciate is that models and their associated
interpretations are closely related to each other, rather like an object
language is related to a meta-language. If we go from the interpretation
to the model we say we are formalising the interpretation or theory; if
on the other hand we are going from the model to the theory we say we are
placing an interpretation on the model.

As far as mathematical logic is concerned, the interpretation we
place on the axiomatic system that makes up the mathematical logic under

consideration, and which is made up of a set of symbols in axiomatic form,
will either be for the purpose of examining the foundations of mathematics,
the purpose of interpreting and analyzing ordinary language, or for the
purpose of describing empirical systems; for the latter two purposes, we
shall call the systems a part of symbolic logic. The fact is though that
the terms 'symbolic logic' and 'mathematical logic' are more or less
synonymous.

     Once we have formulated the logical system, it is important to
appreciate its general properties. Thus we are concerned to draw up an
axiom set and rules of inference to derive the theorems from the axiom set.
Then we look to see that the axioms are independent. If we have axioms
that are not independent, they do not invalidate the logic which we are
using but they are wasteful of effort. We also look to see if the system
is consistent with itself, since we obviously do not want to be able to
draw conclusions and the negation of those same conclusions within the
same system. We also want to look for the property of completeness, so
that we want to know that a formal or axiomatic treatment of Boolean
algebra does in fact give a complete picture of the algebra of classes, it
expresses all the properties we want expressed, such as in the formalisation
of a term, and does not express those properties as valid statements in the
calculus which are not what we intended.

     There is another property we look for particularly in axiomatic
systems and that is the search for an algorithm or decision procedure.
We shall say more about this later, but the basic idea is that an algorithm
or a decision procedure is a shorthand mechanical way of deriving theorems
and showing that a certain string of symbols is a theorem within a system
without having to go through the actual process of proving it by applying
rules of inference to the axioms. If we have such an automatic procedure,
which has sometimes been referred to as computable, then it greatly
facilitates the system and makes it computable in the obvious sense of the
word 'computable'.

     We find out that many axiomatic systems have decision procedures and
many others do not have decision procedures, and we should also mention
that in the building up of the foundations of mathematics, one of the
primary questions which has been asked is whether the whole of mathematics
has a decision procedure. "Is the whole of mathematics capable of being
mechanized?" is another way of putting the same point.

     In the next section of this chapter we shall be developing Boolean
algebra; in the two chapters after that we shall be giving a new
interpretation to the same model where we shall be calling the axiomatic
system the Propositional calculus. After that we shall be looking briefly
at the development of the Functional calculus which is a generalization
of the Propositional calculus and which is essential to the study of
mathematics! This is so because of mathematics' dependence on functions.
After that we shall be looking very briefly at the foundations of
mathematics and finally we shall look at other forms of logical calculi or
axiomatic systems which are used in the analysis of language and the
description of empirical systems. We shall then be returning to the
problem of scientific thinking and semantics as well as the pragmatic
context of arguments and discussions.

BOOLEAN ALGEBRA

Boolean algebra is also called the calculus or algebra of classes, and we have already discussed the basic notion of class, which represents collections or aggregates of things, such as "all red objects", "all round objects" and so on. In this section we shall be discussing the algebra of classes informally, and we shall not derive Boolean algebra as a deductive (axiomatic) system; rather we shall show the formal derivation of the same model as the Propositional calculus.

A basic notion of Boolean algebra is that of class membership. We say

$$a \; \varepsilon \; A$$

and by this we mean "the individual element (or member) a belongs to (symbolized by the Greek letter epsilon (or ε)) the class A".

Similarly

$$a \notin A$$

means "a is <u>not</u> a member of A".

We also have a relationship between classes, symbolized

$$A \subset B$$

which is meant to characterize "class inclusion". This means that all members of class A are included in class B. We can depict the situation by our usual diagram as follows:-

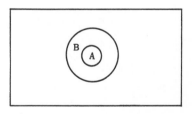

We need to be able to distinguish between class inclusion and class membership. 'Charlie' is an individual and is a member of the class of 'human beings'. 'Charlies' are the class of all people of the name 'Charles' which is included in the class 'human heings'. The whole question is made slightly arbitrary by the fact that classes can of course be <u>nul</u> (have no members) or have one member (a unit class), whereas an individual is to be thought of as one member of a larger group. A unit class and an individual can though, if necessary, be intentionally confounded.

The type of diagram we have shown above is, as we mentioned in the last chapter, sometimes called an Euler-Venn diagram and can be conveniently used to represent class relationships. The rectangle represents the entire universe and A and B, whether overlapping or not, are any two classes

in the universe. We shall be using such diagrams again from time to time
as an easy pictorial aid to logical thinking in much the same way as graphs
and other diagrams can help mathematical thinking.

We can now conjoin two classes A and B, and write this:-

$$A \cap B$$

and by it mean those members of the classes A and B which are common to
both. For example, A is 'all red objects' and B is 'all square objects',
then A ∩ B (read as "A cap B" or "A and B") is the conjunction class of
'all red and square objects". The Euler-Venn diagram is as follows and
shows A ∩ B as a shaded area:-

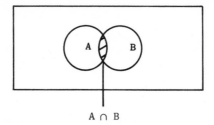

A ∩ B

Similarly A ∪ B (read as "A cup B" or "A or B") is used to define the
disjunction of the classes A and B, where if A is 'all red objects' and
if B is 'all square objects' then A ∪ B is made up of 'all square objects
of all colours, and all red objects of all shapes'. The Euler-Venn diagram
is as follows and shows A ∪ B as shaded:

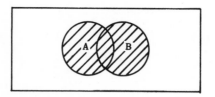

It will be clear that in our discussion of Boolean Algebra we are
using capital letters A, B, ..., N to represent classes, and lower case
letters a, b, ..., n to represent individuals. We shall though in other
chapters use these same letters to represent different entities, so the
reader must beware of a possible source of confusion here. This is made
necessary by the paucity of easily available printable symbols.

Another basic relationship in Boolean algebra is that of negation
(or complementation). We write A' for not-A and represent it in
Euler-Venn diagrams as:-

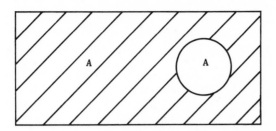

A' is the shaded area, and we say that if A is "all red objects" then A'
is "all objects which are not red". Because A' refers to only one class we
call this a singularly or monadic relation while relations between two
classes such as A ∩ B and A ∪ B are binary or dyadic relations.

Two special classes, one of which we have already mentioned, are the
nul class, which contains nothing and is symbolized by O and the universal
class, which contains everything and is symbolized by 1 (or sometimes I);
the 1 is represented by the rectangle of the Euler-Venn diagram.

We can apply the operation of negation to each of these and naturally
enough we get the opposite, so:-

$$O' = 1$$

$$1' = O$$

and we can also say for any class A that

$$A' \cap A = O$$

$$A \cup A' = 1$$

since clearly a class has no overlap with its negation, and equally clearly
a class and its negation make up everything. It is also clear that we are
assuming here that classes are <u>definite</u> (precisely defined) and we can
always decide whether any individual is, or is not a member of the class.

There are a large number of operations among Boolean classes that are
very similar to those of arithmetic. Thus we can say

$$A = A$$

and

$$\text{if } A = B \text{ then } B = A$$

where all members of A are also members of B and vice-versa. Similarly

$$\text{if } A = B \text{ and } B = C \text{ then } A = C$$

and again we have such relations as:-

$$A \cap B = B \cap A \qquad\qquad\qquad\qquad\qquad\qquad --- (1)$$

$$A \cup B = B \cup A \qquad\qquad\qquad\qquad\qquad\qquad --- (2)$$

$$A \cap (B \cap C) \;=\; (A \cap B) \cap C \qquad\qquad\qquad --- (3)$$

$$A \cup (B \cup C) \;=\; (A \cup B) \cup C \qquad\qquad\qquad --- (4)$$

$$A \cap A \;=\; A \cup A \;=\; A \qquad\qquad\qquad\qquad --- (5)$$

$$A \cap (B \cup C) \;=\; (A \cap B) \cup (A \cap C) \qquad\qquad --- (6)$$

$$A \cup (B \cap C) \;=\; (A \cup B) \cap (A \cup C) \qquad\qquad --- (7)$$

$$A \cup 0 \;=\; A \cap 1 \;=\; A \qquad\qquad\qquad\qquad --- (8)$$

$$(A')' \;=\; A \qquad\qquad\qquad\qquad\qquad\qquad\qquad --- (9)$$

and so on, where there is a close analogy between conjunction and disjunction and multiplication and addition. All the ordinary laws of arithmetic apply in the same way to Boolean algebra.

Let us look at the Euler-Venn diagrams for the relations

$$A \cap (B \cap C) \;=\; (A \cap B) \cap C \qquad\qquad\qquad --- (10)$$

and

$$A \cup (B \cap C) \;=\; (A \cup B) \cap C \qquad\qquad\qquad --- (11)$$

The first is

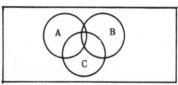

and applies to both the left-hand side and right-hand side of (10). The same applies to the Euler-Venn diagram for (11) which is

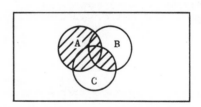

We can also write our classes A, B, ..., N in terms of their individual members a, b, ..., n, so that if $A = \{a, b, c, d\}$ and $B = \{a, b, d, e\}$ then $A \cap B = \{a, b, d\}$. Which simply makes clear that a, b, c and d occur in both A and B, i.e. in $A \cap B$.

Similarly if C $\{a, c, e, f, g\}$ then

$$A \cap (B \cap C) = \{ a \}$$

since a is the only member common to A, B and C.

It follows, of course, from what has already been said that

$$(A \cap B) \cap C = \{ a \}$$

since

$$(A \cap B) \cap C = A \cap (B \cap C)$$

also

$$A \cup B = \{ a, b, c, d, e \}$$

and therefore

$$A \cup (B \cup C) = \{ a, b, c, d, e, f, g \}$$

and also

$$A \cap (B \cup C) = \{ a, b, c, d \}$$

LAWS OF BOOLEAN ALGEBRA

As we have said, Boolean algebra is closely analogous to arithmetic. We shall now look at some of these laws and draw the analogy in full.

First of all we describe what are sometimes called de Morgan's laws, named after their originator.

$$(A \cup B)' = A' \cap B'$$

and

$$(A \cap B)' = A' \cup B'$$

First of all we should notice

$$(A' \cup B')' = (A'' \cap B'') \qquad\qquad --- (12)$$

where $A'' = A$ and $B'' = B$

Here is the Euler-Venn diagram of (12).

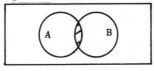

(12) can be re-written

$$(A' \cup B') = A \cap B \qquad\qquad --- (13)$$

We can now take the complements of both the left-hand side and the right-hand side of (13) and this gives

$$(A' \cup B')' = (A \cap B)'$$

and this is

$$A' \cup B' = (A \cap B)'$$

or

$$(A \cap B)' = A' \cup B'$$

as we wrote it above. The other de Morgan law can be proved in exactly the same way.

The more commonplace laws of arithmetic are now to be considered. So in arithmetic

$$a \times (b \times c) = (a \times b) \times c$$

and

$$a + (b + c) = (a + b) + c$$

where a, b and c are "ordinary numbers".

In Boolean algebra we have

$$A \cap (B \cap C) = (A \cap B) \cap C \qquad \text{--- (14)}$$

$$A \cup (B \cup C) = (A \cup B) \cup C \qquad \text{--- (15)}$$

These are called the <u>associative</u> laws of Boolean algebra and they mean that we can write (14) as $\overline{A \cap B \cap C}$ and (15) as $A \cup B \cup C$. This same law of association can, as in the case of arithmetic, be extended to any number of classes, so

$$(A \cap B \cap C) \cap D = (A \cap B) \cap (C \cap D) = A \cap (B \cap C \cap D)$$

and

$$(A \cup B \cup C) \cup D = (A \cup B) \cup (C \cup D) = A \cup (B \cup C \cup D)$$

and so on.

The single distributive law of arithmetic is

$$a + (b \times c) = (a + b) \times (a + c)$$

The equivalent distributive laws for Boolean algebra are

$$A \cup (B \cap C) = (A \cup B) \cap (A \cup C) \qquad\qquad \text{--- (16)}$$

and

$$A \cap (B \cup C) = (A \cap B) \cup (A \cap C) \qquad\qquad \text{--- (17)}$$

The proof of (16) is straightforward:-

$$x \in A \cup (B \cap C) \text{ then } x \in A \text{ or } x \in (B \cap C).$$

If $x \in A$ then $x \in (A \cup B)$ and $x \in (A \cup C)$, and so $x \in (A \cup B) \cap (A \cup C)$. If on the other hand $x \in (B \cap C)$ then $x \in B$ and $x \in C$ so $x \in (A \cup B)$ and $x \in (A \cup C)$ and so $x \in (A \cup B) \cap (A \cup C)$. So it is that

$$A \cup (B \cap C) \subset (A \cup B) \cap (A \cup C)$$

Similarly it can be proved that

$$(A \cup B) \cap (A \cup C) \subset A \cup (B \cap C)$$

and therefore

$$A \cup (B \cap C) = (A \cup B) \cap (A \cup C)$$

The proof of (17) follows along similar lines, but we shall not give the proof here.

In the same way, (1) and (2) show that Boolean algebra is <u>commutative</u> and that means that the order of adding and multiplying is unimportant. The equivalent laws of arithmetic are

$$a \times b = b \times a$$

$$a + b = b + a$$

We now introduce two new operators - and +. A - B is naturally defined in terms of members of A which are not members of B. So

$$A - B = A \cap B'$$

which has the Euler-Venn diagram

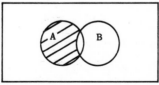

where A - B is the shaded area.

It follows from this that

$$1 - A = A'$$

since

$$1 - A = 1 \cap A' = A'$$

and in particular

$$1 - 0 = 0' = 1$$

Similarly

$$A - B = 0 \text{ implies } A \subset B$$

The Euler-Venn diagram is simply:-

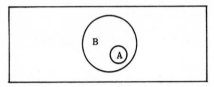

    Another important relation involving the <u>difference</u>, as the - operator is sometimes called, is

$$(A - B) \cup B = A \cup B$$

This follows from the following proof:-

$$(A - B) \cup B = (A \cap B') \cup B$$

$$(A \cap B') \cup B = (A \cup B) \cap (B' \cup B)$$

$$(A \cup B) \cap (B' \cup B) = (A \cup B) \cap 1$$

and

$$(A \cup B) \cap 1 = A \cup B$$

so

$$(A - B) \cup B = A \cup B$$

The + operator is defined

$$A + B = (A - B) \cup (B - A)$$

$$= (A \cap B') \cup (B \cap A')$$

$$= (A \cup B) \cap (A' \cup B')$$

$$= (A \cup B) - (A \cap B)$$

where we can represent the various forms of A + B by the following Euler-Venn diagram.

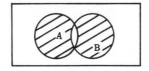

Furthermore

$$A' + B' = A + B$$

We can, in the same way, derive other relationships in Boolean algebra, but we shall not do so, since we prefer to turn to the axiomatic development of Boolean Algebra, which we shall consider in the next chapter, in its alternative interpretation as the Propositional Calculus.

It is of interest to notice, in passing, that we could think of Boolean algebra as a part of a logic, or Calculus of Relations, so that we could rewrite a ε A as MaA, say, where M $\equiv$ ε, and where we can write the "operator" at the beginning of the expression, although it could as easily have been written aMA. Similarly A $\cap$ B, A $\cup$ B, A $\subset$ B, etc. could be written Aab, Oab, Iab, etc. where it seems natural to replace upper case letters for classes by lower case letters.

There is already in existence a Calculus of Relations, and we shall say a little about this in a later chapter, but we can at least notice here how it can be thought of. In fact the word 'relation' is in some sense quite literally intended, since one type of relationship which lends itself naturally to such a description is that of family relationships. Being "the father of", "the sister of" or "the cousin of" suggests immediately the use of relational operators such as those mentioned above; we shall not pursue this matter further for the moment.

BASIC ISSUES INVOLVED

We have assumed quite a lot in this chapter, in our informal discussion of an algebra of classes, and we should clarify some part of the point and purpose of what has been done.

We have assumed the notion of class as being basic and then have discussed operations on classes and relationships between classes. It is being assumed that classes are well-defined and we can always precisely identify a class of objects and its boundaries. In practise many classes of objects have quite hazy boundaries, and we can only say of such classes that they would either not be suitable to be a class of our algebra, or that we would have to decide arbitrarily on definite class boundaries.

The motive which George Boole had in mind in developing such an algebra was based on the belief that the laws of thought could be made precise and mathematical in form. Since those days, arguments have taken place about the relationship between logic and thinking, it being clear that human thought does not always have the precision of an algebra. However it has also been argued that such a logical system can represent idealized thinking, or rather idealized reasoning. The point here is that thinking and reasoning, of course, are not necessarily exactly the same thing.

Use has been made of symbolic logic by philosophers and semanticists, since it is a convenient shorthand and highlights the relationship involved in statements. Logical entailment is the process of seeing what follows from the form or meaning of a statement and this can be conveniently put into symbolic logical form.

The other use of mathematical logic has been to provide a foundation for mathematics and this we shall be discussing later. For both linguistic analysis of arguments, and in order to provide a foundation for mathematical reasoning, the type of symbolic logic needed goes beyond an algebra of classes and we shall take it beyond this ourselves.

The other point to be made clear is that we wish to provide our formal logical systems in axiomatic form, rather than informally. The next chapter will therefore briefly reformulate an alternative inter-pretation of what has been said in this chapter in the form of an axiom system, allowing us to produce our theorems by rules of deductive inference.

THE SYLLOGISM

As a final note in this chapter we will relate Boolean algebra to the syllogism. This should show how compact a symbolic system can be when the full power of its summarizing methods are used.

The entire subject of categorical syllogisms can be summarized by the following three equations:-

$A \cap B' = 0$ and $B \cap C' = 0$ implies $A \cap C' = 0$ --- (18)

$B \cap C' = 0$ and $A \cap B \neq 0$ implies $A \cap C \neq 0$ --- (19)

$A \neq 0$ and $A \cap B' = 0$ and $B \cap C' = 0$ implies $A \cap C \neq 0$ --- (20)

The Euler-Venn diagrams for (18) and (19), which are the most important equations, are as follows:-

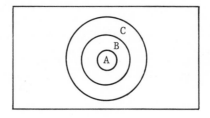

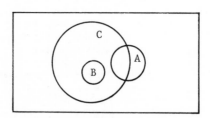

Equation (18) shows that the three propositions:-

$$A \cap B' = O \quad \text{(major premise)}$$

$$B \cap C' = O \quad \text{(minor premise)}$$

$$A \cap C' = O \quad \text{(conclusion)}$$

are all universal affirmative, and hence in the mood AAA. The code word BARBARA (containing the three A's) is sometimes used to represent this set of syllogisms.

Similarly equation (19) represents the syllogisms in the mood AII which are referred to by the code word DARII. The mood is clear since "all B is in C", "some A are in B" and "some A are in C". The Euler-Venn diagrams in each of these two cases make the moods of the syllogisms obvious.

The next step is to eliminate all negative propositions, since we can always replace "No man is tall" (No X is Y) by "All men are short". This means Universal negatives (E) can always be changed to Universal affirmatives (A).

Furthermore we can similarly replace "Some kings are not tall" by "Some kings are short". This means that particular negatives (O) can always be changed to particular affirmatives (I).

Finally since $A \cap B = B \cap A$ in Boolean algebra we do not need to worry about changing the order of the premises to fit in with the various figures. This variation of the order of the premises is often necessary otherwise in the fitting of the syllogisms to the correct figures, which the reader will have doubtless discovered by checking through syllogisms in Chapter Two.

This total reduction process reduces all the categorical syllogisms to BARBARA and DARII (equations (18) and (19)) coupled with equation (20) which simply asserts that the nul class is not permissible in the syllogism, whereas it is of course permitted in Boolean algebra in general.

The hypothetical syllogism is capable of being streamlined in similar fashion, but this is best done after we have developed the propositional calculus, so we shall leave it until a later chapter.

What is important to emphasize at this point is that we are proceeding at each step to ever more powerful logical systems, each of which includes the last, often as quite simple special cases: the power implied by such techniques is very considerable.

<u>SUMMARY</u>

From its beginnings in formal logical systems such as the syllogism, we proceed to more symbolic forms of logic.

The first formal system we consider (although still in an informal way) is Boolean Algebra. Boolean Algebra (developed initially by George Boole is concerned with the logic or algebra of classes. We discuss the laws of Boolean Algebra and show that the syllogism can be represented as a particular case of Boolean Algebra.

EXERCISES

1. Draw Euler-Venn diagrams for the following Boolean expressions:-

    i) $A \cup (B \cap C) = (A \cup B) \cap (A \cup C)$

    ii) $(A')' = A$

    iii) $(A \cap B) \cap C = A \cap (B \cap C)$

    iv) $(A \cap B \cap C) \cap D = (A \cap B) \cap (C \cap D)$

2. If $(a, b, c) \varepsilon A$, $(a, b, c, d, e, f) \varepsilon B$, $(a, b) \varepsilon C$ and $(a, c, f) \varepsilon D$ define

    $A \cap B$, $A \cup B$, $A \cap B \cap C$, $(A \cup B) \cap C$, $A \cap B \cap D$, $A \cup D$, $A \cup B \cup C \cup D$, $A \cap B \cap C \cap D$ and $A \cap D$ in terms of a, b, c, d, e and f.

REFERENCES

BIRKHOFF, G.   Lattice Theory. American Mathematical Society
                        Colloquium Publication. XXV, 1948

BOOLE, G.   An Investigation of the Laws of Thought.
                        London, 1854

BOWRAN, A.P.   A Boolean Algebra. Macmillan, 1966

GOODSTEIN, R.L.   Boolean Algebra. Pergamon Press, 1963

STOLL, R.R.   Sets, Logic and Axiomatic Theories.
                        W.H.Freeman, 1961

CHAPTER 4

THE PROPOSITIONAL CALCULUS

In this chapter we are concerned with developing another axiomatic system called the Propositional calculus. This is the simplest of the so-called <u>logistic</u> systems and is an alternative interpretation of the model supplied by Boolean algebra.

By convention we change the notation of classes represented by A, B, ..., N in our discussion of Boolean algebra to p, q, ..., n in our **discussion of propositions, but where propositions are related to each other** in the Propositional calculus as are classes in Boolean algebra. We shall, similarly, be using different symbols for similar connectives.

Our job is to construct a precise language, and to do this we must use another language which can be made sufficiently precise for our purpose. This more general language will include a large part of ordinary English and symbols that should be capable of being distinguished from the symbols of the precise language, i.e. the Propositional calculus. The general language is called here the syntax language. Theorems can be generated in both the Propositional calculus and the syntax language, and in general we shall be concerned with properties of the Propositional calculus such as its completeness, consistency, and the like, and whether or not there exists a decision procedure.

We shall describe the axioms of the system, the rules of inference and we shall generate theorems of the system. Before we can do this however we need to state the primitive symbols of the system, and we must also remind ourselves that there are various versions of the Propositional calculus in existence. We shall first develop a version in which the primitive symbols are the brackets (,), the horseshoe symbol of "material implication" which we write $\supset$, the constant f (which we shall interpret as falsehood) and an infinite set of propositional variables

$$p, q, \ldots, n$$

which may take suffices if needed. This means that

$$p_1, p_2, \ldots, p_n, \quad q_1, q_2, \ldots q_m, \quad n_1, n_2, \ldots, n_k \text{ etc.}$$

are all propositional variables.

The fact that we talk of brackets, material implication (statements of the "if --- then ..." variety) and falsehood is a reminder that these are interpretations which occur in the syntax language. We are not considering the meaning of the statements of the Propositional calculus in the formal development, but in practise we know that we do in fact have certain interpretations in mind; axiomatic systems are always developed as precise models (or languages) with an interpretation in mind.

Strictly speaking we need a similar set of primitive symbols in the syntax language to the brackets, etc. of the Propositional calculus, which are yet different since they are in a different language. In practise, we need not distinguish the connectives at the typographical level, although we shall use A, B, ..., N for syntax variables to distinguish them from propositional variables.

It is unfortunate that, because of the limited number of convenient alphabetic symbols, we have to use the same variables for Boolean algebra as for our syntax language, but as long as the reader remembers this fact, no confusion should arise.

We now need to consider the rules of formation for the system. Rules of formation are simply designed to distinguish well-formed strings of symbols from those that are not well formed, a point we have already mentioned. In English 'cat' is well formed (we shall use wf for 'well formed' and wff for 'well formed formula') while 'ccc' is not a wf word (or string) in English.

The rules of formation of our first version of the Propositional calculus (which we shall call P) are as follows:-

1. f alone or a variable alone is wf.

2. If A and B are wf (A ⊃ B) is wf.

and no other formula is wf other than those that follow from these rules. This sort of definition is a recursive one, where a recursive definition is one that supplies defining characteristics such as in 1 and 2 above, and then provides a limitation that this is all that is a defining characteristic.

We shall now consider only wff in our discussion, and one of our main aims is how to distinguish those wff that are theorems (or true statements of the system) from those that are not.

We should be clear here that by a true statement of the system, or a theorem, we mean that it follows from the axioms of the system by application of the rules of inference. The axioms are themselves true statements of the system and the rules of inference are also true statements couched in the syntax language. The reader should remember that in P we are formalising the ordinary meaning of the words 'not', 'or', 'and' and so on, and it is this which dictates what we accept as true statements. We shall be saying more about this later.

We can for example define truth (t) in terms of falsehood (f) so that

$$t \rightarrow\ \sim f$$

where by $\sim$ we mean "not" and where by $\rightarrow$ we mean "is defined by" or "the formula on the right may be replaced by the formula on the left". This is an alternative notation to "df." which can be used for definitions, and must not be confused with our use of ⊃ for implication.

In the version of the Propositional calculus P we shall be developing we actually define t as follows:-

$$t \rightarrow f \supset f$$

This is because this is the first of our cumulative definitions and we do not yet have $\sim$ (for 'not') as a defined symbol. We can introduce it straightaway

$$\sim A \quad \rightarrow A \supset f$$

By 'cumulative' above we mean that each definition is assumed by what follows and so that we can assume and use the definition of $\sim$ (for 'not') once it has been defined in the next definition.

We should now mention the t-tables, or truth-tables, which mirror the activity of the operators of P. First of all we give the truth-table for negation, i.e. $\sim p$.

p	$\sim p$
t	f
f	t

Next we look at 'or' and 'and' respectively:-

p	q	pvq
t	f	t
t	t	t
f	f	f
f	t	t

p	q	p.q
t	f	f
t	t	t
f	f	f
f	t	f

by use of the definition

$$p \supset q \; \rightarrow \; \sim p \; v \; q$$

we can derive the truth-table for $\supset$ which is a combination of that for 'not' and that for 'or'

p	q	p $\supset$ q
t	f	f
t	t	t
f	f	t
f	t	t

From these truth-tables we can see the point of the definition $t \rightarrow f \supset f$ whose truth-table is as follows

f	f $\supset$ f
t	f

We now add a list of further definitions:-

$$(A \not\subset B) \; \rightarrow \; \sim . \; B \supset A \qquad\qquad \text{---} \;(1)$$

$$(A \lor B) \; \rightarrow (A \supset B) \supset B \qquad\qquad \text{---} \;(2)$$

$$(A \; . \; B) \; \rightarrow (A \not\subset B) \not\subset B \qquad\qquad \text{---} \;(3)$$

$$(A \equiv B) \; \rightarrow (A \supset B)(B \supset A) \qquad\qquad \text{---} \;(4)$$

$$(A \not\equiv B) \; \rightarrow (A \not\subset B) \; v \; (B \not\subset A) \qquad\qquad \text{---} \;(5)$$

$$(A \subset B) \rightarrow B \supset A \qquad\qquad\qquad \text{---} \ (6)$$

and so on.

The first definition of our list (1) is asserting A (a syntax language variable and thus like B representative of any wff in P) is not contained in B. (2) is concerned with inclusion or (disjunction), (3) with and (conjunction), (4) with equivalence of the form "A if and only if B", (5) with non-equivalence and (6) with "A if B" or class inclusion which asserts that all members of A are necessarily members of B.

THE DOT CONVENTION

We have already made it clear that P has primitive symbols such as f, $\supset$ and brackets (,) is a reminder that we shall often need to use brackets to indicate the order in which operations are to be carried out in P. Thus we have p $\supset$ (q $\supset$ p) to distinguish it from p $\supset$ q $\supset$ p which should be read as (p $\supset$ q) $\supset$ p. This is so because we have a convention of **"association to the left", which automatically brackets off formula to** their left end.

The need for brackets used as above has an analogue in arithmetic where we use brackets for 3 x (4 + 4) to distinguish it from (3 x 4) + 4 which is what would be assumed in the absence of brackets i.e. 3 x 4 + 4.

The priority of operators occurs in P so that $\supset$ takes precedence over v which in turn takes precedence over . which in turn takes precedence over $\sim$.

We also use a dot convention to replace the brackets, although dots and brackets might well be used together. Let us explain our dot convention.

$$p \supset (q \supset p)$$

is written

$$p \supset . q \supset p$$

since

$$p \supset q \supset p$$

would be interpreted as

$$(p \supset q) \supset p$$

Similarly

$$p \supset q \supset p \supset p$$

is read as

$$(((p \supset q) \supset p) \supset p)$$

whereas if we wanted

$$(p \supset (q \supset (p \supset p)))$$

would be written

$$p \supset \cdot q \supset : p \supset p$$

where : takes precedence over . and, of course, :. would precede : , and so on.

    In other words dots are effectively brackets. Look again at:-

$$p \supset \cdot q \supset p$$

we insert a left bracket for the dot and then need its right bracket to properly mate it:-

$$p \supset (q \supset p)$$

But there is also the association to the left rule which means

$$(p \supset q) \supset p$$

is the same as

$$p \supset q \supset p$$

Similarly, combining the two rules we read

$$p \supset p \supset q \supset \cdot p \supset q$$

as

$$((p \supset p) \supset q) \supset (p \supset q)$$

and

$$p \supset \cdot p \supset q \supset : p \supset q \supset q \supset \cdot p \supset q$$

as

$$((p \supset (p \supset q)) \supset (((p \supset q) \supset q) \supset (p \supset q)$$

Sometimes a compromise notation would lead to the writing of this last example as:-

$$(p \supset \cdot p \supset q) \supset \cdot p \supset q$$

The main thing about whatever convention is used is that it should clearly identify the order of precedence of the connectives. That order for us is indicated by the following table which gives priority to a connective in the left column over any connective in a column to its right:-

Coupled to the rule of association to the left, this unambiguously provides the necessary order of precedence (the higher in precedent <u>operates</u> later). So

$$p \text{ v } q.r \text{ is } (p \text{ v } (q.r))$$

and

$$p \supset q \text{ v } r.s \text{ is } (p \supset (q \text{ v } (\sim r.s))$$

where . takes precedence over $\sim$.

This last formula in the dot notation where we omit the dot representing AND and write rs for r.s gives

$$p \supset . q \text{ v } . \sim rs$$

We must now move on to the development of formal proofs, which start with the axioms.

FORMAL PROOFS

First of all we give the axiom set for P.

$$p \supset q \supset . q \supset r \supset . p \supset r \qquad \text{--- (7)}$$

$$p \supset q \supset p \supset p \qquad \text{--- (8)}$$

$$p \supset . q \supset p \qquad \text{--- (9)}$$

$$f \supset p \qquad \text{--- (10)}$$

We now need rules of inference in order to deduce theorems from the axioms. The rules of inference are:-

(1) From A and A $\supset$ B to infer B.

(2) From A to infer $S \begin{smallmatrix} Y \\ X \end{smallmatrix} A \bigg|$ where $S \begin{smallmatrix} Y \\ X \end{smallmatrix} A \bigg|$ means the substitution of X for Y in A of all occurrences of Y.

A formal proof of a wff A is a finite sequence of A_1, A_2, ..., A_n of wff such that every A_1 is an axiom or is obtainable from one or more preceding A_1 by application of one of the rules of inference.

The proving of theorems is by a conventional application of the rules of inference to the axioms. Before we look at a proof we should make a point about the rule of substitution. We must distinguish between <u>successive</u> and <u>simultaneous</u> substitution. For example the simultaneous substitution of p ⊃ q for p and q ⊃ p for q in p ⊃q gives p ⊃ q ⊃ · q ⊃ p. The same substitution done successively with p ⊃ q for p first and q ⊃ p for q second gives p ⊃ (q ⊃ p) ⊃ · q ⊃p. On the other hand where there are an infinite number of variables we can always reduce simultaneous substitution to successive substitution. Thus by substituting r for q, p ⊃ q for p and q ⊃ p for r, we can by successive substitution achieve exactly what was achieved by our previous simultaneous substitution.

We now consider the proof of

$$(p ⊃ · p ⊃q) ⊃ · p ⊃ q$$

A_1.   (p ⊃ q ⊃ ·   q ⊃ r) ⊃ · p ⊃ r   (axiom 7)

A_2.   (p ⊃ p ⊃ q ⊃ · p ⊃ q ⊃ r) ⊃ · p ⊃ r $(S^q_{p ⊃ q}$ in $A_1)$

A_3.   (p ⊃ · p ⊃ q ⊃ · p ⊃q ⊃q) ⊃ · p ⊃ q $(S^r_q$ in $A_2)$

A_4.   p ⊃ q ⊃ p ⊃ p   (axiom 8)

A_5.   (p ⊃ q ⊃q ⊃ · p ⊃q) ⊃ · p ⊃ q $(S^p_{p ⊃ q}$ in $A_4)$

A_6.   (p ⊃ · p ⊃ q)⊃ (p.⊃ q⊃ q ⊃ · p ⊃q) ⊃ ·   (Simultaneous substitution of

(p ⊃q⊃ q⊃ · p⊃ q) ⊃ (p⊃ q) ⊃ · S^p A_1,

(p ⊃ · p ⊃ q)⊃ · p⊃ q $S^q_{p⊃ q⊃ q⊃ ·p⊃ q}$ A_1,

          $S^r_{p ⊃ q}$ $A_1)$

From A_6 we can derive the proof by two applications of <u>modus ponens</u>.

It should be noticed in the above proof that we try by one or more substitutions to achieve a form which has the formula to be proved as the end of a string which has itself been proved. This means the string is A ⊃ B, and if A is proved, then B follows; this is the first rule of inference known as <u>modus ponens</u>. It applies in our proof since A_6 is A ⊃ B, where B is (p ⊃ · p ⊃ q) ⊃ · p ⊃ q and A is itself capable of being broken down into a further form A ⊃ B wherein A is proved and so is A ⊃ B and therefore so is B.

We attempt always to provide, by working back from a desired form, a suitable set of substitutions.

Now to prove p ⊃ p

A_1 p ⊃ q ⊃ . (q ⊃ r) ⊃ . (p ⊃ r)   (7)

A_2 p ⊃ q ⊃ . (q ⊃ p) ⊃ (p ⊃ p) S^r_p A_1

(Notice we now have the sort of end we need to prove p   p)

A_3 (p ⊃ . p ⊃ ⊃ p ⊃ p) ⊃ (p ⊃ p ⊃ p ⊃ p) ⊃ (p ⊃ p)

                                                   $S^q_{p⊃ \ p⊃ \ p}$ A_2

(This retains the end and supplies a better beginning)

A_4 p ⊃ . q ⊃ p   (9)

A_5 p ⊃ . p ⊃ p ⊃ p $S^q_{p \ ⊃ \ p}$ A_4

(This gives us the first part of the beginning of A_3)

A_6 p ⊃ p ⊃ p ⊃ p ⊃ . p ⊃ p

(Since A_3 and A_5 give us a direct application of modus ponens)

A_7 p ⊃ q ⊃ p ⊃ p   (8)

A_8 p ⊃ p ⊃ p ⊃ p S^q_p A_7

A_9 p ⊃ p

(Since A_6 and A_8 give us another opportunity to apply modus ponens)

If we now adopt a new axiom set and call our new version of the
Propositional calculus P*, we have

    p ⊃ (q ⊃ r) ⊃ . (p ⊃ q) ⊃ (p ⊃ r)   --- (11)

    p ⊃ . q ⊃ p   --- (12)

    ~ p ⊃ ~ q ⊃ . q ⊃ p   --- (13)

and should notice that we are now introducing ~ as a primitive symbol.
A proof of the above theorem p ⊃ p in P* is now rather simpler than in P.

    To prove p ⊃ p

A_1 p .⊃ . q ⊃ p   --- (12)

A_2 p ⊃ . q ⊃ p ⊃ p S^q_q p A_1

A_3 p ⊃ (q ⊃ r) ⊃ . (p ⊃ q) ⊃ (p ⊃ r)   --- (11)

A_4 p ⊃ (q ⊃ p ⊃ p) ⊃ . p ⊃ . q ⊃ p ⊃ . p ⊃ p $S^q_{q \ ⊃ p}$ A_3 & S^r_p A_3

Now this is of the form suitable to apply modus ponens since it is

            $((A_2) ⊃ (A_1)) ⊃ p ⊃ p$

We shall spend no more time on proofs in P or P* since we find we have a decision procedure which is readily available and which supplies proofs by much simpler methods.

The reason we have looked at proofs here in the way we have is because it is of some intrinsic interest in its own right, but much more important than this when we come to the Functional calculus, which has no decision procedure, there is no alternative but to use the same method of proving theorems by application of the rules of inference to the postulates.

The decision procedure for the Propositional calculus depends upon the notion of truth-tables, which we have already briefly discussed. Strictly speaking we are talking of t-tables in the object language, although it is to be clearly understood that t and f are to be interpreted as 'truth' and 'falsehood' respectively. Hence we shall refer to t-tables as truth-tables.

Since $p \supset q$ = df. $\sim p \lor q$, we can combine the truth-tables for negation and disjunction, as we have already said, and this gives us:-

p	q	$p \supset q$
t	t	t
t	f	f
f	t	t
f	f	t

In the system P, we had only the one connective $\supset$, so this is the only truth-table needed. However, we can formulate truth-tables for any wff, so for example, the truth-table for $p \supset p$ is

p	$p \supset p$
t	t
f	t

and we can easily see that the case where f occurs in the final column of the truth-table cannot occur here. This is so because p cannot be both t and f together, it is either t or f. Which means that only the limited truth-table for $\supset$ occurs:-

p	p	p ⊃ p
t	t	t
f	f	t

We call such a wff whose truth-table contains only t in the final
column a <u>tautology</u>. Then it can be shown that all theorems of P are
tautologies and all tautologies are theorems. We have therefore acquired
a decision procedure for P now which allows us to decide, by inspection of
the truth-tables alone, whether a wff is a theorem or not.

We have already shown p'⊃ p to be a theorem by both methods of proof.
Let us look next at (p'⊃ . p ⊃ q) ⊃ . p ⊃ q. Rather than reconstruct the
whole truth-table we merely need to see if we can derive a single
combination of truth-values which would make the wff false. For
(p ⊃ . p ⊃ q) ⊃ . p ⊃ q to be false, requires that p ⊃ . p ⊃ q be t while
p ⊃ q is f. p ⊃ q is f if and only if p is t while q is f. Now this makes
p ⊃ . p ⊃ q   t ⊃ . t ⊃ f and that is t ⊃ f which is f and since p ⊃ . p ⊃ q
had to be t to make the whole formulae f, it cannot be made f, and is
therefore a tautology and therefore a theorem.

We need next to look at the proof of the decision procedure, which
is a proof in the Syntax language, and we shall reserve this and our
discussion of consistency, completeness and independence until chapter 5.

BACKGROUND OF THE PROPOSITIONAL CALCULUS

Historically, we should say that the basic elements of the
Propositional calculus are very old, but the modern version which we have
described here is mainly due to Frege in 1879, but also owes something to
Peano. Most of all however the origins of the present versions of the
Propositional calculus, such as we have described in this chapter, are due
to the work of Whitehead and Russell, especially in their work
<u>Principia</u> <u>Mathematica</u>.

Many other logicians have made contributions to the development of
the Propositional calculus, and we should mention at least the names of
C.I. Lewis, W.V. Quine, and the Polish logicians, Tarski and Lukasiewicz,
while Wittgenstein was directly responsible for the development of the
tabular (or matrix) form of truth-tables. The names of Hilbert, Bernays
and Wajsberg should also be mentioned in this context. More recently a
vast amount of literature has appeared on all aspects of the Propositional
calculus and we should refer the reader to the <u>Journal of Symbolic Logic</u>
for a suitable set of references.

Lastly we recognize, of course, in terms of the discussion of our
last chapter that the Propositional Calculus is a Boolean algebra. In
purely algebra terms it is said to form a <u>ring</u> with respect to conjunction
(A ∩ B) and exclusive disjunction (A + B), which are the ring multiplication
and ring addition respectively.

SUMMARY

The Propositional Calculus is the first logistic system which we have described in a formal manner. This involves the use of primitive symbols, definitions, axioms, rules of inference and theorems. The use of truth-tables helps to clarify the relations of the Propositional Calculus and leads into our discussion of its properties in the next chapter.

EXERCISES

1. For practise at both types of proof, you should try your hand at the following examples of either P or P or P*:-

     i)   p ⊃ . p ⊃ q ⊃ q

     ii) (p ⊃ . q ⊃ r) ⊃ . q ⊃ . p ⊃ r

     iii) q ⊃ r ⊃ . p ⊃ q ⊃ . p ⊃ r

     iv) ~ p ⊃ . p ⊃ q

     v)   ~ ~ p ⊃ p

     vi) p ⊃ ~ ~ p

     vii) p ⊃ . p ⊃ q ⊃ q

2. Outline the point and purpose underlying the Propositional Calculus.

REFERENCES

CARNAP, R.   An Introduction to Symbolic Logic and its
                           Applications. Dover Books, 1958

CHURCH, A.   Introduction to Mathematical Logic.
                           Princeton University Press, 1944

COOLEY, J.   A Primer of Formal Logic. New York, 1942

COPI, I.   Symbolic Logic. New York, 1954

KLEENE, S.C.   Mathematical Logic. Wiley, 1967

TARSKI, A.   Introduction to Logic. Oxford University Press.
                           Second Edition, 1946

CHAPTER 5

PROPERTIES OF THE

PROPOSITIONAL CALCULUS

We have, in our version P of the propositional calculus, a logistic or axiomatic system. It now behoves us to look at some of the properties of such an axiomatic system. Among the most obvious properties to look for are consistency and completeness. The former means roughly speaking that we do not want such inconsistencies occurring as being able to prove both a wff and its negation. The latter means, also roughly speaking, that we want P to include precisely what we want formalised and to exclude what we do not want formalised. But these intuitive ways of looking at consistency and completeness are not precise enough for our purpose. We must therefore refine them.

As far as the consistency of P is concerned we have a theorem $P \supset . \sim P \supset q$ and from this we can infer that consistency in the general sense mentioned above is equivalent in P to consistency with respect to $\sim$. To be both general and rigorous, we shall say that any axiomatic system is consistent with respect to any syntactic transformation if upon that syntactic transformation we cannot derive both some theorem A, say, and its negation $\sim A$. In the case of P the syntactic transformation is, of course, that of $\sim$.

By consistency, in other common sense terms we, of course, also mean non-contradictory. We mean to assert that if we have any two contradictory statements in our system at least one cannot be proved.

In a sense the importance of this notion is methodological rather than practical, but mirrors what is fairly obvious and has its analogue in an informal argument where a person contradicts himself. Completeness can be thought of as proving either $\vdash A$ or $\vdash \sim A$ for every wff A. but this is not what we normally want. To explain what we do want requires that we distinguish between <u>free</u> and <u>bound</u> variables. A bound variable is one whose range is precisely defined. For example in the integral calculus the variable x in the formula:

$$\int_0^9 (4x^2 + 7x + 5) \, dx$$

is bound whereas the variable x in the formula:

$$\int (4x^2 + 7x + 5) \, dx$$

is not bound. We say that a variable which is not bound is free. We can now say that for an axiomatic system with no free variables our original notion of completeness holds i.e. that for every wff A, we can assert either $\vdash A$ or $\vdash \sim A$ but not both.

This definition of Completeness, while useful in some cases, does not help us with P, since P has only got free variables. We shall therefore use a further definition of completeness which says that an axiomatic system is complete if for every wff A either $\vdash$ A or the system would be inconsistent if we introduce A as an axiom.

To refer back, as we did with consistency, to everyday discussion we can call a theory or a logistic system complete if of any two contradictory sentences in the system at least one sentence can be proved in the system. We often say of a sentence which has the property that its negation can be proved in the system, then we say the sentence itself is disproved in the system.

In these terms we could say a system is consistent if no sentence can be both proved and disproved in the system. Similarly a system is complete if every sentence in it can be either proved or disproved.

Another characteristic of axiomatic systems is independence, and we say that an axiom of such a system is independent if when it is omitted from the system it is not a theorem of the remaining axiomatic system. Similarly a rule of inference is independent if when it is omitted from the system, some of the theorems of the full system are no longer theorems of the remaining axiomatic system.

We could also say more tersely that for an axiom, x say, to be independent is to say that "x is false" is consistent with the rest of the system. This reduces the problem of independence to that of consistency. This means that if we place an interpretation on the system, all the axioms except x become true, since x is independent.

We now should say a little more, prior to our discussion of the decision problem, about syntactical theorems. These are, as the name implies, theorems in the syntax language.

SYNTACTIC THEOREMS

The so-called deduction theorem asserts the following:-

$$A_1, A_2, \ldots, A_n \vdash B$$

where say B is proved from the hypotheses $A_1, A_2, \ldots, A_n$.

To explain this we introduce the <u>variant</u> of a wff. This is the result of substituting different variables for some (or all) of the original variables, while keeping the original variables distinct. We now say that $A_1, A_2, \ldots, A_n \vdash B$ if there exists a finite set $B_1, B_2, \ldots, B_n$ of formulae of which $B_n \equiv B$ and for every i, we say either (1) B_i is one of $A_1, A_2, \ldots, A_p$ or (2) it is a variant of an axiom or (3) B_i results from B_j (j < i) by substitution, where the variable for which the substitution is made is not one of the set $A_1, A_2, \ldots, A_p$ or (4) B_i results from B_j and B_k by application of <u>modus ponens</u> where j, k < i.

We shall not be dealing in syntactic proofs but this is one syntactic theorem which we include for the sake of illustration.

A corollary of the Deduction Theorem is:

$$\text{If } A \vdash B, \text{ then } \vdash A \supset B$$

This is a special case of the Deduction Theorem where n = 1. The Deduction Theorem itself we can use as a so-called derived rule of inference. We can use it in proofs as follows:-

If we can prove A_1, A_2, ..., $A_n \vdash B$ then by repeated applications of the theorem we get:-

$$A_1 \supset . A_2 \supset . \ldots A_n \supset B$$

The development of syntax theorems is of use in the proofs of the properties of P, but these sort of matters, while of mathematical or mathematico-logical interest take us too far away from logic and its relation to language, reasoning and informal logic.

We come now to the so-called <u>decision procedure</u>. This is in certain terms a machinelike manner for deciding whether a wff within a system is or is not a theorem.

It should be said straightaway that there are only a few deductive systems (logistic systems) for which we can show completeness and consistency and similarly only a few which we can show have a decision procedure (sometimes called an <u>algorithm</u>) and these are usually fairly simple systems.

Emil Post showed that the Propositional Calculus had such a decision procedure which can be expressed as follows:-

In P, every tautology is a theorem and every theorem is a tautology. In the last chapter it may be recalled that in discussing truth tables that a tautology was a truth table in which only t occurred in the final column. Let us look at the truth table for a wff that we know to be a theorem $p \supset p$.

p	$p \supset p$
t	t
f	t

Where it will be remembered that $p \supset p = \sim p \lor p$

Since only t's occur in the final column and we say, by virtue of the decision procedure (for which we shall offer no proof), that $p \supset p$ is a theorem of p.

The reader may wish to persuade himself of the decision procedure method of proof by considering the wff at the end of the last chapter.

AN INTERPRETATION OF PART OF P

We now turn again to the link between the Propositional Calculus and informal logic, since there is a sense in which the formal definition of P is that it formalises the meaning of such symbols as ., v and ~ as 'and', 'or' and 'not'. In fact P can be made to depend on either . and ~ or v and ~ alone.

Even this slim base of two primitive connections was reduced to a simple connective by Sheffer whose famous Sheffer stroke is defined

$$P|q = df ~ p v ~ q$$

The fact that P is a formalisation (or purports to be a formalisation) of basic connectives of ordinary English provides the link with language which deserves our closest scrutiny. We will look first at the concept of material implication or the interpretation placed upon the symbol $\supset$.

Material implication has always been regarded as a central issue of the propositional calculus, since it seems to assert something (if not all) of what is meant in natural language by implication i.e. if --- then ... The problem (or issue) arises because the version of material implication in P of the form

$$P \supset q$$

says "p or not-q or both" and incidently of course does not require that a material (causal) connection exists between the propositions p and q. This therefore does not accord with what we normally mean in everyday conversation by material implication, since we normally think of a statement such as "if I go to Venice for my holiday then I shall certainly be able to ride in a gondola".

A similar state of affairs exists with the inclusive-or of the Propositional Calculus (and Boolean Algebra) since

$$p \lor q$$

means "p or q or both" as opposed to the usual meaning of the word 'or' which of course means "p or q but not both".

The whole question therefore arises as to whether or not the propositional calculus really represents relationships between propositions as they occur, for example, in natural language.

We would certainly not argue that the differences involved between the language of logic and everyday language are complete, although they are open to question. The famous logician Alfred Tarski has drawn attention to the point in question. First consider the example:-

"If you solve this problem, I shall eat my hat"

This affirms a consequence which is almost certainly false and yet we affirm the truth of the whole implication so affirming the falsity of the antecedent. The antecedent and the consequence are in no way connected, so we may be said to have a <u>material</u> rather than a <u>formal</u> implication.

It is clear that we are generalising somewhat the ordinary use of implication in that formal implication is a special case of material implication, in much the same way as "exclusive or" is a special case of "inclusive or".

A great deal has been said or written on the subject of implication and its role in language and logic and **we must,** after one reservation on Tarski's example, look at the matter from a slightly different point of view.

The reservation in Tarski's example is as to the relationship between the antecedent and the consequence in the above example. Consider another example:-

"If Caesar is in Britain then the Dodgers won the World Series."

This is clearly an acceptable material implication and yet there is <u>clearly</u> no relationship of a causal kind possible. In the Tarski example the two statements are at least capable of being causally related.

Look now at the matter from the viewpoint of mathematics. We say:-

"If x is a positive number, then 2x is a positive number."

Or more often we say "From the <u>hypothesis</u> that x is a positive number, we can draw the <u>conclusion</u> that 2x is a positive number." This is a clear case where the second statement can be derived from the first.

Also acceptable however is such a form as:-

"If 3 plus 3 equals 6 then London is a large city"

or

"From the hypothesis that 3 plus 3 equals 6 we can draw the conclusion that London is a large city."

The point by now should be clear and it is that the form of the if --- then ... relationship can be widened from its ordinary meaning of the causal relatedness of the antecedent and the conclusion (all of which relationships are included) to include the wider class of statements which may be materially implicated. As we said earlier, this means that material implication includes formal implication as a particular case.

We should next mention briefly an attempt by C.I. Lewis to provide a definition of implication more in keeping with what we normally mean by 'implies'.

He suggested the following:-

'$\lozenge$ p' means 'p is possible'

'O'   means 'is consistent with'

and we can now define p in terms of its self-consistency. So:-

$$\Diamond \ p = p \ o \ p$$

Similarly for two variables p and q we have:-

$$\Diamond \ pq = p \ o \ q$$

We now use $<$ as a symbol for implication which is defined:-

$$p < q = \sim (p \sim q)$$

which, on application of the above, leads to:-

$$p < q = \sim (po \sim q)$$

Many logistic systems have been derived from the Lewis notion of
strict implication, although most recent ones have tended away from the
notation (partly at least presumably because of printers and typists) used
by Lewis. We shall not in any case follow up this line of argument here
rather we shall now say a few words on many-valued and modal logic.

MANY-VALUED LOGIC

All that we have said so far in this book has presupposed logical
systems such as the syllogism, Boolean Algebra and the Propositional
Calculus having only two values. Or to put it rather differently, the
variables (or classes or statements) involved in such systems are to be
interpreted as true or false. In fact, more formally we might in the
object language use the two symbols 1 and 0, or t and f, but we certainly
intend the interpretation placed on these symbols, in P say, as being
true and false respectively.

In much the same way as geometry can be .thought of in any number of
dimensions so can logic. Geometry is familiar mainly in the 2- and 3-
dimensional cases, but can of course be extended to n-dimensional geometry
and refers to spaces (intuitively acceptable for 3-dimensions and below).
In a somewhat similar fashion we can generalise logic.

We can have 3-valued, 4-valued, ..., n-valued logics. As in geometry
we can simply generalise the formal logistic system. Thus a truth table in
3-valued logic for v could take the following form:-

p	q	p v q
1	1	1
2	1	1
3	1	1
1	2	1
2	2	2
3	2	2
1	3	1
2	3	2
3	3	3

Similarly we can draw up such truth tables involving 3, 4 or more values for all the connectives of the particular logistic system. This can also be extended of course to higher level calculi such as the Functional Calculi (described briefly in the next chapter). The problem of interest here is that of the interpretation we might place on these many-valued logics.

In the case of the 3-valued logic, we could reasonably interpret 1 as truth, 2 as falsehood and 3 as uncertainty. In the case of the 4-valued logic, we might say 1 = truth, 2 = falsehood, 3 = probability and 4 = probability not. To take the example of 7-valued logic, we might reasonably interpret the seven values as: 1 = truth, 2 = falsehood, 3 = almost certainly not, 4 = probably not, 5 = uncertainty, 6 = probably and 7 = almost certainly.

Part of the importance of these many-valued logics lies in the relationship to uncertainty as is represented in language. Statements may be true or false, but our knowledge of their truth or falsity will generally - always in the case of empirical (factual) statements - be uncertain. This represents the important distinction sometimes drawn between truth and degree of confirmation. Statements (or propositions) may be true or false. But our knowledge of their truth is the extent to which they are confirmed. This notion of confirmation itself brings up questions regarding evidence and relevance which we shall be discussing again later.

One question about many-valued logic which we can ask immediately is as to whether it is ever needed other than in the sense of the last paragraph. The answer to this is that the sense of the last paragraph is itself vitally important, but that such logics have a significance over and beyond that. This extra significance is connected with an element of vagueness or uncertainty, not over our knowledge, but about the manner in which we may choose to define situations. Let us consider an example.

"I am in Bristol and it is raining here". This may be clear enough for many purposes (whether or not it is true). But in some cases there are real difficulties that may be encountered. Do we know <u>exactly</u> where Bristol ends and non-Bristol (Somerset or Gloucestershire) begins? The **answer must be** "no". Since although in a broad sense (especially when far removed from the boundaries) we know whether we are in Bristol or not, in a precise sense there are a whole host of places, standing on the borders, where we simply do not know, nor is it well-defined.

We can in the above example always introduce a precise line and say (arbitrarily) you are either in Bristol or you are not and this could apply (by some convention) even to someone who stands astride the boundary. But one sees that in the process of drawing up such conventions one is now increasingly committed to arbitrariness. The alternative is to use a type of description which is capable of accepting more than the two values of traditional logic.

A new kind of logic that has crept into popularity in recent years is called "fuzzy logic". The idea is that which is embodied in what we have just said. The fact is that categories we use as a basis for description are not <u>precisely</u> defined (or delineated). "When are you in Bristol?" "When is a chair not a chair?" and so on. The point being that the classes "Bristol", "chair", (and other such classes) have hazy boundaries.

One particular many-valued logic (also in an obvious sense fuzzy) is the logic of uncertain inference, of the kind already mentioned, where the uncertainty can be given a probability measure. Thus a connection with probability theory (and also statistics) is established. The use of such a logistic system is one where statements of the form $p \supset p$ become $p \supset p$ (p) or $p \supset_p p$, or some such notation where $p = m/n$ say and where n is the number of cases concerned with some event A, say, and where m is the number of cases favourable to that event A; this is the so-called Laplacian measure of probability.

We can perhaps finish this chapter by describing other types of notation which are sometimes felt to be convenient.

The so-called "Polish" notation has some typographical advantages and we will briefly indicate the manner in which it operates.

Instead of writing:-

$$\sim p$$

$$p \lor q$$

$$p \cdot q$$

$$p \supset q$$

we write:-

$$Np$$

$$Opq$$

$$Apq$$

$$Ipq$$

So that the operator occurs at the beginning and has a scope commensurate with whether it is a unary, binary, ternary, etc. operator. This means that we can write:-

$$(p \supset . \ p \supset q) \supset . \ p \supset q$$

as

$$IpIpqIIpq$$

Where the symbol I for "implication" also acts as a syntactical feature explaining where the brackets and/or dots occur.

The interested reader can, for example, rewrite all the formulae used so far in such a "Polish" notation if he feels the need to convince himself of how the translation is carried through.

SUMMARY

We have now analyzed the Propositional Calculus in terms of the characteristic properties of all logistic (axiomatic) systems. These properties include questions of consistency, completeness and the possibility of a decision procedure.

We have particularly discussed material and strict implication, many valued logics, fuzzy logics and have briefly mentioned alternative notations which have been used by different writers.

EXERCISES

1. Explain what is meant by a Syntactical theorem, as opposed to a theorem of the Propositional Calculus itself.

2. Try to explain in simple terms to your own satisfaction:-

     i) Consistency

    ii) Completeness

   iii) Decision Procedures

    iv) **Formation Rules**

     v) Truth Tables

3. Suppose you wished to use a formal many-valued logic to describe your
    knowledge of the empirical world at a fairly common sense level. How
    many values would be convenient to you and how would you construct such
    a language in broad terms? You ought also to place an interpretation
    (e.g. "possible", "probable", etc.) on the various values (or modalities).

4. What advantages has Polish notation over Principia Mathematica notation
    (the general notation we have used in this book)? Scribble down a few
    examples to illustrate the difference.

REFERENCES

LEWIS, C.I. & LANGFORD, C.H.   Symbolic Logic. The Century Co. 1932

QUINE, W.V.O.   Methods of Logic. New York, 1950

ROSENBLOOM, P.   The Elements of Mathematical Logic.
                                    The Dover Books, 1950

RUSSELL, B.   The Principles of Mathematics.
                                    Allen and Unwin, Second Edition, 1950

WHITEHEAD, A.N. &   Principia Mathematica. Cambridge
RUSSELL, B.   University Press, 3 vols. 1910, 1912,
                                    1913

CHAPTER 6

THE FUNCTIONAL AND PREDICATE CALCULUS

The Propositional calculus is, as we have said, concerned with the relation between propositions but cannot analyze propositions into subject and predicate form, nor can it handle functions or quantification, whether over functions or predicates. It is for this reason that we have to generalize on P and P* to produce F (and F_1, F_2, ..., as needed) which is how we will refer to the Functional calculus.

In introducing what have been called propositional functions we can think of a function as in mathematics as a relation R whereby to each object x there is at most one object y such that x has the relation R_2 to y. y is the <u>value</u> of the function for the <u>argument</u> x. $y = x^2$, $y = 3x + x$, etc. are among the infinite number of examples found in mathematics.

A propositional function is a function whose values are propositions. We then say that a propositional function is denoted by a sentence-form such as "x is a man" and from this sentence-form we obtain a sentence by substituting the name of a woman for x. So "Charlie is a man" is a sentence which is also true, whereas if we had substituted Murrayfield for x we would have arrived at the sentence "Murrayfield is a man" which is a sentence which is false. Let us now look at some of the formal construction of F.

It should be made clear that F is a generalization of P and therefore includes all of P as part of itself, so we still have the propositional variables

$$p, q, r, \ldots$$

Now we add individual variables:-

$$x, y, z, \ldots$$

where the variables can be replaced by the name of a particular individual, by which we mean that they refer to individual members of a class. We also have functional variables:-

$$F, G, H, \ldots$$

where all of these variables can take suffices as needed. Such functional variables are of course characterized by mathematical functions for example. The functional variables also have super-scripts, so that

$$F^1, G^1, H^1, \ldots \quad \text{singularly functional variables}$$

$$F^2, G^2, H^2, \ldots \quad \text{binary functional variables}$$

$$F^n, G^n, H^n, \ldots \quad \text{n-ary functional variables}$$

where the superscripts 1, 2, ..., n refer to the number of individual variables which are associated with each functional variable.

Thus $F^2(x, y)$, $F^3(x_1, x_2, x_3)$, and other such expressions may be expected to appear within the formulae of F.

We also use the universal quantifier, $(Ax)F^1(x)$ which means 'for all x, $F^1(x)$' and the existential quantifier, $(Ex)F^1(x)$ which means 'there exists at least one x such that $F^1(x)$'.

The use of so-called quantifiers, such as the universal and existential quantifiers mentioned here represents a big step towards greater generality. This will become apparent in the second half of this chapter when we look at quantification with respect to what we shall call the Predicate calculus, where the operators are to be interpreted in the context of natural-language statements.   In any event, to be able to talk of "all" or "at least one" member of a set is a necessary condition for us to make the logically acceptable mathematical and linguistic statements we require.

F will inevitably have many different sorts of brackets, and is capable of handling constants of a functional, propositional or individual kind.   All the constants can be introduced as individual symbols, or written within some form of properly mated brackets.   In fact, brackets [,] are usually used for propositional constants, braces { , } for functional constants and parentheses (,) for individual constants.   We shall not in fact be much concerned with these technical details, since it is not our intention to pursue a detailed enquiry into the Functional Calculi, least of all from a highly formalized point which is so necessary to the development of metamathematics.

One distinction which is often made is between the pure and applied Functional Calculus.   The pure Functional Calculus contains only variables, whereas an applied Functional Calculus will also contain constants.

The rules of formation for our version of F are as follows:-

1. A proposition variable alone is wf.
2. A propositional constant alone is wf.
3. $A(B_1, B_2, \ldots, B_n)$ is wf if A is n-adic functional variable or constant and B's are individual constants.
4. If A and B are wf A $\supset$ B is wf.
5. If A is wf then B is **wf**.
6. If A is wf and B is an individual variable, (B)A is wf.

It should be noticed here that we are using upper case letters for individual constants and also for syntax-variables.   The context should avoid confusion in these usages.

Some definitions are also given:

$$(Ea)B \rightarrow \sim (Aa) \sim B$$

$$(Aa) \ A \supset B \supset (Aa) \ . \ (A \supset B)$$

$$(Aa) \ (Ab) \ A \supset B \supset (Aa) \ (Ab) \ . \ A \supset B$$

etc.

The axiom set for the first order functional calculus (F^1) is as follows:

From A and A $\supset$ B to infer B   --- (1)

From A to infer (Aa)A   --- (2)

This is the rule of generalization and a is to be read as an individual variable, where we say a is "generalized upon". The list of axioms which is expressed in the syntax language is, as a result, infinite. It can be expressed as:-

$A \supset \left[A \supset B \right] \supset . \ \ A \supset B \supset . \ \ A \supset C$ --- (3)

$A \supset . \ \ B \supset A$ --- (4)

$\sim A \supset \ \sim B \supset . \ \ B \supset A$ --- (5)

$(Aa)(A \supset B) \ . \ A \ \supset \ (Aa)B$ --- (6)

where a is any individual not free in A.

$(Aa) \ A \supset B$ --- (7)

where a is an individual variable, b is and individual variable or constant. We also need to insist that no free occurrence of a in A is in a wf part of A of the form (Ab)C.   B results from the substitution of b for all free occurrences of a in A, i.e. (Aa) A $\supset S_b^a$ A | where the notions of <u>free</u> and <u>bound</u> variables has already been described in our discussion of the propositional calculus.

The following are derived rules of F^1 :-

Rule for alphabetic change of bound variable

If $\vdash$ A then $\vdash$ B where B is formed from A by substituting S_b^a M | for a particular occurrence of M in A, where a and b are individual variables, a is not free in M and b does not occur in M.

Rule of substitution for propositional variables

If $\vdash$ A then $\vdash S_b^a$A where a is a propositional variable and B is any wff in P, provided the bound variables of A are distinct from free variables of B.   An example will help:

In (Ax) (p $\supset$ F(x)) $= \left[p \supset (Ax)F \ x \right]$ --- (8)

we cannot substitute a formula where x is free, since x would become bound at the first substitution position.   If we substituted P(x) for p, we get

$$(Ax)(P(x) \supset F(x)) \equiv \Big[P(x) \supset (Ax) F(x)\Big] \qquad\qquad \text{--- (9)}$$

but this is no longer a logically true formula, since if we substitute P for F and a for x, we get

$$(Ax)(P(x) \supset P(x)) \equiv \Big[P(a) \supset (Ax) P(x)\Big] \qquad\qquad \text{--- (10)}$$

The fourth occurrence of x is the first one to be free and thus allow substitution by a. If we now interpret a as a certain individual and P as a class containing a, then P(a) is true and (Ax)(P(x) is false so $\Big[P(a) \supset (Ax)P(x)\Big]$ is false. Similarly (Ax)(P(x) $\supset$ P(x)) is true, so (10) is not logically true.

Rule of substitution for individual variables

If $\vdash$ A, then $\vdash S_b^a A \mid$ where a is an individual variable and b is an individual variable or an individual constant, a is not bound in A and no occurrence of a in A is a wf part of A of form (b)B. Here is an example:

We can substitute an individual constant or an individual variable for an individual variable, provided no individual variable which is substituted becomes bound at one of the substitution positions. An example makes the position clear. Given:-

$$(Ex) \; Sm \; (x,y) \qquad\qquad \text{--- (11)}$$

where this asserts "there is a number x that is smaller than y". If we now substituted x for the free variable y, we would get

$$(Ex) \; Sm \; (x,x) \qquad\qquad \text{--- (12)}$$

which is false.

Rule of substitution for Functional Variables

If $\vdash$ A then $S_B^C(a_1, a_2, \ldots, a_n) A \mid$ provided that certain conditions for the meaningfulness of the notation $S_B^C(a_1, a_2, \ldots, a_n) A$ are satisfied. This implies the replacing of $C(b_1, b_2, \ldots, b_n)$ everywhere in A by $S_{b_1, b_2, \ldots, b_n}^{a_1, a_2, \ldots, a_n} B$ where this replacement is carried out simultaneously for all sets $b_1, b_2, \ldots, b_n$ of individual variables or constants and such that $C(b_1, b_2, \ldots, b_n)$ occurs in A.

This whole matter of substitution rules in the functional calculus is very complicated and one of the reasons that a search for a decision procedure and alternative forms of such logistic systems has taken place. For the moment, our rather austere statement of the rules themselves will have to suffice, except to add that we are including these details merely to give some feel to those interested in how logistic systems proceed in heading towards their role in the foundations of mathematics. We will now mention the derivation of theorems which occur in F.

The first point to be made is that all theorems of the propositional calculus are also theorems of the functional calculus. Over and above this we may prove theorems in the functional calculus although these are now, except in those cases where we can reduce them to formula in P, rather more difficult to carry out.   The difficulties arise from the fact that whereas it can be shown that F is consistent and complete, it can also be shown that it has no general decision procedure.   The fact that F has no general decision procedure has often been regarded as the fundamental problem of mathematical logic.

The absence of a <u>general</u> decision procedure has led to the search for decision procedures for a whole set of special cases of which the most obvious is that class of formulae which are also formulae of P.   The implications for proof are much dependent upon the success of this search since the alternative, which is made complicated by the many rules of substitution, is to proceed by applying the rules of inference to the axioms as we have already seen done in P.   Let us look though at some of the forms which are relevant to decision procedures.

Let us show first of all a proof (sometimes called a schematic proof) in F^1 :-

$$(Aa)((Aa)A \supset B) \supset .(Aa)A \supset (Aa)B$$

Proof:	Axioms
$(Aa)A \vdash A$	(7,1)
$(Aa)(A \supset B) \vdash A \supset B$	(7,1)
$(Aa)(A \supset B) , (Aa)A \vdash B$	(1)
$(Aa)(A \supset B) \supset .(Aa)A \supset B$	(* below, applied twice)
$(Aa)((Aa)(A \supset B) \supset ((Aa)A \supset B)$	(3)
$(Aa)(A \supset B) \supset .(Aa)((Aa)A \supset B)$	(6,1)
$(Aa)((Aa)(A \supset B) \supset .(Aa)A \supset (Aa)B)$	(6)

*   If A_1, A_2, ..., $A_n \vdash B$ then A_1, A_2, ..., $A_{n-1} \vdash A_n \supset B$

Then the theorem follows from P.

We now turn to a description of the first of two important forms which make it easier to characterize subsets of F which have a decision prodedure.   The first form is called the Prenex Normal Form.   A wff A is said to be in Prenex normal form if it has the following structure

$$(Qa_1)(Qa_2) \quad ... \quad (Qa_r)M \qquad\qquad\qquad --- (13)$$

where a_1, a_2, ..., a are distinct individual variables ($r \geqslant o$) and each of Qa_1 is either (Aa_i) or (Ea_i) and M is quantifier-free formula in which each of a_1, a_2, ..., a_n actually occurs.   M is the <u>matrix</u> of (13) and the remainder of (13) is called the <u>prefix</u>.

We could consider a rendering of the pure functional calculus where there are no constants and the rules of substitution become rules of inference.   Such a calculus is called the pure functional calculus of first order (F^1p).   Within Fp, we can limit ourselves, for most purposes, to formulae in Prenex normal form, or even to a special case of this which is given by formulae in a second form called Skolem normal form.   We must now look at formulae in Skolem normal form.

We can limit most discussions of the functional calculi, certainly for purposes of decision procedure analysis, for example, to Skolem normal form, and this form is where a formula in Prenex normal form has no universal quantifiers preceding an existential quantifier.   We now state Skolem's theorem.

Skolem's Theorem

There is an effective procedure by which, given any wff A, we may find a formula A_o in Skolem normal form such that $\vdash A$ if and only if $\vdash A_o$.

We must now briefly state some theorems and definition which lead us into Godel's Completeness Theorem and other theorems of F.

DEFINITION: A wff of F^1p containing no free individual variables is <u>satisfiable</u> if it is possible to determine a non-empty domain of individuals and to give each of the remaining variables a truth value such that the formula becomes true.

DEFINITION: A wff A of F^1p is <u>valid</u> in a particular domain if A is not satisfiable in that domain.

THEOREM: If a_1 wff in Skolem normal form is <u>valid</u>, it is a theorem of F^1p.

THEOREM: Every theorem of F^1p is <u>valid</u>.

THEOREM: A wff A of F^1p is <u>valid</u> if and only if its Skolem normal form A_o is <u>valid</u>.

Godel's Completeness theorem

THEOREM: A wff is a theorem of F^1p if and only if it is <u>valid</u>.

Lowenheim's theorem

THEOREM: A wff A of F^1p is <u>valid</u> in a given domain if and only if its Skolem normal form A is valid in that domain.

Lowenheim

THEOREM: Every wff of F^1p, containing no free individual variables, which is <u>valid</u> in the domain of natural numbers (or in any denumerably infinite domain) is <u>valid</u> in every non-empty domain.

Skolem's generalization of Lowenheim's theorem

If the members of a denumerable set of wff A_1, A_2, ... containing no free individual variables, are simultaneously satisfiable in some non-empty domain, then they are simultaneously satisfiable in a domain at most denumerably infinite.   Let us now resist the temptation to pursue further this line of approach which leads us further into meta-mathematics.

If we had pursued the matter of functional calculi here in more detail, we should come to deal with functional calculi of higher order and the theory of types.   We shall merely mention here that the second order functional calculus (F^2) differs from F^1 in that it allows quantification of propositional and functional variables as well as individual variables, F^3 introduces new variables and F^4 allows quantification over those new variables, and so we continue on a path towards an axiom system for the whole of mathematics.

Part of the paraphernalia which we need is the theory of types which develops a hierarchy of formal languages in an attempt to eliminate paradoxes in the system; we also use the axioms of infinity and choice.

We should mention before looking at the Predicate Calculus interpretation of our logistic system involving propositional functions, that another kind of logistic system has been produced called Combinatorial logic. These Combinatorial logics were designed in terms of constants only and thus could avoid the complexity of the substitution rules in the Functional Calculi. They proved successful alternatives, yet the price paid was heavy in other respects, and at least as far as mathematics is concerned the rule of substitution seems natural. The interested reader should refer to standard textbooks on mathematical logic if he feels the need to know more about such Combinatorial methods.

PREDICATE CALCULUS

We now introduce predicates

$$P, Q, \ldots, N$$

with suffices as necessary, and also using combinations of upper and lower case letters for predicates where we say

$$P(a)$$

where we might interpret this as "a is a prime number". Similarly we could write

$$Book(a)$$
$$Fl(a)$$
$$Hus(a,b)$$
$$Sm(a,b)$$

which could be interpreted respectively as "a is a book", "a is female", "a is the husband of b" and "a is smaller than b" (usually written $a < b$ in arithmetic).

We can think now of the same connectives as have been employed in the propositional and functional calculus. So we have

$$P(a) \text{ v } Q(b)$$

which could be written

$$(Pa) \text{ v } (Qb)$$

which means "a is P or b is Q or both".

We can of course also have forms such as

$$\left[Doc\ (a) \right] \text{ v } \left[Fl\ (a) \right]$$

which means "a is a doctor or a female or both".

In the conjunctive case:-

$$\left[\text{Doc (a)}\right] . \left[\text{Fl (a)}\right]$$

means "a is a female doctor".   Similarly we have the form

$$\sim \left[\dot{P}\text{ (a)}\right]$$

which means "a is not P".

We can introduce quantifiers into the Predicate calculus so we have forms such as:-

$$(Ax)(Px \lor Rxb)$$

which means "for every individual x, x has property P or x bears relation R to b".

Similarly we have

$$(Ex)(Px \lor Rxb)$$

which means "there exists at least one individual x such that x has property P or x bears relation R to b."

By use of the same definitions as were mentioned in the brief discussion of the Functional Calculus,   we have

$$\sim (Ax)\ Px \equiv (Ex) \sim Px$$

Similarly we have

$$(Ax)(\text{Book}(x) \supset \text{Blue}(x))$$

and

$$(Ax)(Ex)\ Gr(y, x)$$

which mean respectively "All books are blue" and "for each natural number there is always a greater number".

The truth conditions for the quantifiers are of course that a formula or part of a formula referred to by the universal quantifier (its scope) is true for all the individuals to which the universal quantifier applies. In the case of an existential quantifier the formula, or part of the formula, is true for at least one individual referred to by the existential quantifier.

We have already discussed the very important and complicated rules of substitution for both the propositional calculus and functional calculus and these apply in the same way to the Predicate Calculus.

We can now give a few examples of logically true formulae (Carnap calls these L-true) in the Predicate Calculus

$$(Ax)(Fx \supset Gx) \supset \big[(Ax)Fx \supset (Ax)Gx\big]$$
$$(Ax)(Fx \supset Gx) \ . \ (Ax)Fx \supset (Ax)Gx$$
$$(Ax)(Fx \supset Gx) \ . \ (Ex)Fx \supset (Ex)Gx$$
$$(Ax)(Fx \equiv Gx) \supset (Ax)(Fx \supset Gx)$$
$$(Ax)(Fx \equiv Gx) \ . \ (Ax)(Fx \supset (Ax)Gx$$
$$(Ax)(Fx \equiv Gx) \supset \big[(Ax)Fx \equiv (Ax)Gx\big]$$
$$(Ex)(Fx \ . \ Gx) \supset (Ex)Fx \ . \ (Ex)Gx$$
$$(Ex)(Fx \ . \ Gx) \supset (Ex)Fx$$

and although we could extend these examples (for which we offer no proofs) indefinitely, we shall simply content ourselves with restating the syllogism in terms of the Predicate Calculus.

The syllogism can be written:-

$$\big[(Ax)(Fx \supset Gx) \ . \ (Ax)(Gx \supset Hx)\big] \supset (Ax)(Fx \supset Hx)$$

Let us now return briefly to a more informal discussion of the Functional Calculi.

We have described the Functional Calculus (or really Functional Calculi since there are many versions) in very brief outline. This description has been given solely with the object of supplying the interested reader with a glimpse of a route which logic takes in what is historically one of its most important roles to date: to supply a background to mathematics.

The whole picture stems from the classic work of Russell and Whitehead in "Principia Mathematica" wherein mathematics was shown to be (a matter which has not gone undisputed) derivable from logic.

To carry through the derivation of mathematics from logic demands that we supply an axiomatic system of a logistic kind which is sufficiently rich (in symbols, rules of inference and derived rules of inference, etc.) to encompass the features commonly associated with mathematics. This, in particular, requires the inclusion of functions and therefore of functional and independent variables and also quantification. This automatically led to the development of the Functional Calculus. It also requires set theory, but this takes us beyond our present interest.

The use of functions and the paraphernalia of the Functional Calculus can though be given a different interpretation, as we have seen, as a Predicate Calculus. In other words, ordinary language involving individuals and properties can be analyzed logically in a subject-predicate form.

As we have said before, since we are not primarily concerned with mathematics as such, but rather with formalisation, we shall not pursue the mathematical route through the various versions of the Functional Calculi, the theory of types, leading to recursive functions and Turing machines. These are the important signposts in the field of meta-mathematics, but have no sufficient bearing on the process of formalizing our knowledge, and that is our main topic.

Functional and Predicate Calculi, like Propositional Calculi, can be many-valued as well as two-valued, and can in the limit all these systems can become (where the n of n-values tends to infinity) probability logics by interpretation.

But we next turn to a consideration of such formal systems interpreted as empirically descriptive systems and this is part of the essential link between logic and formal (and precise) descriptions. So to our next chapter which is the first of Book II and is concerned with scientific method.

SUMMARY

We have in this chapter simply generalized on the Propositional Calculus, and introduced Functional or Predicate variables and individual variables. We now have the means to analyze sentences and not merely analyze the relationship between sentences (or propositions).

EXERCISES

1. Convince yourself of the need for the Functional Calculus (over and above the Propositional Calculus) if you are to investigate mathematical statements. Give some examples.

2. Write "the lady has a green coat and a brown hat" in the form of a statement of the Predicate Calculus.

3. Write some examples of statements in the Functional and Predicate Calculus which could sensibly be given a three-valued interpretation. Explain the significance of many-valued logics in terms of these calculi.

4. Explain to yourself the way the syllogism is encapsulated by the formula on page 66 of this chapter.

REFERENCES

ACKOFF, R.
Scientific Method: Optimizing Applied Research Decisions. Wiley, 1962

BRAITHWAITE, R.B.
Scientific Explanation. Cambridge University Press, 1953

COHEN, M. AND NAGEL, E.
An Introduction to Logic and Scientific Method. Routledge, 1934

GEORGE, F.H.
Cybernetics in Management. Pan books, 1970

GEORGE, F.H.
Models of Thinking. Allen and Unwin, 1970

GEORGE, F.H.
Science and the Crisis in Society. Wiley, 1970

MORONEY, M.J.
Facts from Figures. Pelican Books, 1951

PART II

LOGIC, PROBABILITY AND PHILOSOPHY

In this part of the book we deal with probability theory
and briefly mention statistics. We follow this by a
discussion of induction. We then move on to philosophical
issues. In particular we discuss philosophy and its
relations to logic, language and behaviour.

CHAPTER 7

SCIENTIFIC METHOD

We have so far been concerned with formal logic and its relationship to ordinary language as well as its relationship to the foundations of mathematics. We have seen that formal logic takes us, in its symbolic form, beyond what is generally required in ordinary discourse. We have also found that the more detailed and precise distinctions and definitions required by science can be catered for in some measure by empirical logic, as we have called it.

Empirical logic, fuzzy logic and modal logic are related to mathematics, probability and statistics which we shall be discussing further. It is also related to science and scientific method generally and since science forms a sort of bridge between logic and empirical descriptions we shall devote the present chapter to an outline description of what scientific method entails.

Science is often thought of as the process of collecting facts. It is certainly true that fact-collecting plays an important part in science, but it is by no means the whole of what is involved. Just as important as fact-collecting is the setting up of theories, theoretical structures, models, etc., which allow the use of both deductive (which we have discussed) and inductive logic (which we shall be discussing). What we must do now is to outline each of the various steps involved in the total scientific process, explaining each as far as is necessary for an understanding of what science entails in the context of the "reasonable man".

It should be made clear from the start that in talking of scientific method, we are taking a global look at the process, and it does not by any means follow from this that any particular scientist at any particular time is involved in the whole of this global process. The chemist doing experiments in his laboratory, or the biologist inspecting tissues under a microscope may only be involved in a small part of the total activity of theory construction and logical reasoning, although often he is more involved than he might appear (even to himself) to be at first sight. It is also true that the scientific steps involved at any particular time in the scientist's work are not always made explicit to the external observer, or are not even always made explicit to the scientists themselves. Our description is normative in that we are describing what we believe the "reasonable" scientist ought to do.

There is still inevitably a lot of debate as to the nature of scientific method, and what we are asserting here is fairly general, and does not dwell on particular (and detailed) arguments. Most of what has filled many books on logic and scientific method has been about the detail of the subject, precisely how hypotheses are confirmed under certain restricted conditions, and precisely what sort of experimental controls

are suitable for some set of observations. They are also concerned with
the nature of evidence, and what makes a statement acceptable as (relevant)
evidence. We are not concerned with that degree of detail in this chapter,
we are only concerned with "broad brush" description of the scientific
processes. The reason for this is that our main aim in this book is to
provide ammunition for the debator and the man who is discussing everyday
events rather than studying some remote aspects of genetics or chemistry.

Scientific procedures can be thought of in terms of two principal
(sets of) operations which can occur in either order and therefore we will
arbitrarily select the deductive procedure first for discussion. Given
a set of assumptions, whether these be set out explicitly as postulates
in a formal system such as the Propositional or Functional Calculus, or
whether they are implicit and merely stated in ordinary language, or
indeed whether they be in some sort of special symbolic form as in
organic chemistry (or biochemistry), they represent the starting point
for the making of deductive inferences. A deductive inference is based
on the language which is used to describe that part of the system we are
interested in, it being obvious that science is partitioned into various
sub-departments all of which are a part of the totality of human
knowledge, but nevertheless are somewhat specialised and often thought of
under their specialised names of chemistry, physics, etc.

The process of deduction is one of drawing logical inferences from
assumptions. From these inferences further statements are generated,
sometimes called theorems in a formal system, which apply to the system
being described. Deduction itself is a symbolic process and refers to the
conclusions that follow from the assumptions. Some deductive inferences
are sometimes made in very complex circumstances and can involve
statistical and probability methods of inference as well as logical ones,
but more of this later.

There are also though logical inferences which can be complicated
when viewed against a background of the syllogism say. Let us remind
ourselves again of particular inference making situations; we use again
our example of Chapter 1.

If there are 366 people in a particular room at a particular time
and we overlook the leap year, then it follows that at least two people
in that same room have the same birthday. This is true because we can
allocate January 1st to one, January 2nd to another, January 3rd to
another, right through to December 31st and after we have exhausted the
365 days and allocated them to 365 people, we are left with a 366th person,
and since we have agreed to ignore leap year, his must be a duplicate
birthday. This is not necessarily asserting anything about the factual
situation, of course, because it may be that all the 366 people were born
on the same day. All it is asserting is that certain things must
necessarily follow by virtue of the way the problem is posed, or described.

It will be noted in our example of deduction that it was dependent on
the semantics of the situation. If the word 'birthday' means the hour in
which you were born instead of the day on which you were born, then the
validity of the argument would fail. It can be the case that arguments
are formal, as opposed to factual as in the case of the one about birthdays.
That is, if we say a implies b and b implies c, then a implies c, is a
formal argument in that it is true whatever a, b and c are, such that the

implication is transitive in the way suggested. If I use a simple
deductive argument such as "I am in Taunton" and "Taunton is in Somerset",
therefore "I am in Somerset", it is obviously true that if Taunton is in
Somerset and I am in Taunton implies I am in Somerset if of the form a
implies b and b implies c and therefore a implies c, whereas the argument
I am the father of x and x is the father of y means I am the father of y,
clearly does not follow in the same way because the relationship is not
a transitive one with respect to implication. But all of this should be
already clear to the reader, and these comments are intended merely as
reminders.

      One has to be careful about using formal arguments for factual
information which do not have the same structure as the formal structure.
Equally, in any sort of factual discussion one has to be careful about
fallacious arguments. Thus we may find examples like "If the (clean-
shaven) barber in the village shaves everyone except those who shave
themselves", if we ask who shaves the barber the answer cannot sensibly
be given because the argument has been stated paradoxically, which suggests
that he both shaves and does not shave himself at the same time. We have,
of course, excluded the possibility, by definition, of his being clean-
shaven; we recognise here merely that certain apparently valid arguments
can often cloak logical fallacies.

      So much for deduction (we have already devoted several chapters to
deductive systems). It is the process of drawing out what is inherent
in a set of assumptions, by logical argument, which may be formal and
concerned with the semantics, i.e. the meaning of the terms being used.
Whatever the deductive procedure involved, the result is a set of factual
statements about that part of the world which in science we are trying to
describe, and these factual statements can be the source of observation
which is designed to test their accuracy.

      It is true in fact that either the assumptions or the statements which
follow logically from the assumptions can both be tested for their empirical
veracity. Obviously science is concerned with collecting true statements
whether they are particular or general, and the point about scientific
method is to try to discover whether a statement is true or not.

      In a sense the process of observation is the most characteristic of
scientific processes since it is systematic observation, and this includes
experimentation, which one thinks of most readily when one thinks of
practical science. The fact that the observations might be well controlled,
either by the design of the experiment and by the use of suitable
statistical controls or whether by suitable apparatus to isolate certain
variables or whether by increasing the power of observation by a microscope
or telescope, does not alter the fact that observation is the critical
method by which the truth of statements is tested empirically.

INDUCTION

      The second stage (this in no sense implies a priority in reality, as
either deduction or induction could come first) of scientific method starts
from observation and goes through the process of induction, which is
sometimes characterised by the name inductive logic. This aims to arrive
at generalisations which are the hypotheses which are broken down into
assumptions which are the starting point for deduction. The following

diagram represents the two processes and their relationship:-

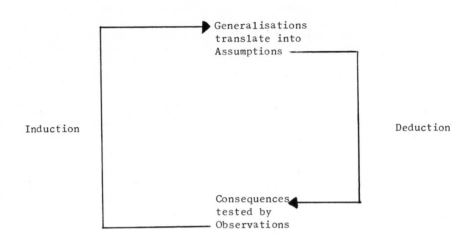

    The process of induction is that of generalising on the particular
and is therefore in some sense the opposite of deduction which is
particularising from the general. Like deduction, it is dependent on
language since knowledge can hardly be thought of as knowledge unless it is
communicable and therefore capable of being stated in some sort of language,
whether symbolic or otherwise, and has the added ingredient, in the case of
induction, of being factual. The basis on which the generalisations are
made is observation. This is an important point because deduction can
cater for statements which refer to nothing in reality at all. Hence much
of mathematics, and certainly potential mathematics such as, for example,
eight-dimensional geometry, and much of logical argument need not refer to
anything that is actually observable, whereas inductive generalisations
are about what is, in fact, observed. Therefore it is not purely linguistic,
it is also "factual".

    An inductive argument would be one of the form "I have seen one duck
and it is white, I have seen two ducks and they are both white, I shall
assume that all ducks are white". We are very careful to say in making
the inductive generalisation that a duck is defined independently of its
colour, otherwise it would be <u>logically true</u> to say ducks are white, and
anything that was in every other way a duck but some other colour than
white would be regarded as not a duck. It is clear that there is no point
in making observations about things which are already logically or
semantically determined. Scientific statements have to be verifiable.
Another way of saying the same thing is to say that science only deals in
testable statements. If you cannot invalidate a statement, it is not
testable. This does not mean that we want to invalidate every statement,
only that if it is not capable of being invalidated, it is not an
empirical statement.

The difficulty of course, with the inductive argument is that it is always uncertain (although hopefully probabilistic), we can never be sure that we have found a true inductive generalisation. There is no way in which we can see all ducks, or be sure that we have seen all ducks, and if we take a typical logician's point of view and talk about seeing all ducks at all times t, which means all the past and all the future as well, then it is clearly impossible to test such a statement. But even if we take the present time alone, there is no way in which we can be sure that we have seen every duck and as a result, of course, all empirical statements can reasonably be said to be dubitable; one could be wrong about the facts they assert.

It should be noticed that the form of these empirical statements is of the kind "If ... then ---" where the first gap "..." is filled by the inductive generalisation and the second gap "---" is filled by the deductive inference. These two interact sometimes in a haphazard way in scientific argument, but essentially it is the integration of inductive and deductive inference, coupled with systematic well-controlled observation, that provides the factual basis for scientific model building.

When we talk about scientific model building, we leave it free to the model builder to use whatever building bricks he likes. The building bricks of numbers has led to a huge edifice of mathematics which is clearly applicable to a very large number of things where quantification applies. There is also a whole field of activity where one is more interested in relationships, particularly logical relationships, where the development of logical models is more appropriate, and many aspects of knowledge where ordinary linguistic descriptions are more appropriate.

When we used the word 'mathematics', we did not mean to imply mathematics was only concerned with numbers or quantification. Mathematics is not easy to define precisely, but much of mathematics has been concerned with number and the quantification that goes with number, and much of the world of physics, for example, has been amenable to that sort of descriptive model, but not all. Some parts of mathematics deal with physical relations, logic or other precise statements which are not numerical.

Model building is essentially part of the scientific process as is the interpretations we place on models, as we have made clear, make them theories. The model is in a sense an abstract structure concerned with relationships etc., whereas the interpretation we place on the model makes it into an empirical theory. This relationship between model and theory is rather similar to the relationship between induction and deduction.

SCIENCE IN ACTION

We will now try to exhibit the activity of the scientist by a caricature, or a sort of fairy story which has been found useful in expounding a description of the scientist at work.

Let us suppose we have a visitor from another planet coming to the Earth, having had a good training in scientific method and therefore being familiar with deductive and inductive inferences as well as systematic observation and well-controlled experiments, and he is sent to Earth to try to find out, in some particular location, say Beaconsfield, what time the shopkeepers open their shops in the morning and what time they close them at night. He knows from the start that he can only observe so many shop-keepers, therefore he carries out what statisticians call a <u>random sample</u>.

He knows that he cannot ask questions of the shopkeepers because they may not tell him the truth, and since we are talking by analogy with science, a physicist cannot ask a particle which he is observing what its velocity and position in space is, for obvious reasons. Therefore he arrives on the Earth, sets up his observation post and observes, say on Monday morning, that they arrive at 9 a.m. and go at 5 p.m. He observes the same on Tuesday and makes the obvious inductive inference that every day is the same. By deduction he then concludes that if every day is the same, tomorrow will be the same, therefore Wednesday will be 9 a.m. to 5 p.m. also. He in fact finds that on Wednesday they work from 9 a.m. to 1 p.m. and therefore this invalidates his hypothesis, and he has to think of another one. He could then suggest that the repetition which he is looking for is exemplified by 9 to 5, 9 to 1, and one sees very clearly at this point what science (and all objective analysis) is about. It is about repetitive patterns which can be observed in the environment. Where we get precise repetition we call the system <u>deterministic</u> and where we fail to find precise repetition, which is in most empirical cases (although we sometimes get fairly near to it) then we are talking about <u>statistical</u> systems. What of course is needed is the ability to <u>forecast</u> with respect to the repetitions.

Our observer returns on Thursday and finds it is 9 to 5, Friday is 9 to 5, so far so good, but on Saturday they work from 9 to 5 again which upsets this hypothesis and it is only a matter of time before he hits on a seven-day cycle, after observing that they do not turn up at all on Sunday. But even this seven-day cycle is not wholly precise as he discovers on the first Bank Holiday he reaches, assuming he was not confused by arriving on a Bank Holiday in the first place.

After several years in Beaconsfield, and it would take him that amount of time, he discovers that the cycle is more nearly a 365-day cycle, but even this is not exactly accurate because Leap Year happens every fourth year and this is the source of a great deal of confusion to him, because the first time he meets Leap Year he might easily think that he had made a mistake in his counting. He would have to stay at least two Leap Years, probably three, before he begins to see that Leap Year is something which happens every fourth year, an extra day is put into 365 making a 366-day year.

In the end it can clearly be seen that the only useful material the visitor has acquired is something which could be the basis of a "Visit Beaconsfield Bureau" to be set up on his own planet, and even this would be subject to error because he could not be sure after he returns to his own planet and says "Well, normally they open at 9 and close at 5" that on a Tuesday this is no longer true. In the second place, of course, he would only be giving a statistical statement about what the majority of people do in Beaconsfield (or what people do in Beaconsfield on the average) because all people do not open and shut their shops at the same time. There are important exceptions like off-licences which require a corollary to the general theory. Nor can he argue that what applies to Beaconsfield applies to any other part of England unless he has actually observed other parts of England. Nevertheless he is performing the vital

and basic act of forecasting or predicting – it is this which is the
essential part of our methodology.

The ability to generalise on data is only true to the extent that you
have sampled the data in the first place, this is a basic principle of
scientific method. So it can be seen from this that the scientist's role
is a fairly complicated one, in which he has got to be statistician,
logician, a very careful observer and documentor of facts and has got to
have a great deal of commonsense as well. Scientists working in specialised
fields do not always have all these qualities, but they are certainly needed
if we are going to apply science to a new field, as in our case to everyday
affairs and rational discourse.

IN GENERAL

What we have said about science is meant to be a straight-forward
account of the sort of steps needed to acquire information which is an
objective as we know we can get it. We accept the fact that we shall impose
personal experience, hunch and the like and must inevitably do so whether we
like it or not.

The most important point that we need to appreciate is the need for a
clear understanding of the nature of both the scientific model and the
theory. We shall now try to maintain the view that the precise approach
of a basically common-sense kind is applicable to knowledge generally and
by such methods we can and should investigate any systems whatever. Our
methodology is designed to produce similar results to the scientist. We can
predict, sometimes understand and sometimes control our environment as a
result of its efforts. Let us say a few words about these important matters.

Prediction is essentially the same as forecasting and involves knowing
(or having some reason to believe) or even just believing that if you
market a product then it will be bought in sufficient quantities to justify
the expense in providing both it and the necessary launching campaign. The
main point of our methodology is to try to provide the evidence for having
the reason to believe rather than merely believing.

The difference between prediction and understanding is a matter of
degree. If you say "If I give a patient medicine A for a spotty chin and
the spots go" then this entails a prediction, and if it happens regularly
it becomes a good prediction, even though I may have no idea why medicine A
has such an effect. All that matters is that it does have the desired
effect. If now I find medicine A has the opposite effect on spotty noses
(i.e. it makes them spottier) and I gradually accumulate more and more
evidence, I can begin to formulate a theory as to why medicine A has the
effect it has, and if this theory is highly confirmed, as in the case of
our visitor to Beaconsfield from another planet, so the feeling of
understanding begins to occur, and so we will say in the end, if the theory
seems to be correct, that we understand the use of medicine A. We mean
we have knowledge of a much greater range of predictability and have
established the principles – the theory – on which the predictions are
based.

From our ability, ideally to understand, or at the very least to
predict – if not absolutely at least better than chance – stems our ability
to control. We are enabled to control those aspects of our environment

covered by the theory – and the model or models.

We are thinking now of course of models of <u>any</u> system – including everyday life systems like a business house, and therefore of <u>any</u> theories that go with them. This is at the very core of all our subsequent discussions.

SUMMARY

Scientific method, which is the essential feature of our methodology, is composed of a number of stages and we have emphasised some of them:-

      1.   Collecting information

      2.   Deductive (logic) reasoning

      3.   Inductive (logic) reasoning

      4.   Formulating hypotheses

      5.   Deducing the consequences of hypotheses

      6.   Testing the hypotheses

Over and above all of these steps, we have to construct models and relate them to theories, where a model is a formalization of a theory, and a theory is an interpretation of a model.

We are also, in science, studying systems. Such models and theories have been used to refer to a whole variety of systems, such as brains and nervous systems, business houses and government departments, social and economic systems, and so on and so forth. In short, almost anything can for our purposes be thought of as a system and subsequently modelled.

EXERCISES

1. Write a brief note explaining the principles of scientific method.

2. What are:-

      concepts

      hypotheses

      generalizations

      axioms

      postulates?

3. Give an example of scientific method in action.

REFERENCES

BRAITHWAITE, R.B.   Scientific Explanation. Cambridge University
                         Press, 1953

COHEN, M. and   An Introduction to Logic. Routledge, 1963
NAGEL, E.

CHAPTER 8

INDUCTION AND HYPOTHESIS FORMATION

In this chapter we will take a more detailed look at the inductive process. We shall look at it not primarily as a philosopher nor mathematician, nor as a psychologist, but from the point of view of the debator who simply wants to get his thoughts clear. We have assumed that induction and deduction are <u>both</u> essential features of clear thinking (which is what we are assuming as being characteristic of the ideal scientist), and that our problem is to consider how they can be made readily available to our human thinkers.

It is convenient to think of induction with respect to various related forms such as Bayes Rule, Inverse Probability, etc. But over and above these corporately developed techniques it is convenient to think of induction as related to sequential processes in a fashion which is reminiscent of learning <u>by acquaintance</u>. It is also though convenient in some cases to think of induction as reminiscent of learning <u>by description</u>.

By learning by acquaintance we mean learning by direct experience of the environment. Learning by description on the other hand implies learning through signs and symbols and especially, of course, through language.

The kind of induction concerned with sequential analysis has, on the whole, been less emphasised than that concerned with atemporal induction, in the end perhaps because the two forms are not really different. It is rather a difference over the means by which the inductions are themselves derived.

Some of the principles involved in collecting data are relatively simple; the simplest is perhaps that of collecting conditional probabilities which refer to the sequence of events a, b, ..., n, coupled to some <u>measure</u> of their frequency of occurrence:

$$p(a/b) = m_1/n_1$$

$$p(a/bc) = m_2/n_2$$

$$p(ab/c) = m_3/n_3$$

$$p(a/bcd) = m_4/n_4$$

---

etc.

By taking longer and longer samples of sequences we can, by use of the measure of conditional probabilities, refer predictively to events of greater and greater length. This is one method of discovering sequential patterns. By such means, we can arrive at new concepts which have been derived from old, and empirical statements and hypotheses derived from concepts. By 'concept' here we mean, of course, much what we mean by a class. 'Green' and 'dog' are concepts, whereas empirical statements are expressions of propositions and propositional attitudes (or beliefs). 'That dog is green" is such a statement, and "all dogs are green" is a hypothesis.

Processes (or sets of events) which are to be thought of as identical, say, are so to be thought whether or not they are symbolised. When symbolised however, some details are omitted <u>from the symbolisation</u> (description) and as a result in general a problem handled purely in symbolic terms is necessarily less complete than one handled directly by acquaintance in terms of direct, non-verbal stimuli. Indeed in either case apparent identity can of course mask differences, and vice-versa.

We must next ask ourselves whether or not all inductive problems are tractable, in principle, in terms of such sequential methods. The answer is uncertain, but for human beings most problems come within the logical hypothetico-deductive (or inductive-deductive) and linguistic complex, and in principle, we can see how these could be handled. The fact that all the events (names) may have been collected before induction takes place does not destroy the sequential nature of the problem. But then, of course, as we have said, the induction itself is not dependent upon the manner of its construction.

EXAMPLES OF INDUCTIONS

Given an ordered set of numbers (i, j, ..., n), our problem is to derive certain general features, if any exist, that draw attention either to similarities between (different) subsets, or to differences between (similar) subsets. When, and if, we give meaning (add "semantic rules") to the members of the sets, interpreting them say as "number of people living in Paris", "number of men in the world", etc., we can proceed along more specific lines of search. Before we do this we should consider the general (abstract) case, where the members of the set can be ordered and the sets themselves can be ordered.

A partially ordered set is:-

$$a_1 > a_2 > \text{---} > a_n$$

or

$$a_1 \leqslant a_2 \leqslant \text{---} \leqslant a_n$$

and a partially ordered set of sets is similarly:-

$$S_1 > S_2 > \text{---} > S_m$$

etc.

where we are concerned with the principle of ordering, obvious in the case of the integers, where we have:-

$$1 \leqslant 2 \leqslant --- \leqslant n$$

etc.

A particular class of analysis by sets occurs if we partition the sets. We can now ask whether specific subsets are significantly different from each other and here statistical methods (see Chapter 9), such as the <u>Difference between Means</u>, <u>Significance of a Single Mean</u>, etc. occur as likely methods to use to answer the proposed questions. We could though ask whether such subsets are <u>correlated</u>. A whole host of statistical methods suggest themselves, as well as simpler heuristic equivalents. The undertaking in general, is indeed, as in the first case, hopelessly uneconomic unless we have some starting "insight" or "heuristic".

If we examine all the possible relationships implied by the above, for even fairly small sets $\overset{30}{\underset{i1}{\times}} S_i$, say, (where $\times$ merely indicates a non-ordered collection of sets), it is clearly an uneconomic undertaking. So as in ordinary scientific research, we formulate hypotheses (heuristics) and test them by the means used above.

The second type of analysis which is obviously relevant is of a stochastic kind. We can consider sequences 1, 2, ..., n at a time of either whole sets or any of the subsets. Such conditional probabilistic stochastic processes are called Finite Markov Chains. Given conditional probability tables and a tree-structure which represents the choices and probabilities we can represent a whole set of problems which can be made more and more complex, by the following conditions:-

1. The choice of a route and its cost may itself change as a function of use.

2. A deterministic problem involving costs, say, may be a probabilistic problem based on uncertainties.

3. Information may be incomplete, even probabilities not all known.

The Dynamic programming technique, which is in a sense a generalisation on stochastic processes, uses the Calculus of Variations for a deterministic (continuous variable) case, and Dynamic Programming for the Stochastic Case. Where the game is a Minimax procedure, as in Games Against Nature, the problem reduces to that of a standard linear programme.

We shall try next to provide a link between the arguments leading by way of concept formation to hypothesis formation.

<u>HYPOTHESIS FORMATION AND INDUCTION</u>

Having concepts and names for the classes to which they belong, or for their collective properties, we can conjoin such concepts and express them as empirical propositions.

We can say, for example, that "some dogs are white" and provided only that the class words 'dog' and 'white' are sufficiently defined, then we can acquire evidence to support (or not) such a proposition.

Evidence can be of the form, " I know some dogs (one dog) and they are (it is) white", and this is sufficient. If the proposition had been "all dogs are white", then, of course, such supporting evidence would be insufficient, and only one non-white dog would be sufficient to disprove the hypothesis.

The problem we have in mind now is primarily that of performing induction and relating that inductive process specifically to hypothesis formation.

We can continue to think of the fairly rough distinction we have made between spatial and temporal extrapolation. So, to take the temporal sequence first, we may consider a set of events depicted by the letters A, B, ..., N. We may now consider the conditional probabilities of one event with respect to the next, e.g.

$$p(A/B)$$

is the probability of B given A and we may supply a measure such as:-

$$p(A/B) = m(= \tfrac{3}{4} \text{ say})$$

where $\tfrac{3}{4}$ is simply the Laplacian probability of B occurring, given that A has occurred; all this being in the light of past experience.

Consider now the sequence of events depicted by the following symbols:-

ABCADABCABCADABCABABACACABDBACABAA

We can construct a set of conditional probability tables for events of length 2 (over only two successive events in time) as follows:-

	A	B	C	D
A	1/13	7/13	3/13	2/13
B	4/9	0	4/9	1/9
C	7/7	0	0	0
D	2/3	1/3	0	0

Table 1.

This clearly implies that given C, for example, A may definitely be expected to follow. From such a table we can, albeit tentatively, draw conclusions about necessary and contingent relations, e.g.

> Given C, A necessarily follows, and
> given D, A contingently follows,
> twice as often as B.

We can also consider events three at a time so we could have, based
on the same events, tables which, given A, B, C or D, shows the frequency
of AA, AB. ... etc. following. Also given AA, AB, ... etc. the frequency
of A, B, ... etc. following could be tabulated. From here we can go on to
consider events of length 4, 5, ... etc.

But let us merely emphasise that this form of sequential analysis is
appropriate to conditional probability tables of length n, and view the
whole matter from a different point of view. The second point of view
involves many-channelled inputs, and the occurrence of individuals.
Suppose we consider eight successive moments of time t_0 - t_7 for a 4-channel
input C_1 - C_4.

	t_0	t_1	t_2	t_3	t_4	t_5	t_6	t_7
C_1		A		A	A		A	A
C_2		B	B	B		B	B	B
C_3	C	C		C			C	C
C_4	D		D				D	

Table 2.

We now see how the concept of individuals arises. It is clear that
(ABC) could be a part of a coherent whole. So that in the three appearances
of (ABC), all the features occur together. The events A, B, and C could
here be interpreted as properties x, y and z and as a result capable of
being interpreted as three appearances of some individual.

Let us consider an example, a dog. A dog is an individual with
properties such as being four-legged, tailed, two-eyed, etc. ...
Name these properties x, y, z, etc. and then we can think of (x, y, z) as
a simplified description of an individual, such as a dog.

In the same way as a dog can present itself, so the class of all
objects, such as chairs, tables, pictures, etc. can be so exemplified. The
problem, which can be treated for expository purposes, in a simplified form,
involving only an unrealistically few properties can be dealt with in terms
as complex as are made necessary by circumstances, or indeed as simple as
circumstances demand.

The argument is that successive events incorporate sets 1, 2, ..., n,
at a time, and also simultaneous events incorporate sets of 1, 2, ..., m, at

a time, involving specific sets (or individuals) which are the basic material of inductive inference. The next step is to show that such inductive arguments as: "given A, B will follow with probability p" or "given A and B, the probability is that the individual K, where K is the set (x, y, z) is present, has probability p". The probability measure may not be available, and the result is that a general uncertainty must remain without necessarily having a particular measure.

It is not difficult to see the principle on which such inductive inferences can be based; so far it is no more than a conditional probability system which can operate over both space and time, and giving a measure to the conditional probabilities.

We now ask the question, does C "belong to" ("is a property of") AB or not? We may say 'yes' in answer if p(AB/C) = 1 and not otherwise. We must distinguish here between properties which are manifestly part of the same object or individual, and those which are not, but are either necessarily or contingently connected.

Our technique so far merely counts properties, and it must also identify individuals. So it should name xyz as X for example where:-

$$X = df.xyz$$

In assessing whether an object is an individual we shall need conventions, since we might for example be unsure as to whether the bell on a bicycle is a part of the bicycle or not. We might indeed have to change our views as to what composes an individual and what does not. However, while this is a point to remember, it is also one that can fairly easily be solved in any particular context, in much the same way as we can reduce many-valued to 2-valued logic by suitable constraints.

So far, we have talked of induction as identifiable with the collecting in some form of conditional probabilities; we must now go beyond this to the more general interpretative statements which we know are also a vital part if induction. Look at some more examples:-

"All cats are white"

"All cats meet in Bristol in June"

"All Irish prople are born with two eyes and two ears"

etc.

Our problem is now not only to develop methods for performing an inductive check, but also to develop methods for both expressing that induction in language, and interpreting other people's inductions in language. We must now look at the matter as a linguistic problem and this takes us into the field of what we have called "Non-Sequential Analysis".

NON-SEQUENTIAL ANALYSIS AND HEURISTIC METHODS

In talking of thinking, we tend to consider the creative activity of deriving hypotheses or "seeing" appropriate deductive inferences that can be made in a problem-solving context. Whereas simple learning, like habit formation, can be thought of as occurring sequentially, we do not as frequently draw attention to the sequential processes in thinking or problem-solving. Perhaps the main reason for this is that whereas we may acquire the information as a temporally ordered process, the basis for such inductions as are made are usually independent of how the information is collected. Let us look for a moment at some well known work in this field.

Newell, Shaw and Simon in the U.S.A. made a detailed study of what they called creative thinking which dealt with those aspects of problem solving which required originality, as opposed to explanation, definition, remembering, etc., all of which come into the day-to-day problem-solver's activities.

Their work has great importance because they were able to show by heuristic techniques (much like the use of inductions) how short cuts in routes to goals (solution) could be achieved by assumptions that facilitated the problem-solving process.

The manner of approach is simple enough in principle and we can illustrate what is called the heuristic principle. If you are an architect and asked to design a building and the building is intended for use as offices, then you can omit consideration of previous designs for private houses, garages, etc., whereas when performing the task algorithmically (by a decision procedure), you might consider every possible building type however irrelevant.

Newell, Shaw and Simon used what they called solution generators, trial-and-error learning and then the formation of hypotheses, often involving working backwards from the solution (deducing sub-goals from goals) where the problem was, for example, to find some proof. They used verifying processes to justify their steps and in this they made a distinction between the context of discovery (cf. induction) and the context of justification (cf. deduction). They were concerned with simulating principles for theorem-proving, and they used the human-like means of substitution and the like. We are more concerned with the delineation (through language) of a problem for which appropriate heuristics have to be sought i.e. hypothesis formation by induction.

Heuristics are, as we have said, generalised rules of thumb or hypotheses and can be used in various ways. Newell, Shaw and Simon simulated the operations of the human problem-solver, but Dr. Samuel at I.B.M. synthesised his heuristics by a set of polynomials. These polynomials could be adjusted by experience. Others have used heuristics to solve aspects of the line balancing problem, and other have used them for decision making. Furthermore, a somewhat similar procedure was followed for scheduling on a production line.

As distinct from these piecemeal efforts, we wish to see heuristics in use in all these ways, operating together, and heuristic generation to occur as appropriate to the solution of a problem.

We must of course remember to distinguish between adaptive and non-adaptive heuristics. This in fact reflects a distinction that is similar to that between "taking a set of Hypotheses" as opposed to testing and, if necessary, modifying those Hypotheses as a result of circumstances; or indeed even setting "new" Hypotheses.

It is in these terms that we see problem solving as a synthetic undertaking. Problem solving is the ability to construct or reconstruct methods used to solve problems and learn new methods and strategies by experience as circumstances demand, especially through verbal description.

We have been careful to distinguish the process of discovering induction (e.g. counting, sequential and non-sequential analysis, Bayes Rule) and the inductive statement itself (the inductive generalisation). This is a type of curve-fitting or pattern recognition operation and we must distinguish the method by which we arrive at the "best-fit", and the formula which we actually adopt as a result of the fitting. Now let us turn to the problem of induction as it has been tackled in a more traditional manner.

INDUCTION AND BEHAVIOUR

To make our underlying assumptions clear it should be said that we are assuming that inside the organism we have the apparatus of language, which is built up through experience, like other learned skills. We assume that language, as we grow up, is increasingly used to refer to our experiences of the external world, and operates together with certain "physiological" or "psychological" occurrences called 'images'.

Language is both descriptive of, and also part of (since it is self-referential) the internal conceptual model (schema); we have an internal model of the world about us and of ourselves, and we as humans are assumed to be aware of words and images often in complex associations. At this level the "mental processes" are thought of as fairly crude and dependent upon associative principles. But underlying these molar "mental processes" are the molecular neural processes which make it all possible. We are certainly unaware of our neurons firing in their various complex patterns, but there is reason to believe that this is what is actually occurring. Since the effect of these complex firing patterns is to suggest a mechanism which worked as if it were a complex and sophisticated mathematical process; it seems reasonable therefore to try to both synthesise and simulate it. We can here use these same mathematical processes for both; they have become, in effect, descriptions of a fraction of the nervous system. The nervous system at this stage could be called 'conceptual' rather than real, although this is a difference which can only be one of degree.

BELIEF FORMATION

We shall now consider belief formation (we shall be discussing this later and in more detail under the name Pragmatics) as the psychological process which is subserved by induction. We are thinking here of beliefs in the same sense as Hypotheses (some of which are heuristics) and being in need of confirmation by empirical evidence. We write:-

$$c(h,e)$$

to be read "the degree of confirmation of the hypothesis h by evidence e" and we will generally identify this with some value p such that $0 \leqslant p \leqslant 1$, so that

$$c(h,e) = p$$

It is clear that evidence in the objective sense will not always apply to our personal beliefs, but will in general apply to rational beliefs, since this is really what we mean by 'evidence' and 'rational'; but we shall need to state some satisfactory criteria for 'rational beliefs'. In doing so, we are moving into well-trod territory, and we must be careful to point out again that our motives in doing so are not always necessarily those of mathematicians, philosophers and logicians who may be interested primarily in mathematical generality or epistemological clarity: both of these things are of interest. Our interest comes somewhere in between the two and involves the pragmatic consideration of acquiring realistic human reasoning abilities.

We shall devote the next section to a very brief summary of the difficulties met so far in the fields of induction and inductive logic.

INDUCTIVE LOGIC

Inductive logic is a system for providing both evidence for the confirmation of inductive inferences. If we say:-

"All dogs are blue"   ... (1)

then if I have seen 256 dogs all of which were blue and no dog that is non-blue, this constitutes evidence to support (1) above.

Difficulties occur in inductive logic for various reasons. The first difficulty arises because some people have felt that seeing a blue non-dog is also evidence for (1). So we must ask ourselves does a particular motor car being red in any way confirm that all dogs are blue?

We shall waste no time over the more technical points of inductive logic, but say merely that a certain support, primarily for syntactical reasons, has been found for the view that such statements as "All dogs are blue" is confirmed by such statements as:-

"Most motor cars are red"   ... (2)

We shall say, however, following the famous Nicode's condition that (2) is irrelevant to (1). We should mention that the problem of relevance as met above is also involved with the use of material implication, which we have already discussed. Material implication it will be remembered is defined as follows:-

$$p \supset q = df \sim p \ v \ q \qquad \qquad ... (3)$$

which is intended to be interpreted as "if ... then ---". This use may be defensible definition of material implication in a syntactical theory, but entails as we have already said that, where p and q are interpreted as statements, one statement may imply another statement even though they are not in any way connected with each other. This is certainly contrary to its use in most human argument.

We shall now say that a statement S_1 is relevant to another statement S_2 if it has a common subject or predicate or if it can be linked by a common subject or predicate.

According to such a notation of relevance any statement directly relevant to (1) must be one of the following form:-

$$\text{"All dogs are ---"} \qquad \qquad \ldots (3)$$

$$\text{"--- are blue"} \qquad \qquad \ldots (4)$$

and similar statements prefixed by the existential operator, i.e. which refer to a class with at least one member, rather than to a universal class. Furthermore, any statement is indirectly relevant to (1) if it has a form which can be traced by the same associative principle such as in (3) and (4). For example "All cats are white" is indirectly relevant to (1) if there exist a finite number of statements of a similar kind linked to it, one at least of which involves the terms 'dog' and 'blue'.

The other vital point about relevance is presumably about causal relations. If, for example, other species of dogs like some wild dogs are thought to be biologically related to domesticated dogs, and if they are blue, then this might be thought to be confirmatory evidence for (1). So we must accept the fact that there may exist causal chains which are not necessarily descriptively or logically complete, although in principle they are capable of being completed. It is assumed, of course, that all such statements as (3) and (4) will not be of the same level of generality; this does not effect the argument.

Briefly we shall now deal with some other related matters. We should separate credibility from probability. We will say that credibility includes probability, and that whenever a statement can be supported by (or confirmed by) an objective (relevant) probability then it comes within our concept on confirmation. It is clear, as a matter of human psychology, that human beings often regard statements as credible on non-objective bases (even indeed though they may be correct) and will sometimes support credible statements on objective probabilistic bases (even though they may be incorrect).

This is inevitable and we accept this as true of any system which is to operate under conditions of uncertainty. We shall however use confirmation as a necessary condition for acceptance, and in general say that the extent of one is proportional to the extent of the other, subject to "risk analysis" being used.

We shall say that inductive generalisations are confirmed by other specific methods such as Bayes Rule, stimulus sampling, Markov Chains, etc., and that this coupled with work on Explanation and Factual Support are all part and parcel of the justificatory process.

We should say here that we are tempted to draw a distinction between confirming theories or hypotheses on one hand and providing a basis for

decision making on the other. This distinction though is in some measure
contaminated by our other main distinction between formal (normative) and
factual (behaviouristic) accounts of decision making. This is especially
important if we compare concept formation as a process of manufacturing
new concepts with Bayes decision taking which presupposes a whole universe
of possibilities from the start.

The above distinction is important on grounds of utility since it
seems that in using heuristic methods, the stimulus-sampling, Markov net
type of approach, which allows easily for the addition of new concepts, is
also more economic to use.

Arguing either from a true (certain) or probabilistic datum, is
another alternative worth mentioning, and worth remembering. Clearly no
empirical data are certain and although we could argue, that a datum could
be a proposition that "has some degree of rational credibility on its own
account, independently of any argument derived from other propositions",
this is not too easy an idea to use in practice, nor obviously useful. This
anyway is hardly an important point for us since our own view is more
nearly that of C.S. Peirce, that we have a set of more or less coherent and
more or less confirmed beliefs, which we regard, in their totality, as our
knowledge and use to provide a basis for inference making. We will accept
therefore probabilistic data as a basis for induction and as a result must
knowingly expose ourselves to the danger of drawing false (improbable)
conclusions.

Heuristics can be manufactured by induction, either by "hunch" or by
description. Whichever way the heuristic is acquired, and we have
discussed many such methods, we are also involved, as we have said,
explicitly in confirmation.

First of all, we may have heuristics which refer to events with "low
risk" and these can be confirmed by experience, at leisure, provided always
urgency is also low. If urgency is high and if risk is high then
confirmation may need to be replaced by (computer) simulation of the events.
This, of course, eliminates the other two categories where urgency is low
and risk is high, or urgency is high and risk low, where behaviour may be
trial-and-error or on the basis of hypothesis, but where action is
immediately needed.

SUMMARY

Induction and inductive logic form a natural link between the
deductive systems described in the first six chapters and scientific
method described in the last chapter. It also forms a bridge with the
remainder of the book which is rather more philosophically orientated.

We could make the most direct link with deductive systems by likening
inductive logic to probabilistic logic. It is indeed the case that a
logistic system which involves a probabilistic inference (or more generally
an uncertain inference) is exactly the same as an inductive system.

Induction itself is much like hypothesis formation as we have seen in this chapter and is therefore closely related to human thinking. It is near the truth to say that a human being is rather like an inductive logical machine. The formation of beliefs, which we shall be discussing later, is very much an inductively based process and is quite basic to pragmatics.

EXERCISES

1. Define (even informally, and without necessarily attempting great precision) 'induction' and compare it with 'inductive logic'. Is there a difference between the two terms? If there is, what is it?

2. Suppose a series of events occurs which we can depict by using alphabetic letters as labels of these events in the following sequence:-

   ababcabdabcabcabdababaabcabcaab

   Can you derive any inferences about the future occurrence of a, b, c and d or any combinations of these letters?

3. It is worth having a try at distinguishing heuristic from algorithmic modes of reasoning. A comparison with induction and deduction could be helpful. Try and write down an answer which you might give in answer to a casual enquiry.

REFERENCES

CARNAP, R.   An axiom system for Inductive Logic. In
                             The Philosophy of Rudolph Carnap (The Library of
                             Living Philosophers) ed. P.A. Schilipp.
                             Open Court 973 - 979

HINTIKKA, J. and   Aspects of Inductive Logic. North Holland, 1966
SUPPES, P.

MORONEY, M.J.   Facts from Figures. Pelican Books, 1951

VON WRIGHT, G.H.   The Logical Problem of Induction. Macmillan, 1957

CHAPTER 9

PROBABILITY AND STATISTICS

In this chapter we shall describe briefly certain aspects of rational thinking and decision taking, which are based on probability and statistics. We shall therefore start with a brief summary of probability and later give an even briefer summary of statistics.

We have no intention of providing here an introductory text on probability or statistics. We shall, however, give some background ideas to help with our brief summary of what follows.

Let p be the probability favourable to the occurrence of some event A, say the probability of a coin coming down heads in one toss. Then let q be the opposite probability. i.e. that the coin will not come down heads, which is of course tails in a two-valued case such as the toss of a coin. We say p_A = m/n where n is the total number of trials and m is the number of times A has occurred and where p_A is "the probability of A occurring".

We can rigorously define a probability so that for indefinitely large value of n, the individual independent possibilities tend to certain limits. In the case of tossing a "proper" (unbiased) coin, by definition each side is equally likely to appear uppermost on each toss. The limits are p_A = 1/2 and q_A = 1/2

$$p = m/_n \qquad \qquad \qquad \text{... (1)}$$

and since

$$p + q = 1$$

$$q = 1 - p = 1 - m/_n = \frac{n - m}{n} \qquad \text{... (2)}$$

We extend this argument to a series of tosses (trials) so that the probability of, say, ten heads occurring on the run i.e. hhhhhhhhhh is given by $(\frac{1}{2} \times \frac{1}{2} \times \frac{1}{2} \times \frac{1}{2} \times \frac{1}{2} \times \frac{1}{2} \times \frac{1}{2} \times \frac{1}{2} \times \frac{1}{2} \times \frac{1}{2}) = \frac{1}{1,024}$. This illustrates the use of the <u>multiplication theorem</u>, where independent probabilities p_1, p_2, ..., p_n are multiplied together to find the total probability of a certain event. q here, say, is the event not occurring and $q = 1,023/_{1,024}$ since $p + q = 1$ which is an instance of the <u>addition theorem</u>, which adds the probabilities of the total number of mutually exclusive alternatives that apply in the definition of any event.

We can now supply an axiom set for probability theory and from this derive Bayes Rule which is one method which is relevant to the sort of inductive arguments which we must know how to use.

THE CALCULUS OF PROBABILITY

Let us write p/h for the phrase "the probability of p given h". The following axiom set is then sufficient to provide a calculus.

1. Given p and h, p/h is uniquely defined.

2. p/h lies in the closed internal (0,1) for all real numbers, i.e. $0 \leqslant p/h \leqslant 1$

3. If h $\rightarrow$ p, then p/h $= 1$, where $\rightarrow$ means "(logically) implies" and where 1 means 'certainty .

4. If h $\rightarrow \sim$ p, then p/h $= 0$, where 0, means 'impossibility.'

5. p . q/h $=$ q/p.h $=$ q/h x p/q.h

6. pvq/h $=$ p/h $+$ q/h $-$ p.q/h

We should note that p/h is a relationship between p and h, where p and h can be thought of as two propositions.

From axiom 5, we can derive the principle of Inverse Probability, which is:-

$$p/q.h = \frac{p/h \times q/p . h}{q/h} \qquad \dots (3)$$

(3) follows directly from axiom 5 by simply dividing each side of the second part of the formula by q/h.

Axiom 5, sometimes called the conjunctive axiom can be very simply exemplified. What is the chance of drawing two hearts in succession without replacement from an ordinary pack of cards? p is the statement "the first card is a heart", q is the statement "the second card is a heart" and h is the fact that there are 13 hearts in a set of 52 cards.

$$p/h = 1/4$$

q/p.h   12/51

$$p.q/h = \tfrac{1}{4} \times \frac{12}{51} = \frac{3}{51}$$

Axiom 6, the disjunctive axiom, can be similarly exemplified. So the above example, the chance that at least one card is a heart is given by

$$\tfrac{1}{4} + \tfrac{3}{4} - \tfrac{1}{4} . \frac{12}{51} = \frac{48}{51}$$

Inverse probability is interpreted in terms of the above example as giving the probability p in the event that q is known to occur. So for the example of choosing two successive hearts from a pack of cards we get

$$p/q.h = \frac{\frac{1}{4} \times \frac{12}{51}}{\frac{3}{4}} = \frac{4}{51}$$

We can interpret inverse probability in more general terms so we say that if p is a theory and q is some statement relevant to p, then we can think of p as being changed by q (either in terms of confirmation or infirmation). The special case where $p \rightarrow q$ and therefore where $q/p . h = 1$ reduces (3) to

$$p/q.h = \frac{p/h}{q/h} \qquad \qquad \ldots (4)$$

The next step is to derive Bayes Rule since this is the basis of so many decision processes and much precise thought, some of which we shall be discussing briefly. Bayes Rule is usually written

$$p_r/q.h = \frac{q/(p_r.h).p_r/h}{\prod\limits_{1}^{n} q(p_r.h).p_r/h} \qquad \qquad \ldots (5)$$

Where $p_1, p_2, \ldots, p_n$ are n mutually exclusive possibilities one of which is known to be true, and where $\prod$ means "the product of" i.e. $\prod\limits_{}^{3} y_i = y_1 \times y_2 \times y_3$ a convenient alternative rendering of (5) is

$$P(H/D) = \frac{P(D/H)P(H)}{P(D)} \qquad \qquad \ldots (5A)$$

where P(D/H) is the conditional probability of an event D given another event H, and where $P(H) \neq 0$.

In terms of our above example of drawing two hearts in succession, for H = "drawing one heart" and D = "drawing a second heart", Bayes in (5A) gives:-

$$P(H/D) = \frac{\frac{12}{51} \cdot \frac{1}{4}}{\frac{1}{4}} = \frac{12}{51}$$

This gives the conditional probability of the second card being a heart granted the first card actually was a heart. We say P(H/D) is a posteriori probability, while P(H) is an a priori probability.

An example of Bayes Rule may help. Two people start tossing a coin, without having given it a prior examination. They agree after one toss (which is heads) that it either has two heads (A_1) or is normal (A_2), so they agree that the situation is defined by

$$P(B/A_1), \ P(B/A_2)$$

for the proposition B which refers to A_1 and A_2 and describes the outcome of tosses.

If a tail occurs $P(B/A_1) = 0$ and if all tosses give heads $P(B/A_1) = 1$, $P(B/A_2) = \frac{1}{2}n$ in any case.

Now suppose first five tosses yield hhtht then $P(B/A_1) = 0$ and $P(B/A_2) = 1/_{32}$ But the two people may disagree about the possibilities of the probabilities (a priori probabilities) A_1 and A_2.   One of them (X) says A_1 and A_2 are equally likely while the other (Y) thinks A_2 is twice as likely as A_1.

i.e.

$$X: \ \ P(A_1) = \ P(A_2) = \tfrac{1}{2}$$

$$Y: \ \ P(A_1) = \tfrac{1}{3} \ ; \ P(A_2) = \frac{2}{3}$$

Now after five tosses the evidence B allows them to reconsider these initial notions about A_1 and A_2.

Bayes Theorem is:—

$$P(A_1/B) = \frac{P(A_1) . P(B/A_1)}{P(A_1)P)B/A_1) + \ ... \ + \ P(A_m)P(B/A_m)}$$

gives

$$P(A_1/B) \ = \ \frac{0}{0 \quad P(A_2)/32} \ = 0$$

for both X and Y and the case for A_2 has collapsed i.e. the coin does <u>not</u> have two heads.

But if B gave the first 5 tosses as hhhhh, this means, by Bayes:—

$$P(A_1/B) \ = \ \frac{P(A_1)}{P(A_1) + P(A_2)/32}$$

Then X: $P(A_1/B) = \dfrac{32}{33}$; $P(A_2/B) = \dfrac{1}{33}$

Y: $P(A_1/B) = \dfrac{32}{34}$; $P(A_2/B) = \dfrac{2}{34}$

So in fact there is little disagreement here between X and Y, and the possibility of the coin having two heads remains.

This example brings out clearly how the application of Bayes Rule (or Theorem) allows the easy change of a priori probabilities in the light of new evidence.   Not that in the above example the matter is wholly settled in the second case because a head may still occur.

Ward Edwards has designed a series of computer programs to test out the effectiveness of Bayes Rule in a man-machine interaction situation. He used a version of Bayes Rule that is a modification of (5) above. This version is called the odds-likelihood ratio form.

Given two hypotheses H_A and H_B and some datum D (comparable to h in the earlier part of the last section):-

$$P(H_A/D) = \frac{P(D/H_A) \; P(H_A)}{P(D)} \qquad \ldots (6)$$

Similarly for H_B, Bayes odds-likelihood ratio form is:-

$$P(H_B/D) = \frac{P(D/H_B) \; P(H_B)}{P(D)} \qquad \ldots (7)$$

Dividing (6) by (7) gives

$$\frac{P(H_A/D)}{P(H_B/D)} = \frac{P(D/H_A) \; P(H_A)}{P(D/H_B) \; P(H_B)} \qquad \ldots (8)$$

We will write (8) as

$$L_1 = L_0 \qquad \ldots (9)$$

L_0 is the ratio of the a priori probabilities for H_A and H_B, and L_1 gives the likelihood ratio, and $P(D/H_A)$ are both a posteriori probabilities. Only the likelihood ratios are needed for the application of Bayes Rule.

Ward Edwards uses this Bayesian property of aggregating information to set up a probabilistic information processing system which he called PIP. PIP works on the assumption that "men can serve as transducers for P(D/H)"; this means that given a situation where information is to be processed and predictions or diagnoses made, then the predictions are evaluated.

Ward Edwards made up a 50 page summary of the "imaginary history of the world from 1964 to 1975". It was such that eight hypotheses were plausible as a result. They were of the form:-

"Russia and China are about to attack North America".

Then at a later date additional information was supplied by sensors to the computer as a result of which the eight hypotheses would be re-assessed. Several likelihood ratios were assessed for each datum, and training occurred with the processing of vast amounts of information over a lengthy period.

The most important result to come out of this experiment was that PIP achieved a greater degree of certainty from the data than did the equivalent human group who acted much like a group of military or political

leaders might. The ad hoc human group was called POP, and two other
variants were called PEP and PUP respectively.

The results indicate clearly enough the advantages of using Bayesian
methods over human judgment. Since the time of Ward Edward's original work
a great deal more research has been done on applications of Bayes Rule
which makes its use in military and other decision processing absolutely
essential. Bayesian statistics is a method sometimes used for adaptive
stock control for this reason, and we might give some consideration to
Bayes Rule (as well as simpler methods like exponential smoothing) for
adaptive stock control of spares.

An example (of a military kind) makes clear one possible use of
Bayes Rule.

If X_1 is the decision to select missile A, and X_2 to select missile B,
where additional information has been acquired and where the possible
outcomes are a_1, a_2, a_3 and a_4.

We have, by Bayes, for any decision d_1 or d_2:-

$$\sum_{j=1}^{n} c_{1j} P(X/a_j) . P(a_j)$$

	a_1	a_2	a_3	a_4	X_1	X_2
d_1	10m	30m	0	0	2m	8m
d_2	0	0	110m	20m	12m	3m
$p(a_j)$	$\frac{1}{4}$	$\frac{1}{4}$	$\frac{1}{4}$	$\frac{1}{4}$		
$p(X_1/a_j)$	0.2	0.2	0.8	0.8		
$p(X_2/a_j)$	0.8	0.8	0.2	0.2		

$d_1 X_1$ is

$$\left[(10 \times 0.2 \times \tfrac{1}{4}) + (30 \times 0.2 \times \tfrac{1}{4}) + 0 + 0 \right] M = 2M$$

and similarly $d_1 X_2$, $d_2 X_1$ and $d_2 X_2$. If we sum the two minima in the X_1 and
X_2 columns, we have £5M as a total regret figure. Earlier the regret was
£10M and now with additional information (this means additional development
in an R and D phase) we have a £5M regret and can spend, as it turns out,
up to £5M to ensure an 80% probability of accuracy. We can, of course,
build up whole tables in this way.

We now look at Bayesian Models from a slightly different point of view. We can think of Bayesian Models as models of deliberation.

DECISION PROCESSING

In the first instance we define a desirability matrix as describing the ideal combination of events. For example, if we wish to have steak with chips, this will have a greater rating than having steak with boiled or roast potatoes. The desirability gives the relative weighting of some quality with respect to some others. Thus we might write a desirability matrix for steak in Column 1 with beef in Column 2, with chips in Row 1 and boiled in Row 2 and roast in Row 3. We shall assume that boiled and roast potatoes are equally acceptable to go with fish. We thus have:-

$$\begin{pmatrix} 1 & 0 \\ 0 & \frac{1}{2} \\ 0 & \frac{1}{2} \end{pmatrix} \qquad \text{--- (10)}$$

In practice, of course, an empirical analysis of tastes in a community might throw up something totally different. A matrix such as the following seems quite likely:-

$$\begin{pmatrix} .88 & .06 \\ .08 & .48 \\ .04 & .46 \end{pmatrix} \qquad \text{--- (11)}$$

Alternatively, and considering the idealized desirability matrix, we might have included negative numbers giving:-

$$\begin{pmatrix} 1 & -1 \\ -1 & 1 \\ -1 & 1 \end{pmatrix} \qquad \text{--- (12)}$$

where -1 means completely unacceptable.

Suppose now we think of the probability matrix as suggesting steak and fish as equally likely (we obviously do not control the choice). Then we have probability matrix

$$\begin{pmatrix} \frac{1}{2} & \frac{1}{2} \\ \frac{1}{2} & \frac{1}{2} \\ \frac{1}{2} & \frac{1}{2} \end{pmatrix} \qquad \text{--- (13)}$$

Now we multiply equivalent entries in the probability matrix (✻ stands for the unusual element-by-element form of multiplication) and one of the desirability matrices (we shall take the last of these).

$$\begin{pmatrix} 1 & -1 \\ -1 & 1 \\ -1 & 1 \end{pmatrix} \; ✻ \; \begin{pmatrix} \frac{1}{2} & \frac{1}{2} \\ \frac{1}{2} & \frac{1}{2} \\ \frac{1}{2} & \frac{1}{2} \end{pmatrix}$$

$$= \begin{pmatrix} \frac{1}{2} & \frac{-1}{2} \\ \frac{-1}{2} & \frac{1}{2} \\ \frac{-1}{2} & \frac{1}{2} \end{pmatrix}$$

Adding the rows gives

$$\begin{pmatrix} 0 \\ 0 \\ 0 \end{pmatrix}$$

Here no one choice of potatoes is better than any other in this case. If we had a desirability matrix:-

$$\begin{pmatrix} 0 & 1 \\ -1 & 1 \\ -1 & 0 \end{pmatrix} \qquad\qquad \text{--- (14)}$$

then we should have had:-

$$\begin{pmatrix} 0 & 1 \\ -1 & 1 \\ -1 & 0 \end{pmatrix} \; ✻ \; \begin{pmatrix} \frac{1}{2} & \frac{1}{2} \\ \frac{1}{2} & \frac{1}{2} \\ \frac{1}{2} & \frac{1}{2} \end{pmatrix}$$

$$
= \begin{pmatrix} 0 & \dfrac{1}{2} \\[2ex] \dfrac{-1}{2} & \dfrac{1}{2} \\[2ex] \dfrac{-1}{2} & 0 \end{pmatrix}
$$

giving

$$
\begin{pmatrix} \dfrac{1}{2} \\[2ex] 0 \\[2ex] \dfrac{-1}{2} \end{pmatrix}
$$

so that now the choice of chip potatoes in Row 1 becomes the best choice according to this type of Bayes application.

We can of course deal just as well with events which are not equiprobable, and we can deal with desirabilities which are not completely specified. In any case, of course, as with all applications of probability theory, it seems that the greatest single difficulty lies in establishing the appropriate numerical probabilities.

The rationale of the technique is easy enough to understand since to put the matter crudely, highly desirable and very likely events are the first choice. Then we weigh desirability against probability of occurrence and leave out the undesirable and the unlikely. In other words, if I wish to eat a good meal at a good restaurant I would choose a very good meal at a very convenient restaurant as opposed to a superb meal at a hopelessly inconvenient one.

We shall not discuss further the technical apparatus which occur in the full range of possible applications. We can though make the point that such methods, which are closely related to forms of probabilistic logic, are open to all sorts of practical difficulties in application, although such difficulties are by no means insuperable.

Decision processing along these lines could be of use in distinguishing different options where effectiveness and cost are the two principle components.

The problem of accurate estimating of costs is not itself solved by such methods; for such estimating we need to look elsewhere - to simulation models, extrapolation from past records, some sort of curve-fitting procedure, or econometric models. Exactly the same argument applies to our next example of "Games Against Nature".

GAMES AGAINST NATURE

Another type of decision processing sometimes called "Games against Nature" are very similar to those we have just discussed. We consider various strategies under various conditions of uncertainty, subjective estimates of probability and the like. Here we come close to psychological theories and pragmatic models. It should be noted that we are assuming that "objective" and "subjective" probabilities are on a continuum, i.e. that probability is a special case of credibility.

To illustrate the viewpoint by a simple sort of example, consider that the rows of the following matrix represent states of nature which are all equally likely. Consider next the choice of a column you would make, being ignorant of which is the relevant row. Here is the matrix

$$\begin{pmatrix} -1 & 1 & 0 \\ 2 & 1 & 0 \\ -1 & -1 & 0 \end{pmatrix} \qquad \text{--- (15)}$$

If we use Laplace's strategy, we take the arithmetic mean of each column, and select the column with the highest mean; in this example, column 2 is thus selected.

If however, we were playing the optimist's strategy, we go for the column with the maximum payoff, and that gives column 1 as the solution. If you are a pessimist, you consider which column loses you least in the event of your being wrong, and the answer is now column 3.

A further factor which affects the strategy followed is the size of the units. If the integers about refer to single pounds (sterling) then your maximum loss is £1. If it referred to thousands of pounds, then you could lose £1,000. As the size of the prize and the risk goes up, so the decision may change along a sort of continuum between extreme optimism and extreme pessimism. Let us look at the matter again now explicitly as risk analysis.

RISK ANALYSIS

We shall indicate in quite simple terms the nature of risk analysis, since the ideas have already been partially explained. In intuitive terms, we are concerned with the taking of a risk, such as a gamble on a horse. Clearly we may be prepared to risk a few shillings and not worry if we lose; equally clearly if we are instructed to put several hundred pounds on a horse, we should worry considerably and, lacking any other information, we might be tempted to back the favourite, because of the odds which would imply a minimum risk. If we were allowed to back more than one horse we might put a substantial amount on three different ones in an attempt to minimize the risk entailed. We are supposing in this latter case that we are not so much concerned with winning - since we are being forced to place our bet - but are more concerned with avoiding losing, since we cannot really afford the money; the risk is really too great.

The above situation, which may occur in a whole variety of ways, is the key to such things as business investment, designing a new ship and other similar such activities. Our aim is to show how, while making a decision to carry out a business undertaking, we can minimize our risk.

First look at a simple example in matrix form:-

$$
\begin{array}{cc}
& B_1 \qquad\qquad B_2 \\
\begin{array}{c} A_1 \\[20pt] A \end{array} &
\left(
\begin{array}{cc}
0 & 100 \\[20pt]
1 & 1
\end{array}
\right)
\end{array}
\qquad\qquad \text{--- (16)}
$$

Suppose we take a "utility pay off" view of these numbers, and suppose we say that the numbers represent £0, £1 and £100 respectively. Suppose you have to play for A and your choice is between A_1 and A_2, and you do not know whether B_1 or B_2 is correct, which would you choose?

We say that to maximise your utility you choose A_1 because then you can win £100 which is clearly the maximum possible pay off. But if we think of this problem in terms of regret as in the last section, i.e. the extent we shall regret the loss if we are wrong, the matrix becomes:-

$$
\begin{array}{cc}
& B_1 \qquad\qquad B_2 \\
\begin{array}{c} A_1 \\[20pt] A_2 \end{array} &
\left(
\begin{array}{cc}
1 & 0 \\[20pt]
0 & 99
\end{array}
\right)
\end{array}
\qquad\qquad \text{--- (17)}
$$

which is derived by subtracting each value from the maximum value in the same column, i.e.

$$
\begin{array}{cc}
& B_1 \qquad\qquad\qquad B_2 \\
\begin{array}{c} A_1 \\[20pt] A_2 \end{array} &
\left(
\begin{array}{cc}
1 - 0 & 100 - 100 \\[20pt]
1 - 1 & 100 - 1
\end{array}
\right)
\end{array}
\qquad\qquad \text{--- (18)}
$$

which, of course, gives you the above values in (17), and still leads to the choice of A_1.

In general, of course, we can consider cases of varying probabilities, whereas those above were considered to be equi-probable. This argument is identical with that of the last section viewed from a slightly different point of view. But if (15) were substituted for (19) the argument would be more or less the same. Many different strategies are possible, and we must make a comparison between three of them to show how this choice may occur.

$$
\begin{array}{cc}
& B_1 \qquad\qquad\qquad B_2 \qquad\qquad\qquad B_3 \\
\begin{array}{c} A_1 \\[15pt] A_2 \\[15pt] A_3 \end{array} &
\left(
\begin{array}{ccc}
0 & 3 & 0 \\[15pt]
2 & 2 & 0 \\[15pt]
1 & 1 & 1
\end{array}
\right)
\end{array}
\qquad\qquad \text{--- (19)}
$$

Suppose the columns B_1, B_2, B_3 are all equiprobable, which A would you choose where the pay off is in £'s? Maximum utility suggests A_1, since £3 is the maximum pay off, minimum regret is derived as before, giving the matrix (20):-

$$
\begin{array}{c}
 \\
A_1 \\
\\
A_2 \\
\\
A_3
\end{array}
\begin{array}{ccc}
B_1 & B_2 & B_3 \\
\left(\begin{array}{ccc}
3 & 0 & 3 \\
\\
0 & 0 & 2 \\
\\
0 & 0 & 0
\end{array}\right)
\end{array}
\quad \text{--- (20)}
$$

so you would clearly choose A_3 to minimize your regret. A third strategy might be to choose A_2 since this (sometimes called Laplace's Strategy) could be supported by the view that it gives the maximum average pay off. The average of the three rows of (19) being 1, $1\frac{1}{3}$ and 1 respectively.

There are other more complicated strategies but these are sufficient for our illustrative purpose. Now if we take matrix (19) and change the value of the pay off from £'s to millions of pounds much as we changed (15) to (16), would you still bet the same way?

You now stand to lose - or fail to win - up to £3 million. If you now translate (19) into a new matrix (21), which satisfies all the same conditions the point becomes even more obvious:-

$$
\begin{array}{c}
 \\
A_1 \\
\\
A_3 \\
\\
A_2
\end{array}
\begin{array}{ccc}
B_1 & B_2 & B_3 \\
\left(\begin{array}{ccc}
-1 & 2 & -1 \\
\\
1 & 1 & -1 \\
\\
0 & 0 & 0
\end{array}\right)
\end{array}
\quad \text{--- (21)}
$$

The same strategies exist and the pay offs are relatively the same, but now you have to risk losing £1 million. This will almost certainly have the effect of moving your choice from A_1 as first choice, overlooking A_2, and moving to A_3, where you cannot lose anything. The fact that you cannot win anything is no longer the most important factor.

To summarize the situation, we shall say that it is fairly obvious that the choice of strategies to be used is a function of the size of the risk, and we must use this technique as a result of some quantification of the data wherever that is possible (and we can always use subjective probabilities) and whenever we are asked to take any decision which entails risk. Once again our example, using Bayes, was precisely along these lines.

THEORY OF GAMES

        No summary of probability theory in our context of rational discourse,
would be complete without some (even if brief) mention of the Theory of
Games. This approach to game playing situations is concerned primarily
with one-off games, or games where a decision is made and the consequences
of the decision are not obviously sequential.

        It is, when viewed as a problem of linear programming - equivalent to
game theoretic situations - as a process of seeking maxima and minima where
the differential calculus cannot be used.

        We want in this section to avoid describing the technical terms
associated with these special branches of mathematics and concentrate, as
we have done so far, on simple examples, showing their use.

        In general terms, we talk of n-person games where n people are involved,
so contract bridge is a 4-person game and patience is a 1-person game. We
say such games are zero sum if when viewed as a gamble what one person wins
another loses and there is no residue. We need strategies and solutions.
If we were considering contract bridge we should also need to talk of
coalitions, but we shall restrict our discussion to games without coalitions.

        Consider a simple example of a 2-person zero sum game, with a simple
pay off matrix. The numbers in the matrix are, as usual, the pay offs to
the recipients, A by rows and B by columns.

        Let us again consider a simple pay off matrix:-

	B_1	B_2	B_3	B_4
A_1	18	3	0	2
A_2	0	3	8	20
A_3	5	4	5	5
A_4	16	4	2	25
A_5	9	3	0	20

        This time, we do not have a "game against nature" but a game between
two "intelligent" people (the theory itself deals with any number of
intelligent people, i.e. n-person games).

        If A_2 is chosen by the A-player and the B-player chooses B_3, then the
B-player pays £8 to the A-player. Let us look at the matter from A's point
of view. If A knew what B would choose the problem would be simple, but
this is not the case, so A must assume that each will think of the others
best choice in the light of each other's maximum ability.

A's choice is governed by:-

If B chooses:	B_1	B_2	B_3	B_4	
A must choose:	A_1	$(A_3$ or $A_4)$	A_2	A_4	--- (22)
A's pay off is:	18	4	8	25	

B's choice is governed by:-

If A chooses:	A_1	A_2	A_3	A_4	A_5	
B must choose:	B_3	B_1	B_2	B_3	B_3	--- (23)
A's pay off is:	0	0	4	2	0	

Now A sees from this that he can be sure of the following:-

A chooses:	A_1	A_2	A_3	A_4	A_5	
He is <u>sure</u> of:	0	0	4	**2**	0	--- (24)

So A_3 is the maximum pay off that can be guaranteed A for B:-

B chooses:	B_1	B_2	B_3	B_4	
He is <u>sure</u> of	-18	-4	-8	-25	--- (25)

So it is clear that provided both are optimal players, A must choose A_3 and B must choose B_2 and (A_3, B_2) is the so-called "solution of the game". The solution is, of course, a combination of the optima for both players in a 2-person game.

If there is any reason on either side to believe that their opponent's play is less than optimal - and this might be gauged over a series of games - then the solution might be improved. However, marketing (and planning) tends to be a "one-off" type of activity and although some experience is possible, it must by the nature of things be very limited. What in practise happens is that we assume what is usually called the <u>minimax</u> (or <u>maximin</u>) strategy.

A generalisation of game-theoretic methods called Dynamic Programming has been developed, and this consists of specific techniques for arriving at decisions and optima in sequential situations. Since this has not been seriously developed as a practical technique, we shall consider a particular case which has been extensively developed, that of stochastic processes.

STOCHASTIC PROCESSES

A special case of Dynamic Programming which is of special importance to logical and rational thinking as well as to decision making is known as a Stochastic Process. Before we give examples of Stochastic Processes,

let us say that they play an important part in the inductive process,
particularly insofar as they are so often the basis for inductive
generalisations.

A Stochastic Process is a random series, which can be represented by
a series of symbols - A, B, C. They occur in a purely random way, and
for which a definite probability can be associated with the occurrence of
each symbol. Thus for the following table:-

A	$\frac{1}{4}$
B	$\frac{1}{4}$
C	$\frac{1}{4}$

a series such as:-

BCCCBCABCCAA

ABCACBCACBCC

is typical; the longer the series the more likely it is to conform to the
table, unless, of course, the table is derived from the series. The process
of generation can be carried out in either direction. When carried out in
the former way, which entails deriving the table from the series, it is a
process of learning. If the series leads to the table, we refer to the
fractions in the table as probabilities and say that the fraction, or
probability, associated with each letter of the alphabet is the ratio of the
occurrence of that particular letter to the total number of letters
occurring.

We can generate more complicated cases from these beginnings, so that
we may have a table of conditional probabilities extending over two
successive events. As an example, using the same alphabet A, B, C alone,
consider:-

	A	B	C
A	$\frac{1}{2}$	$\frac{1}{2}$	0
B	$\frac{1}{4}$	$\frac{1}{4}$	$\frac{1}{2}$
C	$\frac{1}{3}$	0	$\frac{2}{3}$

which may generate a series such as:-

AABCABCCCAABABABBCCCCAABBC

and so on. It will be clear that the fact that 0 occurs in two places
ensures that A can never be followed by C and C can never be followed by B.
If, on the other hand, the table represents the series, what was 0 at any
instant may become a positive fraction, since the future is not necessarily
the same as the past.

The rules of English can be reassembled in such a table, either for
the order of letters or for the order of words. Probabilities can be
associated with either the letters or the words although for reasonable
English a weighting will have to be given to the context of the discussion.
Thus, matters in a particular context will take on special probabilities
relative to that context. For example, in a book on rugby the letters
"ba" with one space to follow is likely to have a heavy probability towards
"r", whereas a book on cricket is more likely to be a "t".

This contextual property is that of statistical homogeneity and can
be utilised in a special way. Different authors tend to build up slightly
different vocabularies and as a result it is possible to carry out
statistical tests to establish the authors of anonymous works by finding
out the frequency with which certain words occur. Such a test of vocabulary
tends to be as discriminating for each author as a test of fingerprints.

Such stochastic methods as we have said have a direct bearing on
learning (induction) and we can guess therefore are relevant to language,
semantics, etc. which we shall be discussing later.

STATISTICS

We have in this chapter in the main discussed probability theory,
where probability distributions involve the probability of some event
(or events) occurring. A probability distribution is one where we know
all the relevant possibilities and can apply probabilities to them. This
applies, for example, to the throwing of dice, the choice of cards from a
pack and indeed the selection of any objects from a finite set where the
contents are already known.

Bayes Rule could be seen to apply to a situation where the contents
are not fully known initially and where the probabilities change in the
light of new information.

Now we can go one step further and deal with any contents (we shall
call them collections or distributions of events) even if the details of
the full "population", as it is usually called, is never known. What we
can do is sample the population and carry out various tests and comparisons
on the sample to see what the probability is, for example, of them being
representative of the whole population.

There are various statistical techniques which are mostly based on
the so-called Normal Distribution. A very high percentage of variables
(e.g. the height and weight of men and women etc.) are "normally
distributed". We can then take these samples and test them as being
significantly different from each other, highly correlated with each other
and many other things besides. This is no text book on statistics, so we
shall merely make the point here that all causally related events are

highly correlated, but all highly correlated events are not necessarily connected at all, let alone causally connected. Similarly we can use the test for the "significance between means" to decide whether the chances are that any two groups (taken at random say) have significantly different characteristics in certain respects. By such means we could test, for example, the likely difference between an Englishman's and a Welshman's knowledge of rugby football.

The use of the word 'significance' in statistics is a reminder that we are talking in terms of probabilities and therefore of possible error. We mean to place odds on a difference being "real" or a correlation being "real" and we can take any odds we choose. If it is vital that we are not wrong in such as case as estimating likely strains in the design of an aircraft we shall look for a much higher level of confidence (better odds) than if we are deciding to take a raincoat out with us in case of rain.

The whole of statistics is relevant to the rational thinker and the debator since it plays a role which is closely analogous to logic. It allows you to reason from cause to effect or in other ways draw inferences of an uncertain kind. The fact that they are uncertain is usually inevitable by the nature of things and in no way detracts from the importance of these methods for clear thinking.

The rational man needs to understand at least logic, scientific method, probability theory and statistics. At any rate these are the main ingredients of rationality we have discussed so far - so more is yet to come.

SUMMARY

We have, in this chapter, described probability theory in terms of an axiom set, from which we have derived Inverse probability and Bayes Rule. Bayesian methods have then been illustrated in the context of decision making.

Decision making, like planning and problem solving, (all very similar in their logic) are very much a part of what the rational man needs to know something about.

Statistics (closely related to probability theory) is also described briefly, since statistical methods are also methods for drawing inferences, as was clear from our discussion of scientific method.

EXERCISES

1. What is the difference between probability theory and statistical theory? Explain the difference in a manner which convinces yourself, and also try to decide the connection between the two.

2. If you drew five cards from a normal pack of fifty-two playing cards, what would be the probability that they were:-

    i)   all hearts

    ii) all knaves

    iii) three diamonds and two clubs

    iv) two spades, one heart, one club and one diamond.

3. Is uncertainty over an event the same as the probability of some event occurring? Explain to yourself the answer to this question.

4. What is the nature of "doubt" and "certainty" in terms of knowledge?

REFERENCES

CARNAP, R.	The Logical Foundations of Probability. University of Chicago Press. Ed. II 1963
CHANCE, W.A.	Statistical Methods for Decision Making. 1969
GOODMAN, R.	Probability. English Universities Press
JEFFREY, R.C.	The Logic of Decision. McGraw Hill 1965
REICHMANN, W.J.	Use and Abuse of Statistics. Methuen 1962
WHITE, D.J.	Decision Theory. George Allen and Unwin, 1969

CHAPTER 10

LANGUAGE AND PHILOSOPHY

Philosophy is concerned to a great extent with language and logic (and certainly with clear thinking). It is not really very easy to say where philosophy starts and semantics and pragmatics (these we still have to discuss in detail) end, or whether we should regard philosophy as being within pragmatics or pragmatics within philosophy. This particular matter refers to a rather more general debate as to the precise relation between science and philosophy; this is something with which pragmatics is especially concerned.

It has certainly been argued that the <u>theory</u> of signs is not a part of philosophy, although the use of signs is an appropriate subject for philosophical analysis. In fact we might say that philosophy is roughly speaking concerned with the questions that arise over <u>meaning</u> and <u>truth</u> in language, but it is also concerned with ontology, which is the study concerned with what exists. There is also the study called Theory of Knowledge (sometimes called epistemology) and ethics which is a part of philosophy. We can also include political philosophy and possibly social philosophy, and perhaps even other sub-divisions as well.

To follow up the ontological question of existence, if we ask ourselves such questions as "do atoms really exist?", we have a problem that can be regarded quite readily from the semantic point of view. This is so because the phrase 'really exist' or merely the word 'exist' is very far from being clear (or unambiguous), at least this is so in the rather word-splitting world of philosophical discourse. If we asked whether dragons or eight-legged horses exist, of course, we would find it easier to deal with the existence problem, because presumably we would have no reasonable doubt as to what these were, but only whether anyone had ever seen them; in fact we would think that they were mythical. Even here though we can run into difficulties with the precise minded philosopher who may say "how do you know that they do not exist?", to which we can only reply that we think it unlikely and have never heard of anyone having seen them and so on. Indeed our two examples are not quite the same, since a dragon is avowedly mythical, while an eight-legged horse is not and could conceivably exist as a result of some (unhappy) genetic mutation.

Should we get irritated with the arguer who keeps asking us <u>how we know</u> whatever we claim to know, we should admit that sometimes we are <u>inclined</u> to take things for granted and philosophers, logicians and pragmatists have been quick to point this out. So let us ask about the existence of something that seems reasonable or plausible. Do black tigers exist? To answer this question might merely entail looking, and if this is so, it is not so much a matter of philosophical but of scientific interest. It is a matter of confirming or otherwise the truth of such an empirical statement.

In this sort of circumstance, we must be clear about the definitions
we use. We might have said a tiger by definition is a yellow and black
animal, so the very possibility of having a purely black tiger is thereby
excluded by the very act of definition. Such a technique removes questions
such as "are there black tigers?" from the empirical domain and makes them
purely analytic.

So it is that the philosopher, the semanticist and the scientist
(pragmatist) get involved in the same problems. On the other hand, of
course, when a scientist is looking through his microscope or his telescope,
or doing some sort of chemical or physical experiment in the laboratory,
he may merely be checking something such as the change of colour in a
liquid, or measuring the speed of an object, or performing some act that
takes him right away from the field of language. He never gets wholly
away though, because he must be able to communicate his findings, and this
requires language and language can, quite clearly, mislead as well as inform.
The philosopher may question and doubt as much as the pragmatist. He may
ask what you mean and, like the pragmatist, ask you how you know; he too
deals with matters that take him away from ordinary language when he is
thinking of some logical justification for a belief he holds, or when he
is asking himself whether he holds certain beliefs or not, or again, when
he is concerned with mathematical or symbolic logic. Actually, it is clear
that it is more difficult for the philosopher to get away from language
than the scientist, and neither can ever do so completely. The reason the
philosopher cannot get away from language is because, as Wittgenstein has
said, so much of philosophy is a critique of language.

It is clear that pragmatics (and especially the part of pragmatics
which is concerned directly with semantics) is concerned with the evolution
of languages, their development and the change of meanings of words, and
the actual physical process of talking and listening, and these are not
much the concern of philosophers, although they are to some extent the
concern of scientists. So finally it may be said that semantics overlaps
with philosophy and science with perhaps as a matter of historical fact a
stronger association with philosophy. Pragmatics, on the other hand, is
probably rather more concerned with science.

WITTGENSTEIN'S PHILOSOPHY OF LANGUAGE

For Wittgenstein, philosophy is a critique of language, or as Russell
has put it

> "Wittgenstein's analysis of language is concerned with the
> conditions which would have to be fulfilled by a logically
> perfect language."

But Wittgenstein, like so many other philosophers, thought of the analysis
of language from a very particular viewpoint.

This special viewpoint denied the philosophical usefulness of knowing
anything about the history of language, and required only that a language
be analyzed from a logical point of view. Wittgenstein, as we have said,
was concerned with a logically perfect language which implies a language
in which it would be easy to see the logical relations between different
statements, and one in which all the logical relationships could be

completely utilized. Natural languages such as English and French fall
short of the ideal language in at least two respects.

1. They <u>allow</u> sentences which are "meaningless" combinations of
    symbols, and

2. Words used in these languages can be both vague and ambiguous.

So a perfect language must repair these defects at the very least, and
this presents a very serious problem. A problem of providing a formalisation
of a kind by no means yet achieved. Indeed, as Professor Max Black has
said:-

> "The defect in their (most linguistic analysts) answers
> is not in the character of their method but in the fact
> that their fragmentary and appropriate conclusions are
> presented as if they were complete analyses."

But before we try to see more clearly what Wittgenstein was attempting,
let us look at this more general point about the logical use of language.
If you are asked, for example, to define crucial terms like 'meaning' and
'truth', it would have to be by using other words. A definition is divided
into the definiendum (that which is to be defined) and the words that are
to be featured in the definiens (that which defines). The definition is a
relationship such as between two words that are synonymous or rules which
govern the proper use of terms. A definition provides a way of distinguishing one word from another rather than seeking synonyms; therefore we shall
avoid argument for the present by saying that the definition is made up of
words, where the words involved tell a person what a word <u>means</u>. So that,
for example, we say "Explanation means a description of a set of events
which precede the event to be explained, or involves a general description
of principles of which the thing to be explained is a typical case". This
in fact is not so easy, particularly for words like 'explanation' and
'definition' themselves.

We could next try to define a term with respect to what we could do to
measure or observe it; so for the word for 'temperature' we might say it is
what we measure if we place a thermometer in a liquid. This is the essence
of an <u>Operational Definition</u> which we previously referred to in Part I.

We are saying that explanations and definitions in philosophy are of
the form "meaning is ..." and "truth is ..." where what follows each
sentence stem must not depend on something which is a mere description of
how the idea of meaning and truth came about as a matter of historical fact.

Wittgenstein was not only concerned with whether or not we can develop
a logically perfect language. He was also concerned with the structure
represented by language. In the first place he said that "every possible
proposition is legitimately constructed" and other such comments which
seemed to suggest that we must not seek to impose a logic on language but
rather we should accept language as a starting point for a logical
investigation. Language in other words is the given starting point, and
we should now work from there to try to look behind language to understand
the structure of the world which language depicts.

The important idea of language representing structure is one that was followed up by Count Alfred Korzybski, and relates to the notion of logical form. Of the form of propositions, Susan Stebbing has said:-

> "The form of a proposition is what remains unchanged although all the constituents of the proposition are altered."

The interesting idea involved here is similar to that embodied in the notion of a map or a visual similarity that may exist between a description and a structure. The difficulty with this, in general, is that the map-analogy is over-strained if it is made to incorporate all aspects of all natural languages. In Wittgenstein's writing, words like 'structure' are not in fact explicitly defined.

The words 'symbol' and 'sign' are two further words which precipitate discussions in semantics and pragmatics, so let us look now at the way in which Wittgenstein uses these terms. The distinction between token and type is important, and such a distinction is also made by Wittgenstein where he means to distinguish between the word 'mountain', say, each time it is used and different words like 'mountain' and 'river' when they are used. Thus 'mountain' used twice are two different tokens of the same type, while the words 'mountain' and 'river' are two different types. Wittgenstein seems to use the word 'symbol' to designate tokens of the same set, while 'sign' can be used for either a token or a type.

Wittgenstein then argues that the organization of the types in a language is more or less an accident, while the organization of the symbols is a result of logical structure. In practice it is important not to confuse logical and grammatical distinctions as, since we can see clearly enough, to do so would be much the same as to rename all the components of a complicated structure such as a jet engine, believing that by doing so the relations between them was somehow changed. On the other hand, we need to be careful about this distinction, and we shall be saying more about it in the next section of this chapter on Russell's linguistic analysis.

The next point about Wittgenstein's views, which relates him closely to the group of semanticists and philosophers called pragmaticists, and thus to pragmatics, is the sense in which he insists that languages must be related to language users, and that the proposition is the basic unit of meaning, and that names (words) occur only in propositions when they have meaning. In his words, "only in a proposition has a name meaning". He further says that the rule for using a word such as 'language' is not a statement about the way in which the word is used in the language in question and he insists on distinguishing between rules of usage and statements about usage. This is in some ways similar to the distinction between analytic and synthetic propositions. We are, however, going to argue that the rules of usage can be regarded as a formalisation of an empirical description of usage.

Wittgenstein develops the idea of a context of meaning, implying, as do the pragmaticists, that propositions occur together making a "more complete picture" of what is entailed by the utterer of the sentences.

So we may summarize Wittgenstein's views, albeit oversimply, by saying

1. That language is made up of sets of propositions.

2. That words only occur meaningfully in propositions.

3. That meaning must be explained to us by the users of propositions.

4. The criterion of the kind of symbol to which a token belongs is the manner in which the token is used.

5. The way to recognize the symbol in the sign is to recognize its significant use.

6. That words (or names) stand for objects and have the objects as meanings.

7. That propositions represent possible states of affairs and to verify a proposition we must compare it with reality, and finally,

8. The structure of the proposition repeats the structure of the reality it describes.

We should perhaps add that we must doubt that the objects (referents) of words have meanings; rather it is the concept of which a particular object is an exemplar or particular token of a token-type. We shall not comment further on the difficulties over the word 'structure' but simply note its vagueness. It will be clear that in spite of Wittgenstein's pragmatic leanings, he was not implying anything as extreme as "science should replace philosophy", but we should rather try to understand language from a more social and biological point of view. Wittgenstein depended on a further distinction we must now make.

Wittgenstein said of propositions that they assert the existence of a state of affairs but they show the logical form of reality; 'saying' or 'asserting' is one thing, and 'showing' is another, so that any proposition, let us call it p, is such that if p can be said, means that p is empirical, if of course it is not nonsense, whereas to say that p shows but does <u>not assert</u> is to say that p is not empirical. In other words, p may be "Lions are bigger than rats" and p is said and is empirical, but if I say "Lions are yellow and black creatures with ... etc." then I am showing. The point of this distinction is to deal with the difficulty that the lion must be defined independently of its properties if it is to be investigated as having some new property. Mathematics, according to Wittgenstein, is made up of such <u>showing</u> statements which are tautologies and assert nothing whatever, merely show relations between defined entities.

We should say next something about <u>logical structure</u>, since it is closely related to the idea of <u>logical form</u>, which is a way of constructing propositions or sentences such that there is some form present independent of what is being asserted. For example, in saying that "Jack is short", "David is hot" and "Bill is light" implies some sort of similarity of form between the three sentences, quite independent of the fact that they all assert different things. It is like saying $x \rightarrow y \rightarrow z$ regardless of the values of x, y and z and regardless of whether they are apples, oranges or anything else. This is what Susan Stebbing implied by distinguishing form from content.

Logical form has been the source of a lot of argument and is difficult
to define, but Wittgenstein tries to define logical structure, by saying
that it must have a logical form, which for him means that terms must be
in the same sort of relation to each other, so that "Jack is Bill's brother"
is a different form from the three sentences above. Also the names or
words put into the sentence form must be of the same kind and category.

Perhaps we can finish our brief resume of Wittgenstein's view of
language with a quotation from one of his books:-

> "But now it may come to look as if there were something
> like final analysis of our forms of language, and so a
> single completely resolved form of every expression.
> That is, as if our usual forms of expression were essentially
> unanalyzed; as if there were something hidden in them
> that had to be brought to light. When this is done the
> expression is completely clarified and our problem is
> solved.
>
> It can also be put like this: we eliminate misunderstandings
> by making our expressions more exact; but now it may look
> as if we were moving towards a particular state, a state
> of complete exactness; and as if this were the real goal
> of our investigation."

This shows shades of the "ideal language".

RUSSELL'S LINGUISTIC ANALYSIS

Another person who has made a major contribution to linguistic analysis
is Bertrand Russell and we should briefly look at the contributions he has
made and the stance he has taken up with regard to linguistic questions.

In the chapter on "the philosophy of logical analysis", Russell says:-

> "It gradually became clear that a great part of philosophy
> can be reduced to something that may be called "syntax",
> though the word has to be used in a somewhat wider sense
> than has hitherto been customary."

In fact, the widening of the word 'syntax' as used above involves its
extension to include semantics, and indeed as Russell suggests elsewhere
it should be extended to include pragmatics.

The theory of descriptions is central to Russell's view and he uses
this to illustrate the above quotation. A description is a phrase such as
"The present King of France" where the phrase designates a person by a
property he possesses, or may possess, rather than naming him. This
creates a problem of meaning, since we assert the existence of something
even though the designation of the description is nul.

The classical example used by Russell is that of "Sir Walter Scott"
and "the author of Waverley", which he analyzes as:-

"There is an entity c such that the statement 'x wrote
Waverley' is true if x is c and false otherwise; moreover
c is Scott."

and "the King of France does not exist" comes out as:-

"There is no entity c such that 'x is the King of France'
is true when x is c, but not otherwise."

In fact a part of the difficulty here is bound up with the fact that the
designation of a term is not the same as its meaning, if by 'designation'
is meant the class of objects to which the term applies.

Again Russell makes the point that there are some things which cannot
be adequately expressed by means of descriptions substituted for proper
names. Thus, of course, as Woodger has pointed out, it is incorrect to
say that "Sir Walter Scott" and "The author of Waverley" are synonymous.
There is a clear sense in which Sir Walter Scott was much more than the
author of Waverley, and being the author of Waverley merely expressed one
aspect of his being; it is, as it were, one of the properties of Sir
Walter Scott.

Russell himself developed the theory of types in order to try to
remove the ambiguity over terms and their substitutability. It is clear
that the reflexive application of terms requires some sort of restriction
upon what can be substituted for what in a statement format. This state
of affairs is particularly clear in the development of symbolic logic
where in building up each new type it must consist of n-adic propositional
functions, with fixed n, and with each argument in order restricted to a
certain fixed previous type, and so on.

This method can be used to distinguish the type of different terms
and disallow some of the substitutions such as those involved in the theory
of descriptions. The difficulty involved in applying even this simple
theory of types is that we can continue to make finer and ever finer
distinctions of meaning and in the end even two occurrences of the same
term in a different context might cause them to be designated as different
types. We should mention in passing that Russell also proposed a so-called
Ramified Theory of types, which he used in Principia Mathematica, which
involved even more complex subdivisions. It has generally been argued that
the simple theory of types was adequate in its formal capacity, and that
in the context of ordinary language, we would argue that the general notion
of a theory of types is sufficient to ensure an awareness of possible
ambiguity. If, however, it is taken to its limits it has the undesirable
consequences that might lead us to say that no two terms ever mean the
same thing.

Max Black has attemped to resolve this difficulty by re-interpreting
the theory of types, by applying it to words rather than entities, so that

"L is of the same type as K" is a fact and

"M is not the same type as K" is a fact

are re-written with L, K and M designating words, and then follows the
conclusion that L, K and M are syntactically similar. This though leaves us

still in the position that the identification of different word types is
not, in ordinary English, context free. So the gain implied is at best
only slight.

This discussion bears in some measure on belief statements. Hilary
Putnam had said of Rudolph Carnap's notion of <u>intensional isomorphism</u>
that it is inadequate. .Carnap's definition (1947) of intensional
isomorphism is as follows:-

> There is a sentence B in the semantic system S such
> that (1) B is intensionally isomorphic to B^1 and
> (2) some person X was disposed to an affirmative
> response to B, and where B^1 is the proposition
> asserted by B.

Let us take one of Church's examples.

> "Columbus believed the world to be round"

We find B in the above definition is intensionally isomorphic to 'the world
is round' and Columbus was disposed to an affirmative response to B.

Putnam tries to generalize the Carnap definition and suggests:-

> "Two expressions are intensionally isomorphic if they
> have the same logical structure, and if corresponding
> parts are L-equivalent."

Putnam believes that it is the logical structure of the statements
that distinguishes "All Greeks are Greeks" from "All Greeks are Hellenes".
This is reminiscent of Russell's distinction between logical and syntactical
structure. The present author has argued that such belief statements are
most properly analyzed in pragmatic terms.

Thus it is that the distinction between "proper use" and equivalent
references are the things that really matter if two beliefs are thought to
be intensionally isomorphic to each other. In other words, to use symbolic
terminology:

> Bfa
>
> a = b
>
> Bfb

where Bfa is some such statement 'Jones believes that fa' and Bfb is some
such statement as 'Jones believes that fb'
and we shall conclude

> Bf(a = b)
>
> (Jones believes that a = b)

In other words, there is absolutely no problem to solve if we accept the
two critical conditions of a pragmatic kind which apply in such situations.
This implies that the references of the two terms or phrases are the same

and that regardless of the way the phrases are translated or expressed in
statements, that the person who utters them believes the references to be
the same. If the person uttering the statement merely believes two terms
to have the same reference when they do not, then he is mistaken and the
belief statements are not equivalent. If on the other hand the two terms
or phrases refer to the same thing and they are believed not to by the
person making the statements, they still do not amount to equivalent belief
statements because the operative word is 'belief' which makes it clear the
context of the logic is a pragmatic one. Thus it is that the necessary
and sufficient condition for equivalent belief statements is that the two
terms or phrases have to have the same reference and the people uttering
the statements have to believe that they have the same reference. This is
all that can be said about the logic of belief statements in this regard
and makes it clear that Carnap's original version of intensional isomorphism
is essentially right as it stood.

Finally in this section we should at least mention Russell's notion
of an "ideal" language (something which was also considered by Wittgenstein
and Carnap). The basic idea is that there should be a way of expressing
a description (such as the neutrality implied by the theory of descriptions)
which is epistemologically and ontologically neutral and which is a logically
perfect language. Carnap thought of such a language as expressing the
logic of science, while Russell thought of it as expressing true descriptions
of reality. It seems certain that no such language exists or could exist,
but this is no reason for not trying to develop the concept of a language
that is as near ideal (free of ambiguity and epistemological and ontological
preconceptions and misconceptions) as possible.

THE PHILOSOPHY OF ORDINARY LANGUAGE

G.E. Moore has argued that the use of terms such as 'meaning', 'truth',
'real', 'same', etc. is not something that requires explanation of the kind
that might be involved if I were teaching a foreigner the meaning of such
terms, since I am assuming that I am speaking to people who already know
the English language, and I assume they understand the meaning of the terms
'truth', 'real', etc. as well as I do.

Moore makes the assumption that philosophers are not saying that these
terms have some special meaning, rather they are saying that they mean the
same for philosophers as they do for everyone else, and the problem is
simply to say what they mean. In other words, we know what they mean
already but it may not be easy to say what it is that they mean. Moore's
own words are helpful:-

> "Obviously there can be no need for me to explain to
> you the meaning of the word 'real', in the sense in
> which it might be necessary for me to explain its
> meaning if I were trying to teach English to some
> foreigner who did not know a word of the language."

Philosophers might argue that philosophy differs from semantics in
that philosophers are not concerned with small differences of meaning, but
with major differences between meanings. Again, as Moore puts it:-

>"Of course I am presupposing that you do know the
>English language; and, since you do know it, you
>already know the meaning of the word 'real' just
>as well as you know the meaning of any of the words
>by the help of which I might try to explain it to you."

This being so, the fact that we can carry on in everyday life quite
successfully and talk about real things shows that we have no major
differences of opinion. This same argument does not, of course, apply to
precise discussions of the kind so often found in modern science, where
small differences in meaning may prove to be quite crucial.

Moore is arguing that we are not interested in finding out what these
and many other words mean; rather we are concerned with something different,
as Moore himself puts it:-

>"namely I wish to talk about - the property or properties
>that wish to assert that a thing possesses when you say
>it is real."

The difficulty here is getting at a good way of expressing the question,
yet it can be seen to be different from the question that asks 'what is
real?' and then 'please define it'. Moore is asking for an enumeration of
the properties implied by words like 'dog' or 'cat' and the differences
between the two sets of properties which mark them off as a dog and cat
respectively.

Moore's ontological view of the world is a form of Realism because he
asserts that to say that the world is not real is to talk nonsense. In
other words the world is precisely real, that is one thing we can be sure
of, and to deny this would be to deny the ordinary use of the word 'real'.

It is easy to misunderstand Moore's sort of argument, but it seems
reasonable to say that what is being done is to argue that most people
understand correctly the meaning of words, and that language correctly
depicts the world - Wittgenstein seemed to be saying something rather
similar - and that our only interest is to try to clarify our meanings to
ourselves. Certainly it is not easy to clarify meanings for others, and
Wittgenstein said that in fact the bulk of his own attempts to clarify
semantic problems were themselves illegitimate. This is part of the self-
contradictoriness that seemed to be inherent, according to Wittgenstein,
in his own system of analysis.

Moore, however, would accept that words like 'real' may have two or
three meanings and be used in two senses and this - these are major
differences which are soon revealed in discussion - can be ironed out and
difficulties of argument quickly cleared up. In this respect he agrees
with Wittgenstein, but believes there is nothing self-contradictory in his
own view which essentially attempts to produce the commonsense thinking
and forms of analysis of the "man in the street".

As far as we, as pragmaticists, are concerned, we would accept Moore's
approach as adequate at one level of abstraction, but inadequate at the
levels of more precise detail. His own more detailed analysis comes near
the "classical" analysis in terms of ordinary language which is typical of
the period in which Moore wrote.

We should take the opportunity at this point to mention very briefly the work of Gilbert Ryle and we should say straight away that Ryle's views are in many ways similar to those of Wittgenstein and Moore and also representative of what we called above the "classical" form of analysis. He is also very much concerned with proper meanings in ordinary language.

Ryle's main book "The Concept of the Mind" made great play of the fact that the word 'mind' was used as if to describe 'the ghost in the machine'. It was like looking at all the colleges of Oxford University and saying at the end "Well, now where is the University?", or looking at a car and saying "Yes, I see the piston and cylinders, but where is the performance?". Category mistakes such as these are really a matter of asking the wrong questions about things, questions which can be seen, by those possessing the answer, to be inappropriate. They are in some ways reminiscent of those paradoxes and difficulties that demand the use of the theory of types.

The question as to whether 'mind' is a category mistake is one over which Ryle has made a big issue, and there is some reason to believe that it is quite true that to ask the same sort of questions of mind as one asks of body is almost inevitably doomed to inviting mistakes. Ryle's viewpoint can be gleaned from the following quotation:-

> "Overt intelligent performances are not clues to the workings of minds, they are those workings"

IN SUMMARY

We will finally consider the general nature of statements. We must look at a well-known distinction often drawn between <u>analytic</u> and <u>synthetic</u> statements. This distinction has often been quarrelled with, and we shall mention in this respect Quine's view. Quine says:-

> "Modern empiricism has been conditioned in large by two dogmas. One is a belief in some fundamental cleavage between truths which are analytic, or grounded in meanings independently of matters of fact, and truths which are <u>synthetic</u> or grounded in fact. The other dogma is <u>reductionism</u>: the belief that each meaningful statement is equivalent to some logical construct upon terms which refer to immediate experience. Both dogmas, I shall argue, are ill-founded. One effect of abandoning them is, as we shall see, a blurring of the supposed boundary between speculative meta-physics and natural science. Another effect is a shift towards pragmatism."

We are wholly sympathetic with the view that Quine expresses and it represents one of the reasons that we are developing pragmatics as, among other things, an alternative base to "classical epistemology" for the investigation of knowledge. We shall not discuss Quine's analysis in detail, but merely deal briefly with the differences between analytic and synthetic statements. Quine sets out to show the various attempts to define 'analytic', all of which are inadequate. The following represent typical definitions of 'analytic':-

S is analytic if and only if:-

      (1) S is true in all possible worlds.

      (2) Not-S is self-contradictory

      (3) S is true by virtue of meaning and
           independent of fact.

      (4) S can be reduced to a logical truth
           by definition.

      (5) S is analytic-in-L.

The Liebnizian notion of 'true in all possible worlds' says nothing in effect, since it merely asserts that "the truths of reason are those which could not possibly be false." To say something is 'self-contradictory' is to appeal to a concept as much in need of explanation as the word 'analytic' itself, and to appeal to meaning is to suffer the same criticism as in the case of self-contradictoriness. We shall briefly look now at the notion of meaning.

Meaning is not to be identified with naming or reference, at least not in the ordinary sense, as we have already seen from our summaries of Russell and Wittgenstein. 'The King of France' has meaning but no reference, and the same applies to 'griffin' and other "mythical objects'. 'Evening Star' and "morning star' refer to the same body, but still mean something different, as do 'Sir Walter Scott' and 'the author of Waverley'. What then is the meaning of a term?

If we were taking a pragmatic view of meaning we should emphasize the meaning of statements as expressed by sentences, and not the meaning of terms at all, and in this we seem to have the support of both Russell and Wittgenstein. But if we are to deal with the meaning of terms we have to take one of two courses. We either distinguish the intension (connotation) of the term from its extension (reference or denotation), or we talk of the extension and imply the concept, rather than the physical exemplars. Whichever way we try to solve this problem we are though clearly dealing with a matter at least as complicated as analyticity itself.

Let us now look briefly at definitions. Contrast the two statements S_1 and S_2, where

      S_1 = No unmarried man is married.

      S_2 = No bachelor is married.

We would accept S_1 as logically true, since it asserts something of a form which is true for all substitution for the word 'married'. This is not however true of S_2 since this presupposes that two terms 'bachelor' and 'unmarried man' are synonymous, and synonymity is as complex a concept as analyticity.

Similarly we cannot depend upon definition (which in one form is similar to synonymity) since this too is vague. We are not sure what we

are doing when we are defining terms, since the lexicographer provides
definitions only after usage has been established, and usage is essentially
pragmatic. Finally we can dispose of analytic-in-L since it merely
presupposes the meaning of 'analytic'.

In a sense all this is really just a particular case of a more general
argument we are pursuing which asserts that formal and factual activities
are not wholly separate. Let us though now look at some further aspects of
statements. So far as sense datum statements (protocols) are concerned,
they assert something about immediate impressions and immediate awareness,
e.g. "I have an impression of redness" (S_3), which emphasizes the role of
the observer but does not invite any corroboration of the equivalent
empirical statement "I see something red" (S_4). The empirical statement
S_4 can be verified (i.e. confirmed or informed) by other empirical statements, although all such statements are, as we have seen in our brief
discussion of confirmation and truth, subject to error. S_3 may not be
subject to error but is only not dubitable by virtue of not asserting
anything "public" (i.e. verifiable) and this attempt to provide "certainty"
is what renders it useless.

We should bear in mind here that we are primarily concerned with
formal axiomatic systems (languages) and that such systems may be more than
syntactically formal, they can have semantic rules (rules of designation),
as has been made clear by Carnap. We are concerned with language and
knowledge, although we may feel that what cannot be expressed in language
cannot be known.

We shall say no more at this point about philosophy, philosophers and
language, although in later chapters such as that on perception, we shall
be bearing in mind the philosopher's approach and be referring back to
some of the ideas dealt with in this chapter.

We have built up our discussion around particular approaches to
language, and what we have seen is that language is handled by philosophers
in a very different manner from the way it is handled by linguists,
grammarians, lexicographers and psychologists. The philosopher's interest
comes somewhere "in between" syntax and pragmatics and is near to semantics.
The semantics to which it is near, however, is most often the analytic and
informal approach of Wittgenstein, Moore, Ryle and Russell (the particular
philosophers we have considered) rather than the formal approach of
Carnap. At this point we shall conclude the chapter.

SUMMARY

We will attempt no further summary of the analysis of the relationship
between language and philosophy. We should merely emphasize that for many
philosophers the analysis of language is the central feature of philosophy.
To this extent at least language is related through philosophy to logic.

EXERCISES

1. What is the difference between the meaning and reference (intension and extension) of terms and propositions?

2. Can you define all the terms you use in a discussion or debate? Explain the central problem of precision in discussion and the dangers of circularity.

3. Liken language to a map and whatever language describes to a territory (which is itself not language in any shape or form); how best do you relate one to the other and always remember which is which.

REFERENCES

AYER, A.J.   Language, Truth and Logic. Oxford
                      University Press, 1936

AYER, A.J.   The Foundations of Empirical Knowledge.
                      Macmillan, 1940

BRAITHWAITE, R.B.   Scientific Explanation. Cambridge
                      University Press, 1953

BROAD, C.D.   Scientific Thought. Harcourt Brace, 1923

BROAD, C.D.   The Mind and its Place in Nature.
                      Kegan Paul, Trench, Trubner & Co., 1925

CARNAP, R.   Foundations of Logic and Mathematics.
                      Encyclopedia of Unified Science, 1, 3,
                      Chicago University Press, 1939

CARNAP, R.   Introductions to Semantics. Chicago
                      University Press, 1942

CARNAP, R.   Meaning and Necessity. Chicago University
                      Press, 1947

GEORGE, F.H.   Epistemology and the problem of perception,
                      LXVI, Mind, 491 - 506

LEAN, M.E.   Sense-Perception and Matter. Routledge and
                      Kegan Paul, 1952

MOORE, G.E.   Some Main Problems of Philosophy. Allen and
                      Unwin, 1953

PAP, A.   The Elements of Analytic Philosophy. Macmillan
                      1949

PRICE, H.H.   Perception. Methuen, 1932

QUINE, W.V.   From a Logical Point of View. Harvard
                       University Press, 1953

RYLE, G.   The Concept of Mind. Hutchinson, 1949

RUSSELL, B.   Our Knowledge of the External World.
                       W.W. Norton, 1929

STORER, T.   The philosophic relevance of a "Behavioristic
                       Semiotic". Phil. Sci., 15, 3,1948

WOODGER, J.H.   Science without properties. B.J.Phil. Sci.,
                       2, 7, 193 - 216, 1951

CHAPTER 11

EPISTEMOLOGY

In this chapter in fact we dwell on "what we know" and "how we know what we know". This also links up with questions of ontology and what exists. We shall start by considering the nature of perception. To emphasise the distinction we are making with a psychological or physiological approach to perception, we make it clear that our own discussion is about the philosophical problem. This leaves us with some doubt as to how independent all these problems really are.

THE PHILOSOPHICAL PROBLEM OF PERCEPTION

It is often said that the philosopher's interest in perception is not the same as that of the psychologist, or of any other empirical scientist. The philosopher is usually described as analysing perception in so far as it is essential to the foundations of knowledge, especially our knowledge of the so-called external world and of such things as physical objects. So it is that philosophers are mainly interested in the question of what is perceived and the reliability of the perception. The psychologist, on the other hand, is interested in how perception takes place, what processes are involved and what the system which is carrying out the perceiving looks like; the cybernetician is also primarily interested in this latter category.

Price has stated the task of the theory of perception to be that of examining the experiences of seeing and touching and also of examining the beliefs that they seem to carry with them, e.g. that such things as material objects exist. Price says that the other senses could equally well be examined, and it is only the relatively greater importance to perception of seeing and touching that is the reason for their choice. He also expresses the characteristic philosophic view that in this basic examination we cannot utilize our knowledge derived from scientific investigations which, being empirical, are themselves dependent on perception. This leads to a description of the process which we might label 'visual perception', which refers our knowledge to our intuitive experience and the use of natural language.

It is also part of our purpose in this chapter to show that the attempts of such epistemologists as Price and Broad to solve the philosophical or logical problems of perception are based on a confusion in which they create as many problems as they solve. In taking up this position we shall support a view somewhat similar to that espoused by Lean about the treatment given to perception by Broad, but differing in many important respects.

The principal theme is the contrast between the causal and the logical theory. The difficulties that this engenders is exhibited by the limitations placed on the natural language from which we start. This is so because any language we use is constructed on the basis of, mainly conscious, epistemological and ontological assumptions about reality. No one wishes to

assert that we cannot abstract the logic of an argument from its factual
content, or perhaps more precisely, distinguish logical from non-logical
statements (although we have seen that this can be awkward). Our problem
comes nearer to the question of whether we can find any "absolute"
criterion of distinction between the formal and the factual.

The accepted distinctions between the logical and causal theory of
perception are our starting point. The reason for accepting this distinction
is seen to lie in the notion that the epistemologist's problem is to produce,
not a causal explanation, but a neutral description of all knowledge which
would serve as a logical foundation for the empirical sciences. It is
supposed that an unwanted circularity would arise if appeal were made to the
very sciences whose appropriate foundations we seek to supply. Thus it is
that all scientific theory is deemed irrelevant to this approach to
perception. It seems likely that the whole of the argument suggested by
Price and Broad springs from the distinction sometimes made between so-called
formal and factual matters. That the distinction is only a matter of degree
seems to be a better interpretation of the facts.

A result of denying this particular dualism between formal and factual
matters leads, as both Quine and White pointed out, to just the sort of
merging of scientific and philosophic ideas being urged in the particular
case of perception. Alternatively we might regard the argument to be over
the methods available to us to justify certain, or all, of the beliefs we
hold.

There are, of course, many starting points for such analyses, and it
is therefore possible that what we finish with will be regarded by some
people as something very different from what such epistemologists as Price
and Broad have attempted. Indeed we are dogged by lack of agreement over
criteria about what epistemologists should be doing.

One view that is fairly clear has been expressed by Thomas Storer:-

> "Briefly the view here adopted is that epistemology (theory
> of knowledge) is philosophy; distinct from either the formal
> or factual sciences. Philosophers have made contributions
> to science generally, but that which is unique in their
> work, and thus distinguishes philosophy, is found only in
> the epistemological considerations of these men. Philosophy
> of science (as theoretical methodology of the special sciences)
> and logic are parts of science. And history of philosophy
> is part of general social science. Epistemology, however,
> is not a separate science. It is a precursive investigation,
> preliminary inquiry, that anticipates the current level of
> scientific discovery and common sense opinion."

Storer is in fact tilting at any attempt to provide formal (philosophical)
explanations in factual (scientific) terms. He represents, in short,
precisely the opposite view to that expressed by Quine.

There is a problem that has occupied philosophers and which might
though reasonably be called the philosophical theory of perception. This
is clearly about our senses and about sense-perception, which underlies
anything that we can subsume under the word 'knowledge'.

It is almost a universal assumption that there is an external world
and that there are physical objects. What is the basis for these
assumptions and what is their relation to our sensory information? In
discussing this problem, we might start by making some statement to the
effect that we see something real or see real things, as opposed to cases
where we "see" something which we do not take to be real, or is not real.
The notion of reality implies that we may be able to touch it and use
other senses to confirm its presence; it has continuity in both our own and
other's experiences; we say a chair is real if we can sit on it, and if it
has certain other properties which may be observed by the tactual senses,
etc. We have on some basis to distinguish these two types of experience,
and we may start, as Realists have done, by assuming the existence of
material or physical objects which are independent of the existence of the
organisms which observe them. This is purely an assumption and one which
cannot be proved, if proof by direct observation is required. At the same
time we may say that we have no reason to doubt the truth of the assertion
that there are things that exist independently of us.

We should say a few words here about proof. By a proof we mean, as
we have said, in a formal system a finite sequence

$$f_1, f_2, \ldots, f_n$$

of formulae which are either axioms, or derived from the axioms by the
rules of inference. However, we also use the word 'proof' in the above
sense of 'supplying evidence' to encourage a belief in something or confirm
some statement or hypothesis. A proof in this second sense is similar to a
causal explanation and is subject to what has already been said earlier
about evidence.

It should be explicitly noticed now that as we start to describe
(rather than explain, if we can make this distinction) the process of
perception as introspectively viewed, we are using a natural language
which has been built, not upon epistemologically neutral notions, but upon
primitive forms of beliefs about the world. Thus we may quickly notice
implicit assumptions about classifications, and the distinction between the
observing apparatus and what is observed, and more seriously the notion
that the things we see are supposed to have properties such as colour,
shape, etc. It should also be noticed that in talking of 'describe' and
'explain' we are trying to contrast the construction of a conceptual
framework, independent of all causal explanations, with a causal explanation
itself. The difference is doubtless mainly one of degree. It should
further be noted that the very idea of distinguishing an observer from
what is observed must be regarded as an empirical (scientific) assumption.

In this world of primitive assumptions, based on a somewhat primitive
language, we try to refine our terminology to deal with considerations
which are not normally considered, e.g. finer distinctions and broader
generalisations. Thus it is that we try to play safe and introduce a
neutral term 'sense-datum' for what we perceive where perception is that of
which our consciousness is aware.

In fact, the notion of sensory organs, even sensory faculties, underlying perception, is inferential and not by any means 'given'. But it is
impossible to describe acts such as perception without making inferences of
some sort, and this description in fact is couched in terms of a language

we expect other people to understand. Leaving this matter aside for the
time, it is an empirical fact that theorists such as Price, Broad, and
Moore, are soon brought to ask rather odd questions about these neutral
terms. For example, they come to ask: to what do these alleged sense-data
belong? Are there such things as unsensed sense-data? What is the nature
of perceptual consciousness, by virtue of which we are acquainted with
sense-data? And so on and so forth.

   Now it seems that in asking these questions we are going beyond our
search for a neutral description and are back in the situation of seeking a
causal explanation. At the same time, Broad and Price insist that we must
rely on direct observation alone and cannot appeal to evidence from empirical
data. To take the first question then: How are we to discover to what the
sense-datum belongs when all we are directly aware of is the sense-datum in
a context of other sense-data? The Naive Realists lay themselves open to
obvious difficulties in answering this question by saying that what we see
are the surface of physical objects. The cases of Illusions and Hallucin-
ations seem to give the lie to this answer; no conditions of physicality
can be stated that allow us to believe that a sense-datum always implies
the existence of an empirical object. The point to notice, however, is
that it does sometimes do just this. So we may be persuaded that sense-data
are sometimes indicative of the presence of physical objects, by almost any
conditions of physicality, while sometimes they are not.

   There are also other cases where we have every reason to suppose the
actual existence of some colour patch, rainbows, shadows, irradiated dust
particles and the like, which may not be obviously material objects but
which are not necessarily illusory either. Physical evidence, which we are
not allowed to introduce into the supposedly logical question, could tell
us by virtue of well-validated explanatory principles exactly what some of
these cases involve. However, our interest at this stage should be turned
to the point that we do not have to discuss the question of 'to what do the
sense-data belong?' To say that the sense-data belong to the surface of
physical objects, even where we might agree that physical objects might
be said to exist, is to beg the whole point of the neutral terminology
intended. If we were permitted to utilize our knowledge of physics, if only
for the purpose of better describing the perceptual process in a neutral
manner, we should soon say that the sense-datum (we would probably refer to
it as the appearance) connected with physical objects is a function of at
least a light source, the physical object, and a visual system. In fact,
to ask where the sense-datum belongs is seen to be an unreasonable, and
certainly a non-neutral, question. Equally unreasonable seems to be the
question of whether or not there are unsensed sense-data, which asks whether
something which is an intrinsic part of the act of sensing can exist
independently of the act. It is obvious when we are armed with the
scientific evidence, that we are in fact asking if the word should be used
to apply to a property of an object, our retina, visual cortex or whatever,
and of course we know this to be a silly question.

   Let us now look at another view of the perceptual problem. We shall
consider what Arthur Pap has said on the philosophical problem of
perception. He couches the problem as follows:-

          "Can it ever be the case that what we perceive is
          identical with the physical object and its physical
          properties as 'it really is'?"

It should be noticed that the monists and dualists would first disagree with the phrase 'really is', since for the monist perceptions are all there are, and for the dualist there is the question of stating the conditions for the reality of an object as opposed to our perceptions of it.

In this last matter, as Lean hints, there is a part of the creation of the very problem that the sense-datum theorists construct themselves. They do so by introducing the very dualism which they turn to and regard as a problem; this is true of Broad's, Price's and Moore's versions of sense-datum theory.

Let us now look at the Dualistic Phenomenalism of Broad. It is sufficient for our purpose here to note that he, like Price, acquires a logical problem, wherein he denies the relevance of empirical evidence in the form of the laws of perspective, and the findings of physiological psychology. Broad sees the logical question as arising over the apparent inconsistency of perceptual appearances. Thus the physical object looks different for various observers and also looks different for the same observer at different times.

Broad's difficulties then take on rather a remarkable form as has been well shown by Lean. Broad argues that if we are to accept the commonsense view that the objective elements in perceptions are the parts of physical objects, we are then committed to one of three possibilities: (i) That physical objects both change and do not change their properties. (ii) That we must distinguish the apparent from the real characteristics of sense-data, or (iii) We may deny the view that the objective element really is a part of a physical object. Actually, Broad seems to adopt the third view. But this difficulty is manufactured by Broad himself in the first place when he introduces the notion of objective elements of the perceptual situation. As to the other two possibilities:- (i) is ridiculous since the basic notion of contradiction is offended; how could we, from appearances alone, arrive at the idea of inconsistencies, if appearances are all that we are directly acquainted with? Obviously if our languages fail to account for, or give an inconsistent description of appearances, then it is our languages that are inadequate by the Phenonemalists's own showing. (ii) is inadequate as Price has rightly said; to introduce 'apparent' and 'real' into the compass of our 'sense-datum' language convention would be disagreeable because it would defeat its very purpose. Actually, common sense has no trouble with this problem, since the appeal to the non-allowable laws of perspective, without the added clarifying facts of empirical science in the form of physiological psychology, clear the matter up immediately; this sort of explanation is permitted in the causal theory, but not in the logical theory.

Now there are other matters we should consider that help to explain the extraordinary state of the logical problem of perception. We should argue as does Max Black that the very notion of a sense-datum language is an error in the first place. Such a private method of using terminology does not come within the confines of what are normally called languages, precisely because it cannot communicate information about the empirical world, but this is a point we have sufficiently made already.

It does not matter what the nature of the empirical world is, other than it should involve public designation or description. Ostensive rules are at the roots of communicable signs and the sense-datum language cannot be given ostensively. Sense-data are necessarily private to individuals, since if you deny their privacy, you deny their indubitability which has, in fact, been the villain of the whole peace.

The search for indubitability is misdirected because to have indubitable basic statements is to tie the notion of the basic statement to the non-communicable. Thus we find an indubitable element only to discover that it is useless.

Yolton has discussed the question of the <u>given</u> and pointed to the difficulties experienced by Russell in separating the epistemological given from the psychological given. The simplest solution would seem to have been to drop the distinction altogether, and with it the idea that there are two such sources of information open to us. The fact is that sense-data are not explicable except in the framework of a public physical object language in the first place.

Now let us return to the general problem generated in philosophy. We must proceed with special care at this stage. There is very little doubt that Ayer and Lean have been correct in drawing attention to the primarily verbal nature of the problem and if the problem is one of consistent description of the perceptual process, then this is a truism. However, in practice our language has, by its primitive and complex historical background, committed us to certain ontological and epistemological assumptions, such that when we introduce words such as 'sense-datum' and claim incorrigibility for sense-datum statements or for protocols or basic observation statements, as they are sometimes called, we lose claim to the neutrality of our usage. What, in any case, can be meant by using a term in a 'neutral' manner? But above all when we join with Price in asking 'to what does a sense-datum belong?', the notion of a neutral terminology seems ludicrous and the danger of hypostatisation looms close.

Whether or not Broad, Price and Moore have or have not created their own problems is really of no importance. The fact is that we do not wish to deny anyone the right to approach any problem in his own way and it is possible there is a logical problem of perception; but this being the case it does not follow that we cannot use our knowledge of empirical science to fill in those parts of the picture which are necessarily incomplete without it. The whole purpose of empirical science is to fulfil just this aim. Another way of stating this last point would be to say that there is a logical (the word 'logical' is not altogether well chosen) problem of perception (and all matters in all linguistic or symbolic systems) in that it appears to need to conform to certain fundamental logical rules (e.g. contradiction, identity, etc.) but if the theory is intended to do more than illustrate these principles of logic, it will not involve strictly non-empirical means alone, and so the questions asked by the epistemologists like Price, Broad and Moore are not logical, but empirical questions, which therefore require empirical answers. Indeed in general (as opposed to a particular case) we doubt the very distinction between description and explanation originally used, and this even applies to a conceptual framework for perception as opposed to causal explanation of it.

It is clear that knowing the empirical facts does not solve the "philosophical problem" of perception, but a knowledge of the structure of the process we seek to describe is obviously essential to our choice of language, and our attempt to find appropriate descriptions; the notions of perspective, for example, do quickly clear up our many confusions over 'appearances'. Our trouble has been the deep-rooted belief in certain epistemological priorities and a failure to observe that linguistic description involves empirical assumptions about the world.

Thus the language of properties which is often so misleading leads to inadequate description because of the inevitable, and as it happens, wrong epistemological and ontological interpretations we associate with the term. This is saying that we cannot have a neutral terminology for this or any other job. The marks that mathematical logicians use are neutral (this may be a significant part of the confusion) but these marks have to be interpreted to be of any use to communicate information, and then their neutrality is lost.

It should be noticed here the similarity that exists between the argument presently discussed and the work on the relationship between models and theories. When we formalise we try to eliminate all empirical meaning (factual data) and expose only the logical structure (formal data). The trouble, as ever, is the fact that language ceases to be a language (have empirical reference) when purely formal, and when factual takes on some of the (unconscious) empirical assumptions of the interpreter. Hence a language of 'properties' encourages the view that objects have properties which are observer-independent. This can be a very misleading way of describing events, where properties are perhaps better thought of as part of the relation between observer and observed.

Price says clearly that you cannot use science to explain problems of an epistemological kind, as this would involve an unwanted circularity. Perhaps it is that you cannot use logic for analogous reasons, since the basic level of perceptual description may be the level of our fundamental notions of logic itself. There are in any case various ways in which investigations may be carried out, and it seems, as Quine has said, that there is no reason to give one of them some sort of priority; there would be no sanction for doing so.

If we drop the idea of <u>certainty</u> and accept the notion that our knowledge can never be more than more or less probable, and we return to the acceptance of the direct relevance of empirical science to philosophy, our language it seems, would commit us to precisely this, by virtue of the fact that our language is already based on certain empirically founded interpretations.

All the above, perhaps especially the last paragraph, may seem particularly unsatisfactory to many, and if the matter were left there, without giving a brief illustration of the relative simplicity of our problem in practice, the cause for dissatisfaction may reasonably remain. Let us therefore consider some of the well-known examples of problems in perception, and give what is a form of semantic solution, abstracted from, but wholly dependent upon, the pragmatic facts.

Before we start, let us note that we must of course have some rule for distinguishing the real from the imaginary. It is a commonplace that we can do just this, otherwise our notions of illusion or hallucination would not have arisen. The fact that any particular distinction also depends on probabilities, and cannot be certain, is also commonplace, and since our system is inevitably tied to assumptions we shall make explicit whatever ontological and epistemological criteria seem most appropriate at any time. Our notions of physicality will thus be based upon the latest information physics can give. We will explicitly use the magnifying glass to investigate the magnifying glass and remain explicitly aware of just this fact. In the same way an investigation of the eye occurs in science which depends on the use of the eye. We must always start any investigation on the basis of some assumptions as well as some unanalysed terms.

Let us now consider an ordinary circular coin such as a 'new penny'. There is clearly a difficulty in describing a penny in any language. We say that it is a round, firm, disc-like, brown etc., coin. We may indefinitely enumerate the appearance of the penny which may vary indefinitely although it will never vary for any one person except in a temporal continuum. We are aware that we are independent observers of an independent physical object which we may expect to vary as the context of the viewing varies. Thus we fully expect to see a penny appearing elliptical, and even as a thin rectangular band when the edge is presented. These simple facts are part of our common experience. Where we have to be careful is to attribute a clear meaning to the words we use, and be in a position to distinguish a word that records a mere appearance and one which records an appearance and also implies a reality. The fact that this is all corrigible is to be noted.

We should also notice that the above argument should not be wholly limited to the visual sense modality. We are now in a position to assert, as does Ryle, that we may misuse such perceptual terms, even indeed without anyone knowing it. We may use for the above division 'see' and 'seem to see' and mean to assert physical existence only in the first case. In other words, we use 'see' incorrectly if we are not in the presence of some material object, and should instead say 'sense' or 'seem to see'. We cannot reasonably insist as does Pap that since 'sense' is a transitive verb we must sense something; this is to get tangled up in the sort of semantic or syntactic web which says if there is a word for it, it must exist.

To return to our penny, the plain fact is that no one feels that there is much mystery in a penny appearing elliptical; indeed we should regard it as mysterious if it did not do so under certain circumstances. There should be no mystery about generalisations from experience, except that they may be inconsistent. The essential point that we should notice here is that it is difficult to distinguish a generalisation from a statement of direct observation.

Indeed our point has been that there is no way of distinguishing a statement in a public language which is meant to convey only the directly observed facts from a statement which interprets the facts; or again it makes no sense to talk about direct observation statements, if sense-datum statements are what is meant. The sensory element is not, as Ryle has correctly pointed out, the whole of the observation process, thus the notion of interpretation and generalisation is wholly bound up in a public statement. But only language can be mysterious on this account. No one regards it as odd that parallel lines appear, from certain angles of viewing, to converge. Indeed as in the case of the penny, we should regard appearing to converge and look elliptical as essential to the entities that we call 'parallel lines' and 'pennies'.

From the above two paragraphs, as well as what we have said previously it should be clear that there has been an uncritical use of 'properties of objects' or 'properties' as well as 'material objects'. We are not confused when we regard the process as a triadic relation within which a variation of any one of the variables changes our 'perception' or 'sense-datum'. So the answer to the question: 'to what does the sense-datum belong?' is either (1) that the question is not meaningful because a sense-datum cannot be rightly said to belong to anything, or (2) that sense-data can be said to belong to a triadic relationship which we call 'perception', and which is subject to certain inductively founded generalisations such as the laws of perspective and the data of physiological psychology.

The whole problem is really to decide on where we start an analysis or explanation, and in what way (philosophical) analysis differs from explanation. We are asserting the difference is really not clearcut and that analysis and explanation go hand in hand.

We should now consider another well-known example; that of a stick partially immersed in water. The stick will in general appear bent when placed half in water and half in air, or indeed in any two media which differ in their refractive indices.

One way of using the word 'illusion' would now be to say that the actual properties of the stick differ from the perceived properties. We may simply mean that the tactual perceptual cues will differ from the visual ones and this would constitue one sense of the word 'illusion'. We do not, and should not, expect to see the stick as straight. There is in fact no confusion here between the belief and the visual appearance; we may say that what causes the stick to appear bent is the different refractive indices of water and air.

The whole matter of Broad's inconsistent appearances is made clear if we heed what the psychologist and physiologist tell us about the complex nature of the process we are discussing. We may regard this problem on one hand as merely preserving a proper distinction between the uses of various terms referring to sensation and observation. Thus the physiologist reminds us that we are referring to complex neural procces which will require the semanticist to maintain careful verbal distinctions, devised with one eye on the states or acts to be described and one on the language used for description. The well-known category mistakes, analysed by Ryle, are essentially those warned against here. The point is that we do not want to draw a hard and fast line between science and philosophy. That is, we cannot discuss merely semantics at any given time, since the language analysed semantically is the language already used to describe certain non-verbal designata and their more or less complex relations. Thus the distinction is made between a physiologist who performs operations of observation and records these observations in a language, and the semanticist who can analyse these verbal records, but not without regard for the designata the physiologist has been attempting to describe. Thus when Ryle starts his introduction to 'The Concept of Mind' with the words:-

"This book offers what may with reservations be described as theory of mind. But it does not give new information about minds."

This is the position of the semanticist since he does not perform the
operations of observing the designata that the physiologist performs. But
he cannot reformulate 'the logical geography of the knowledge which we
already possess' without reference to the designata described as well as
the language used to describe it. He is not investigating merely logical
truths as might a mathematical logician; he is investigating the logic of
and the clarity and adequacy of factual descriptions.

So our epistemological problem is to decide how best to arrange or
categorize certain events from the point of view of description. We should
always bear in mind that the distinctions we make, or the categories we set
up are always relevant to certain goals we have in mind, or contexts in
which we are placed or in which explanations are needed. The language has
to refer to the empirical data and also be internally consistent. We may
elect to say 'I see a material object X' and this would be a perfectly good
simple convention for many purposes. Thus if I said it when there was no
material X there, I should simply have made an error. There may of course
be no certain way of finding out whether or not an error has occurred, in
just the same way as there may be no way of ascertaining the truth of a
proposition; this will not impair our findings.

There is another use of 'illusion' which involves the misinterpretation
of a 'sense-datum'. We might mistake a distorted for a normal room, and
indeed this can be shown to happen. This last example could be the result
of the ignoring (or suppressing) of relevant cues, either by the active
organism or by the special conditions of the environment, e.g. such as when
it is specially manipulated by an experimenter. So we begin to understand
the nature of the problem and realise the inadequacy of talking of a purely
logical approach.

Broad's actual repudiation of empirical data, in the discussion of the
laws of perspective, says of the problem of the penny:

> "Our question is as to the compatibility of these changing
> elliptical appearances, however they may be correlated
> with other facts in the world, with the supposed constancy
> and roundness of the physical object."

We must agree with Lean that the laws of perspective are in fact directly
relevant to just this problem, and Broad's confusion seems merely to rest
on a too narrow interpretation of the words 'round' and 'constant'. To
put it briefly, a coin is round, and of constant shape, will appear of
various shapes relative to the angle of observation. This is simple and
obvious and does not require, or in any way depend upon, a logical solution,
any more at least than any solution to any problem whatsoever needs to
satisfy certain logical criteria.

At this point we can claim that the so-called logical problem of
perception, which is supposed to involve the apparent inconsistencies in
appearances, or in the use of sense-datum, is to be regarded as either
trivial or a pseudo-problem, or a question merely of linguistic usage which
depends on what is to be described.

Apart from the above it is however clear that the word 'sense-datum'
has in fact been used in many ways, since the question 'Does the 'sense-
datum' exist whether or not it is being sensed?' is, as we have already

noted, based on the intuitive distinction made between an object and an
observer, and the promotion of the question asking whether we regard the
'sense-datum' as having an existence in the observer or in the object. It
seems clear that we need to know something of the empirical facts before
we can find an adequate verbal description of those empirical facts and it
does not make any sense to say that this is purely a logical matter.

The appearance of an object, e.g. a penny will be said to be a function
of its relation to a light source and an observer. If the light source is
allowed to change in any of a variety of dimensions (brightness, colour,
etc.) then the appearance or sense-datum of the object will generally vary
also. Similarly, if the observer changes his position with respect to the
object or the light source the appearance will change. The sense-datum we
must remember is supposed to be a neutral word to avoid saying that the
object has changed and yet it indicates that the appearance of the object
may have. Thus we can mean that a sense-datum is what we say we see or
perceive according to our intended meanings of these terms; if so, we must
remember that our only evidence for having had a correct perception is on
the basis of probabilities which are referred to subsequent consistencies
as a result of the perceptual categorisation. In short we infer that we
are in error about the facts if no one agrees with us about them, if our
other senses give us inconsistent information, or if our subsequent behaviour
based on our perception turns out to be inadequate.

We may say, if we wish to use words in such a way, that our sense-datum
was of a man (say), but the fact is that it was an ape. Or since this may
merely be regarded as the giving of different interpretations to the same
sense-datum, we may say that to us it was green and to everyone else it was
red. But are these examples really different? We cannot separate the
interpretation we place on some object itself, regardless of words. We
can find ample evidence from experimental psychology that supports this
assertion and there would be no point in ignoring this evidence; rather we
should be sure that our problem of description is facilitated by such
evidence.

In this situation we see again that the word 'sense-datum' has more
than one meaning. If we say that it is what the observer merely records,
which is claimed by some to be the <u>certain</u> element in knowledge, then
clearly it would not do to identify it as belonging to physical objects in
all cases. If we are correct in our perceptions, however, we assume that
the presence of a physical object (taken in a broad sense as anything
reflecting photons of light) was necessary to the perception.

Perhaps the final word on the so-called logical theory of perception
is that there are many solutions which are relative to either our
ontological or linguistic assumptions. They depend on the assumptions made
about the world, and the rules that guide the use of the intended meanings
of the terms used. It is in the matter of usage that we have a convention
which talks about real objects, and so on. We have a mode of description
which attributes properties to objects or things and which has an ontological
commitment that wholly and inevitably overthrows the intended neutrality of
our descriptions. We are as usual faced by the problem of 'meaning' and
this is routed in all language.

The arguments from Illusion depend on our ability to recognise the
difference between a wild and a non-wild perception, which suggests that we

actually know when a sense-datum is not representative of, or caused by,
an external physical object. It may, of course, be caused by an external
state, but the false interpretation is a function of the internal structure
of the organism. Thus a consideration of the broader context of the questio
almost immediately gives us a solution. This whole study drives one to
agree with Professor Boas' conclusions, when he said:

> "The trouble with epistemologists is that they think that
> knowledge goes on in detachment from the total context in
> which it occurs..."

In this section of this chapter we have in fact directed our attack
against confusions involved in the so-called logical theories of perception,
especially against the users of the so-called sense-datum language. The
reason for this is because they, more than any others, have laid emphasis
on the logical nature of this problem. The position taken up is in general
agreement with Lean's condemnation of the Phenomenalist viewpoint; not
only in Broad's, but also in Moore's and Price's forms. Furthermore, while
one can agree with Lean that Broad and the Phenomenalists in general generat(
the problems they wish to solve, it should be emphasized also - a point
rather neglected by Lean - that their main troubles stem from the nature of
the incorrigible 'given' from which they start, and from a belief that they
can deliver themselves of a terminology under the guise of verbal neutrality
that is in fact - and this is especially obvious from the questions that
they subsequently ask - committed to a particular epistemological viewpoint
or a particular ontology or both. It also seems that the wrongly named
sense-datum language is in fact only intelligible within the compass of
some prior, realist terminology.

There are many good reasons which have already been mentioned why
Phenomenalism is deemed to be a thoroughly inadequate interpretation of the
problems of perception. The sense-datum language may have appeared at first
sight to be a convenient form of description, but turns out to be wholly
inadequate by virtue of its failure to be a language at all, and so has no
advantages over the languages of appearances of the public kind, but does
have insurmountable disadvantages. We know all we know from appearances,
and we make, on the basis of these appearances, just whatever assumptions
are necessary to make appearances consistent, and that is precisely the job
of empirical science. We are all of us committed to some interpretation of
the world in answering any question about the world; our choice is between
the naive-implicit and naive-explicit assumptions of such as Broad and
Price, or the explicit and sophisticated assumptions which are in keeping
with the findings of modern science. What Price and Broad have usefully
demonstrated for us is the inadequacy of Phenomenalism, and the hopeless
lameness of talking of the logical question of perception when the questions
asked are empirical. There are problems of language and problems of
empirical fact and our job is to investigate the two together.

We have used the problem of perception to further the argument that
any factual-form dualism is arbitrary, especially in the field of
epistemology. The significance this has for our general reader is to serve
as a reminder that whereas philosophical rumination about what we know and
how we know it is greatly to be encouraged we cannot wholly separate this
from experimental science and the discovery of empirical facts about the
world in which we live. Such activities are as important to our debator as
is logic.

SUMMARY

We have dealt with epistemology as the analysis of knowledge - what we know and how we know what we know. Perception is clearly a central issue and we have tried to show that this is a process which is not merely logical but also capable of psychological and physiological analysis.

EXERCISES

1. How do you know what you know is correct? (i.e. certain or indubitible)

2. How should you use the word 'know'? Advise an enquirer about the care he should take and try to advise him what he should mean.

3. What is knowledge? Explain to an untutored friend what you mean by the word 'knowledge'.

REFERENCES

CARNAP, R.   Introduction to Semantics. Chicago University Press, 1942

CARNAP, R.   Meaning and Necessity. Chicago University Press, 1947

GEORGE, F.H.   Semantics. English Universities Press, 1964

PRICE, H.H.   Thinking and Experience. Hutchinson, 1953

QUINE, W.V.   From a Logical Point of View. Harvard University Press, 1953

RUSSELL, B.   Our Knowledge of the External World. London, 1914

RUSSELL, B.   The Analysis of Mind. London, 1921

RUSSELL, B.   Philosophy. New York, 1927

RUSSELL, B.   An Enquiry into Meaning and Truth. New York, 1940

RUSSELL, B.   Human Knowledge: Its Scope and Limits. George Allen and Unwin, London, 1948

RYLE, G.   The Concept of Mind. Hutchinson, 1949

CHAPTER 12

A PRAGMATIC THEORY OF BEHAVIOUR

Before we discuss formalisation let us outline a theory of behaviour which we can use as a "guinea pig" for our process of formalisation. For our purpose here, it does not matter whether you agree or not with the effectiveness or usefulness of the theory since all we are concerned with is whether it makes an appropriate example of formalisation in action; we hope that it does. We shall call our pragmatic theory of behaviour a Theory of Signs. But even before we come to our Theory of Signs, we shall make a few general statements about the general nature of Pragmatics.

In talking of knowledge and how we know and what we think we know we should conclude that we cannot obtain any certainty regarding knowledge, if we are talking of what is public or communicable knowledge. We can achieve a kind of certainty only about our own feelings and impressions and these are, at least to the extent that they are certain, private and uncommunicable.

The observer is imprisoned to some extent in his own private world and can only derive so much from his contact with reality. In talking this way we are maintaining a realistic ontology, even though we may still accept that what we are aware of (or capable in principle of being aware of) is the sufficient basis for much of science and scientific discourse. We should also bear in mind that science is thought by us to be mainly concerned with trying to answer specific questions about specific issues in a specific context and not merely being a seeker after truth.

We are therefore inclined to say that the epistemologist should consider what the scientist is asserting in so far as it may help his own cause. It may be that a scientific approach to a subject based on assumptions and known to be dubitable, could nevertheless throw light on attempts to explicate questions such as those concerned with meaning and truth.

Pragmatics (Morris, 1946) is the study of the inter-behavioural responses within which discourse occurs. Semantics is a special case of pragmatics concerned with meaning and Syntax is a special case of semantics concerned with formation rules, or what is acceptable in grammatical terms. These three disciplines are closely inter-related, and pragmatics is in one sense a study of psychology and in another sense a study of cybernetics. What distinguishes these two senses is whether or not the approach is simulatory or synthetic.

Pragmatics (as well as syntax and semantics) can also occur in either of two modalities, pure or descriptive (Carnap, 1939; Sellars, 1947a, 1947b). There is little doubt that syntax and semantics can be thought of as either pure or descriptive ('applied' is a synonym for 'descriptive') since we can have a normative approach to each and we can study each as a

science. How do people actually use words and what do they mean by them?
Pragmatics has been a source of some discussion in this context since it
has been suggested that it can never be other than descriptive. We feel
that anything that can be described can be formalised and that anything
that can be formalised can also be the subject of a description or an
interpretation.

Although working under the name semantics, the work of Ogden and
Richards (1923) and Korzybski (1933) are really in the Carnap-Morris sense
of the term offering a theory of meaning which is in the field of pragmatics.
The Ogden and Richards view is closely associated with conditional response
theory and first saw the light of day in the early 1930's. They were
setting out in effect a theory of signs or perhaps in their case more
accurately a theory of symbols. We can at this stage roughly distinguish
a symbol from a sign by saying a symbol is something like x when used in
an algebraic equation or a letter of the alphabet say, and therefore can
be make to signify anything we like whereas a sign is something which
specifically signifies something; natural signs are things like smoke which
signify fire and language signs are words (in themselves symbols) or
sentences which have specific meaning, however difficult it is to define
what that meaning is.

Ogden and Richards were concerned in their scientific theory of
meaning primarily with what they called interpretation; acts of interpretation are involved whenever you read a book or hear words spoken, and
the process of interpretation is a sort of decoding process where the
statements heard are translated into concepts or ideas.

'Basic interpretation' is a term used by Ogden and Richards to refer
to interpretations that cannot be broken down any further. They are the
equivalent in the world of meaning of the smallest particles of physics.
Let us look now at an example of how Ogden and Richards saw the process of
meaning take shape. Consider a man who strikes a match; the striker has
an expectation of seeing a flame on striking the match; the interpreter,
who of course may be the same person as the striker, but is in any case an
observer in his role as interpreter, watches expectantly and thinks of, or
certainly may think of, the flame emanating from the match. The actual
striking of the match is a referent, the conceptual process of thinking
about it or expecting something to happen is the reference (the having of
the concept) and an adequate reference refers to a referent which actually
happens which can be symbolized by a word. Let us take another example:
a referent can be a dog, say, and the thought of the dog is the reference
and the symbol which refers to the referent is the word 'dog'.

As far as they went Ogden and Richards gave a fairly convincing
theory of meaning, but it seems that they did not go far enough to include
the subtleties of meaning encountered in the more sophisticated uses of
language.

Korzybski following on in some measure where Ogden and Richards left
off, emphasized the hierarchical nature of language and drew attention to
the fact that the physical world was distinguishable from the conceptual
world which was again distinguishable from the levels of language which
described both the conceptual and the physical world. There is of course
a sense in which the conceptual world is part of the physical world, as

indeed are the words used to describe either. He then went on to distinguish
the immediate descriptive level of terms which referred directly to
physical events or relationships and then words which referred to words
and words that referred to words that referred to words, and so on.

Korzybski pointed out that terms are many-meaninged ('multi-ordinal'
is the word he used for this) and that they mean different things on
different levels of abstraction and in different contexts. He regarded
the process of abstracting as fundamental to the use of language and the
case of a great deal of misunderstanding about the nature of language. He
contrasted languages with maps, and had what was rather similar to a
Wittgensteinian (1922) view of language as a pictorial thing. In other
words, a linguistic description is a sort of verbal picture of the
environment. This leads Korzybski to say that all our knowledge is only
knowledge of <u>structure</u>. All we can know are structural relationships
which exist in the empirical world.

Korzybski makes the point that modelling, of which language is a
particular kind, is self-referential; it refers to itself just as words
can refer to themselves. But no model can ever be as complete as the
thing being modelled, since if it were it would be the original rather than
the model. Korzybski draws the obvious conclusion from this that we must
be extremely careful, and we have agreed about this time and again, to
distinguish between words and the things the words represent. Most
logicians regard this as self-evident and hardly worth making a major
issue out of. However the fact remains, and here Korzybski was absolutely
correct (Crawshay-Williams, 1957), that in spite of the fact that we
recognise explicitly that things or events and the words used to describe
them are different we nevertheless often fall into the trap of forgetting
that statements and the things that statements are about are different.
It often happens that it is thought that the use of a word automatically
implies the existence of some equivalent and this is not necessarily so.

We now come to the modern theory of signs which owes its origins
primarily to the work of C.S. Peirce (1931-35) and Charles Morris (1946).
Both had a common purpose in supplying science as a foundation for a
theory of knowledge and all felt it could be done through the behavioural
background specifically associated with language signs. The main
difference between the work of Ogden and Richards and Korzybski on one
hand and the work of Peirce and Morris on the other is that the latter is
rather more general in being concerned with other sorts of signs besides
language signs, and it is for this reason that they have called their work
'pragmatics', and the former have called their work 'semantics'.

'Semiotic' is the name that was originally chosen by C.S. Peirce to
categorize this particular scientific study of signs. Sometimes it was
referred to as 'Semiosis' (this was Peirce's usual choice in fact) and
sometimes more recently, particularly with respect to the work of Morris,
it has become known as 'Behavioural Semiotic'. We shall use pragmatics to
cover all these different versions of what is really a theory of sign
behaviour.

Peirce, in christening the subject 'semiosis', thought of it as the
study of signs, sign processes, sign-mediation and other context
relationships existing between people, particularly with respect to their

trade in signs and symbols both with each other and with the environment.
A mental process, for Peirce, was a sign process. The 'representamen' as
he called it is something that is a mental event and it is also the
representation of a thing or object for which it stands. It is exactly
what Ogden and Richards called a thought or reference and we have tended
to call a concept or conceptual process. Signs are representamens of
human minds used by them and manipulated by them in representing through
language the world around themselves. This is indeed a sort of model
building process.

Morris defines a <u>sign</u> as follows:-

> "If anything A is a preparatory stimulus which in the absence
> of stimulus-objects initiating response-sequences of a certain
> behaviour-family causes a disposition in some organism to
> respond under certain conditions by response-sequences of
> this behaviour family, then A is a sign."

This definition has the obvious merit of distinguishing a sign from the
referent or the denotatum, or whatever it is that the sign refers to. The
referent itself is a goal object whereas a sign itself is not; also it is
clear that signs can be understood without an immediate behavioural
response to that sign. This is the whole point of internal mediation of
the organism under the heading Disposition to Respond. In other words,
we realize that all behavioural changes will not be immediately apparent
in performance, which is something we knew from the original discussions
and dispute between Hull (1948, 1952) and Tolman (1932, 1952) leading to
the revision of Hull's earlier theories.

One thing to be added to what has been said already is the fact that
when we talk about lexical signs (signs produced by lexicographers), as
we might call them, we are talking of dictionary definitions and we see
how difficult these are to think of other than as empirical. They also
have something of the conventional about them. We are saying in effect
that words have meanings by virtue of conventions; these conventions may
or indeed may not represent what is empirically used by the majority of
people, this is a matter that can only be determined by empirical
investigation (Arne Naess, 1951).

Let us consider again the distinction between <u>sign</u> and <u>symbol</u>.
<u>Black clouds</u> are a sign of rain and 'rain' is a symbol for rain, and
certainly it is true that in describing rain it is only a sign for me by
virtue of already being a symbol. But this need not make the sign theory
of meaning circular as some (H.H. Price, 1953) have argued, since we would
argue in turn that symbols <u>are</u> signs and signify (albeit by convention).

We will now turn to a brief description of a pragmatic theory of
signs which has been developed (George and Handlon, 1955, 1957).

A THEORY OF SIGNS

The pragmatic theory of signs to be described centres around the notion
of a <u>belief</u>. It is suggested that a belief be thought of, in the Peircian
manner, as "that which disposes the organism to think and perhaps to act".
Belief is here used as a <u>theoretical term</u> (a sort of logical construct)

and can be thought of as being represented by any empirical statement. In
other words, any statement that asserts a fact, a relationship, an
attitude etc., and implies that its holder believes it to be true is to be
thought to hold that belief.

    Beliefs are in fact considered to be relatively permanent states of
the central nervous system, although that is not necessary to the theory.
In everyday terms, beliefs are those stored memories whose contents specify
for the organism what may be expected to happen (S_2) if certain behaviour
(R_1) is performed under certain stimulating circumstances (S_1). Since
at any given moment the organism's behaviour is a function of a relatively
few of the totality of its stored beliefs, we shall call those beliefs
which are actually influencing behaviour at any given instant of time
expectancies ($E(R_1 - S_2)$)'s. Beliefs may be converted into expectancies
through the action of the activating state (S_1). This activating stimulus
state is a conjunction of motivational stimuli (Sm's), stemming from the
motivational state (M) of the organism and of the stimulus complexes (S*s).
It is the activating stimulus state which is the effective part of all the
potential stimuli in the environment. Its effectiveness springs from
active searching and selection on the part of the person as well as
environmentally given.

    Both the Sm's and S*s are sub-classes of the class of stimuli that
have been associated with particular beliefs. Sm's are, of course,
primarily (although not entirely) internal to the organism, while the
S*s may be either external or internal. One possible sub-class of S*s
(the relation may actually be one of overlap, class exclusion or class
inclusion) is the class of modifying motivational stimuli (MM's) which
are capable of changing the internal motivational state (M). This
motivational state, which is seen as being derived from two factors,
drive (D) and urgency (U), may act to determine the size and nature of the
range of the expectancies transformed from the relevant beliefs.

    When a range of expectancies has been transformed from the totality
of relevant stored beliefs by the activating stimulus state (S_1), the
range of expectancies is scanned. This process of scanning leads to the
"selection" of a single expectancy whose correlative response (R_1) is
the one that will be subsequently emitted. The "selection" of the single
expectancy during the scanning process is made in terms of (a) the strength
of the belief underlying the expectancy and (b) the valence and value
of the expectancy. Valence and value, in turn, are a function of the
anticipated reward and the anticipated effort involved in the projected
response, the value of the act or object is the invariant feature while the
valence is its value in a particular context.

    The emission of the correlative response (R_1) associated with the
chosen expectancy follows automatically upon the selection of that
expectancy. This response will either be followed by the anticipated
outcome (S_2), in which case either a confirmation of the correlative
belief will take place, or it will not, in which case a falsification
of the belief will follow. This whole process, beginning with the
transformation of beliefs into expectancies by the S_1 and ending with
confirmation or falsification, is called the general behavioural unit (GBU).
As far as problem solving is concerned this ends with either 1) the
solution, 2) a substitute solution or 3) abandonment. As far as

learning is concerned this is an on-going process, and where "thinking" is involved, as it will often be in both problem solving and learning, series of GBU's occur. They will be concerned with signs (including symbols and images).

While the interactions of the above variables are too complex to be presented in any adequate detail here, a few further points should be made. Which beliefs are converted into expectancies depends upon the previous association between certain stimuli and certain beliefs. Beliefs are thus acquired by contiguity - the association in experience of activating stimuli (S_1's) with means outcomes (R_1 - S_2's). Such experiences may be direct ones, wherein physical energy changes, forming the basis for the stimuli, emanate from that event about which the organism acquires beliefs. But many beliefs are learned indirectly through the use of symbols, where the emanating energy changes from the event do not in any direct fashion determine the beliefs about that event.

Thus, knowledge may be acquired either through <u>direct acquaintance</u> or through <u>description</u>. Apart from their acquisition, beliefs may be <u>strengthened</u> (through confirmation) or <u>weakened</u> (through falsification), either by description or by direct acquaintance, by going through the steps of the general behavioural unit (GBU). The relation between this theory of signs and our discussions of explanation in science (Chapter Seven) is fairly clear.

Motivation is not only an important factor in the determination of the range of expectancies elicited for scanning, but it also plays an important role in the selection process through its indirect effect upon the valence, and on its value. Further, motivation operates to determine the speed of selection as well as the speed and strength of response elicitation.

There are other behavioural units called the <u>perceptual behavioural units</u> (PBU's) which are closely related to GBU's, and are necessary to them, as far as the person's transactions with the environment are concerned. For every GBU there must exist a PBU to categorise the originally registered <u>activating stimulus state</u> (S_1). A PBU is also necessary to identify the <u>outcome</u> or <u>goal</u> (S_2) to allow assessment of <u>confirmation</u> or <u>falsification</u>. It is clear that a PBU must precede every GBU and must also follow every GBU if environmental transactions are concerned. The exception is in the conceptual processes, where thinking and problem solving are concerned; here GBU's might follow each other.

We next come to a whole set of theorems and assumptions regarding the detailed nature of motivation (George and Handlon, 1955, 1957; George, 1963), and we shall not discuss this sort of detail in this chapter. We shall instead next compare further the PBU and the GBU. In general, the form of the PBU is similar to that of the GBU. After proper encoding, certain of the stimuli impinging on the central nervous system are capable of transforming beliefs into expectancies; then, through the process of scanning, one of the expectancies is selected, and a response ensues. But there are certain important differences between the details of the GBU and the PBU that must be noted.

1.   The first difference concerns itself with the nature of the
final response (R_1). In the PBU the R_1 is the covert response of
categorising or classifying the impinging stimuli. Such a response
is best thought of as occurring entirely within the central nervous
system, and as not necessarily involving conscious awareness. In
contrast, the R_1 of the GBU may be any number of different actions,
some of them overt and some covert.

2.   We must distinguish between the contents of the beliefs of the
PBU and those of the GBU. In the PBU, beliefs concern themselves
with such cognitive actions as seeing, hearing, tasting, etc. - in
general, those activities which have traditionally come under the
rubric "sensation and perception". They involve the action of the
central nervous system as the organism "apprehends" its external as
well as its internal, environment. Perceptual beliefs can be
expressed as conditionals of the form: if the impinging stimuli (the S_1)
have been categorised as C_1 (the R_1), then the subsequent impingement
by other stimuli of the categories C_2, ..., C_n (the S_2) is likely to
obtain, with some probability p. What the conditions are under which
these probable impingements will take place also forms the content of
perceptual beliefs - or, more precisely, the perceptual meta-beliefs.

          For convenience's sake, we shall consider all those beliefs that
are concerned with the perceptual categorisation of events to be
perceptual beliefs, and all others general beliefs. That such an
arbitrary division as this is only a temporary verbal convenience
will be appreciated when we now note the close relationship between
GBU's and PBU's.

3.   In the GBU, in order for an activating stimulus state (S_1) to
transform a belief into an expectancy, it is first necessary that
the S_1 be perceived. By perception, of course, we mean the action of
a categorising response which is the R_1 of an immediately preceding
PBU. That is to say, in order for a GBU to take place it must be
preceded by a PBU. On the other hand, in the PBU, in order for an
S_1 to transform a perceptual belief into a percetpual expectancy we
must arbitrarily assert that it is not possible that the S_1 be
preceded by a categorising response. Thus, for the PBU, given a
particular S_1, those perceptual beliefs that are associated with the
S_1, will immediately and automatically be converted into perceptual
expectancies. This transformation will take place without the S_1's
being first perceptually categorised. The only categorisation
involved is the R_1 which ends the PBU.

4.   Since there may be more than one perceptual belief associated
with a given S_1, the question arises as to which of the beliefs
converted into perceptual expectancies will be selected. Such a
selection will lead automatically to the categorising response, R_1,
of the PBU. We have seen that in the GBU the selection of the
expectancy which leads automatically to the R_1 is a joint function
of (a) the value and valence of the expectancies which have been
transformed from beliefs, and (b) the strength of the beliefs
correlative with these expectancies. In the PBU, however, while
these three factors of value, valence and belief strength also
operate to select a single expectancy, it is the latter that seems to

play the more important role. This does not mean that value and valence are not important, especially when the stimulating circumstance (S_1) is ambiguous and when motivation is strong; but, on the whole, the strength of the perceptual belief is primary in the selection of a particular perceptual expectancy leading to the R_1 of the PBU. By strength of perceptual belief we mean, simply, the degree or strength of association existing between a particular S_1 and a particular perceptual belief.

5.   Unlike the GBU, the final step in the PBU is not an <u>outcome</u> or <u>goal</u> (S_2) which is then followed by another PBU leading to a categorising response, for this would now involve us in an infinite regress. Rather, the PBU ends with an R_1, the categorising response. This perceptual categorisation may, however, be subsequently confirmed or disconfirmed; and this, in turn, will lead to the strengthening or weakening of the correlative perceptual belief through confirmation or falsification. Such confirmation or falsification may take place in two ways. First, the outcome (S_2) of the response (R_1) of the subsequent GBU may either confirm or falsify the veridicality of the previous perceptual categorising response. Secondly, a subsequent PBU, because of the content of the organism's belief system, may be categorised as being either compatible or incompatible with the previous PBU in question. And this, in turn, may bring about a confirmation or falsification of the previous PBU, leading to the strengthening or weakening of the correlative perceptual belief. It should be noticed that perception is normally regarded as <u>certain</u> by the organism and is not thought of as requiring confirmation.

We must distinguish between beliefs regarding perceptual <u>events</u> and beliefs regarding perceptual <u>rules</u>. We might also talk of perceptual beliefs regarding <u>rules about rules</u>. Another way of distinguishing these various levels of perceptual beliefs is to call them "beliefs", "meta-beliefs" and "meta-meta- beliefs", etc.

Let us now continue our examination of the PBU in detail. We have previously defined the activating stimulus state (S_1) as "... that state of the central nervous system which is capable of transforming specific beliefs into expectancies" and we have considered the S_1 to be made up of stimulus complexes ($S*s$) plus stimuli arising from motivational states (Sms). But in order to specify more precisely the functioning of the S_1 in the PBU, it is convenient to partition S_1s into three subcategories: (a) cues,   (b) clues and (c) signs.

We shall postulate, as part of the connotation of the words "cue", "clue" and "sign", that they refer to the organism's <u>use</u> of certain stimuli <u>after</u> they have been associated with specific perceptual beliefs. Thus, we shall consider cues, clues and signs to be a subclass of the class of activating stimulus states (S_1s) rather than, say, a subclass of stimulus complexes ($S*s$) or motivational stimuli (Sms). For we wish to make it clear that cues, slues and signs have their functional basis not only in events external to the organism, but also in events internal to it, such as beliefs, attitudes, motivations, etc.

1.   CUES (Cus):   A subclass of the class of activating stimulus states
                    (S₁s) which stems from objects or events, either external
                    or internal, which are being apprehended directly by the
                    organism through knowledge by acquaintance.

    Cues from external events may be modified by internal Sms stemming from concomitant motivational states. Conversely, cues from internal events may be modified by S*s stemming from concomitant external events.

2.   CLUES (Cls): A subclass of activating stimulus states (S₁s) which
                    stems from the context, ground or surround in which
                    the apprehended object or event, either external or
                    internal, is embedded. The apprehension of a clue by
                    the organism is direct, i.e. through knowledge by
                    acquaintance.

    Unlike cues, clues are not apprehended in and of themselves; if they are experienced at all, they are experienced in conjunction with cues, and they usually exert influence upon the apprehension of the concomitant cue, and vice versa.

    Clues, then, are S₁s which inform the organism about some events or objects other than themselves. Such information may have to do with such "objective" matters as the size, colour, shape, location in space, etc. of objects as well as such "subjective" matters as pleasantness, attractiveness, harmfulness, etc. Such information as is given by clues may or may not, of course, be veridical.

3.   SIGNS (Sns): A subclass of the class of activating stimulus states
                    (S₁s) which the organism, through the acquisition of
                    beliefs, has learned stand for other stimuli.

    As can be seen by the definition, signs are closely related to clues, since they are a subclass of S₁s which are concerned with objects or events other than themselves. But, unlike clues, which must always appear with the object or event about which they yield information, signs may give information about objects or events which are not simultaneously present. In this sense, clues may be considered to be a kind of subclass of the class of signs.

    As we see from the above definition, signs may come to stand for, or be substitutable for, or come to represent, objects or events to the organism which are not now present. In fact, under special circumstances, they may come to stand for events or objects which can never be known directly (i.e. through knowledge by acquaintance) by the organism. Thus, though the information the clue conveys is always about an object or event known through knowledge by acquaintance, in the case of signs this need not be so. This is particularly true of signs that are encountered in language which are used in formal and informal education to convey information about objects or events which may never be directly experienced by the organism. Cues as well as clues may, of course, act as signs under special circumstances.

    This is by no means a sufficient analysis of signs, since that part of the definition which says they "stand for", itself requires a great deal of further explanation.

The first step in our further explanation is to define a <u>symbol</u>.

4.   SYMBOLS (Sys).   <u>A subclass of the class of signs (Sns) which have</u>
                       <u>specific reference to concepts (or beliefs) and may</u>
                       <u>also have external referents in the form of physical</u>
                       <u>objects.</u>

Symbols are thus arbitrary or conventional in that they are like words
or sentences. But as words they may signify either internal states or
external objects, relations, etc. As sentences, it is the symbols (as words)
which form the sentence, and the sentence which signifies the concept or
belief. The meaning of the sentence is then to be thought of as its
signification (to the concept or belief).

In Price's example of "the cat is in the cupboard" (S_1) the sentence
clearly signifies this for the utterer or a listener. That he may not
believe what is signified is clear, since we are not saying that
signification disposes the utterer or hearer to believe in S_1, only to form
a belief <u>about</u> S_1 (which may lead to action). We can now add to our
vocabulary <u>signals</u> as standardized signs, sometimes symbolic in form, and
<u>images</u> which are <u>internal signs</u>, and are the equivalent to cues and clues
in the environment.

Objects and events about which cues and clues convey information can
be experienced only directly, while the object and events about which
signs convey information can be experienced either directly or indirectly.
Knowledge <u>about</u> cues, clues and signs, however, may be acquired either
through knowledge by acquaintance or knowledge by description.

The breaking down of S_1s into the above subclasses may often turn out
to be rather arbitrary; nevertheless, it is believed to be a convenient
way of describing the various functions of the activating stimulus state
in the PBU.

Often, when we apprehend an object or event, we are not able to
categorise it completely or fully, to our satisfaction, at the first
attempt. Instead, we may first categorise it one way and then another,
and so on. We may, of course, take into account each one of our "abortive"
categorisations to form a concatenation of interpretations from which
we construct our final categorising response. Or we may make use of
further in-coming information from the object or event itself. Or,
finally, by examining our past experiences, through our perceptual beliefs,
we may try to "remember" what this object or event "might be". We then
arrive at a categorisation upon which we are prepared to act, insofar as
we are relatively sure that our categorisation is a "correct" one.

As with Bruner et al (1956) we think of such categorising behaviour
in cognitive activities such as problem solving as having the following
advantages:-

1.   It reduces the complexity of the environment.

2.   It is a means of identification.

3.   It reduces the need for learning.

4.   It is a means of action.

5.   It permits the ordering and relating of classes of events.

From this we see that we can look upon the perceptual process as central to problem solving and as consisting of a finite series of interpretations: I_1, I_2, ..., I_n, where I_n is that interpretation or categorisation upon which the organism is prepared to act. In the limiting case, the series of interpretations may of course be only two - I_1, I_2, or even merely I_1. The series of categorisations may take place extremely rapidly, and it is only on relatively rare occasions that such a series is slow enough and perhaps difficult enough so that we become conscious of the process.

It is therefore necessary, for any complete description of the perceptual process and conceptual process, to make allowances for such a series of interpretations or categorisations. We shall, therefore, distinguish between what we will term the provisional categorising responses (PCRs) and the final categorising responses (FCRs), the latter being of particular interest since it forms the S_1 of the subsequent GBU.

The final stages of such cognitive acts as problem solving, as opposed to the processes of perception, may be terminated by the solution, etc. This is no longer to be thought of as an on-going process as is the case in perception and learning which is terminated only by sleep (partially) or death (totally). Before termination of, or even the application of, an expectancy to a cognitive situation, we may expect to find the notion of risk also being involved.

The basic question is "What am I risking by taking this course of action rather than that?" and although one may risk delaying a solution, by testing a hypothesis which is either not the most probable or has not the best range for elimination purposes, there is no question of overall life-and-death type of risk considerations involved.

IN SUMMARY

In this chapter we have tried to develop two aspects which are relevant to the main theme of the book.

The first aspect is to provide an alternative (or complementary) approach to knowledge from that provided by epistemology. This is relevant to our own theme, in conjunction with epistemology, since a basic understanding of knowledge and how we know what we know must be relevant to any fairly basic question in science and its precise description, especially ours which is much concerned with the observer-observed relationship.

The second aspect is to provide an account of a system which has intelligence (i.e. a human being) since a formalisation of this can be taken as a description of an artificially intelligent system.

The methods of formalisation, quite naturally carried through by way of automata theory, are outlined and in some measure developed in the rest of this book.

An alternative notation to the one we have used in our theory of signs, which has some advantages, is to refer to a CBU (Conceptual Behaviour Unit) and a PBU and take collections of PBUs and CBUs into GBUs. But this is not a matter of great importance.

EXERCISES

1. Explain the distinction between syntax, semantics and pragmatics. What is the difference between each of these in terms of "pure" and "descriptive" modes?

2. How does formal logic, philosophy and psychology relate to the distinctions mentioned in the first example of this exercise?

3. When asked to "pass the jug of water" and you pass the "can of oil", what does your interlocutor (who asked you to pass the water) conclude about you?

4. What are signs and symbols: give an explanation to yourself that you find convincing. Especially consider how they relate to each other.

5. How do you react to the advice "how are you so sure you are right?" Do you adopt a decent tentativeness when you are actually trying to discover something (we excuse you these constraints if you are merely "doing down" an adversary)?

REFERENCES

BLACK, M.   Language and Philosophy. Cornell University Press, 1949

CRAWSHAY-WILLIAMS, R.   Methods and Criteria of Reasoning. Routledge and Kegan Paul, 1957

GEORGE, F.H. and   Towards a general theory of behaviour.
HANDLON, J.H.   Methods, 25 - 44. 1955, 1

GEORGE, F.H. and   A language for perceptual analysis.
HANDLON, J.H.   Psychol. Rev., 64, 14 - 25, 1957

GEORGE, F.H.   Cognition. Methuen, 1963

KORZYBSKI, A   Science and Sanity. Science Press, 1933

MORRIS, C.W.   Signs, Language and Behaviour. Prentice Hall, 1946

OGDEN, C.K. and   The Meaning of Meaning. Harcourt-Brace, 1923
RICHARDS, I.A.

WITTGENSTEIN, L.   Tractatus Logico-Philosophicus.
                         Routledge and Kegan Paul, 1922

PART III

FORMALISATION

The first part of this book was concerned with an
introduction to logic, common sense and logical thinking,
especially as it applies to scientific and rigorous
thinking. Part II of this book dealt with probability
theory and philosophy in the main and finished off with
a discussion of Pragmatic theory of behaviour which we
use as our major example of formalisation in action in
Part III.

CHAPTER 13

APPLIED LOGIC

In this chapter we deal for the first time with an application of the methods which have been outlined in the last six chapters. What we now do is use formal (sometimes axiomatic) systems for the description of aspects of the "real world." But before we do so we must develop one more formal system: the Calculus of Relations. Our development is however informal.

THE CALCULUS OF RELATIONS

A relation is something that exists between two or more of a set of individuals or between classes, or between individuals and classes. In mathematics we can talk of ordered pairs of numbers and, for example, we can define the class of all ordered pairs (x, y) such that the relation R holds between all x and y. We have already defined a function as a relation R, say, such that Rxy for each x and at most one y, where y is the value of the function for argument x.

More generally, we can talk of ordered n-tuples of numbers and functions of n variables. This permits the derivation of the whole of classical mathematics, when we assume a suitable domain and an axiomatic foundation for arithmetic. Recursive functions are the ultimate expression of this generalized mathematics, but we can develop all of intuitionistic mathematics by a calculus involving constants alone. Such logics are called Combinatorial and are instanced by the so-called Calculi of Lambda-Conversion.

We can represent dyadic relations by diagrams such as in Figure 1.

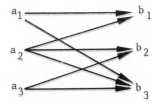

Figure 1.

which represents the set of relations

$$Ra_1b_1$$
$$Ra_2b_2$$
$$Ra_1b_3$$
$$Ra_2b_1$$
$$Ra_2b_3$$
$$Ra_3b_2$$
$$Ra_3b_3$$

This could also be represented as a matrix called here the R-matrix

R	b_1	b_2	b_3
a_1	1	0	1
a_2	1	1	1
a_3	0	1	1

We can now think of our calculus as a Structure Matrix, (showing the connectivity between elements like neurons in a metwork), while the function matrix (telling us the <u>state</u> of the network) is then a measure of the probable relation, so that

$$Ra_1b_1 \rightarrow Ra_1b_1 (p) \rightarrow Ra_1b_1 \ (\tfrac{1}{3}), \ \text{say}$$

So for an arbitrary set of probabilites the R-function matrix may read

R	b_1	b_2	b_3
a_1	$\dfrac{1}{3}$	$\dfrac{1}{3}$	$\dfrac{1}{3}$
a_2	$\dfrac{1}{10}$	0	$\dfrac{9}{10}$
a_3	0	$\dfrac{3}{4}$	$\dfrac{1}{4}$

The notion of Structure and Function Matrix here have a special interest in that they can be interpreted as a branch of the theory of automata. Such a branch is known as logical nets, and we shall be saying more about this later. The structure matrix describes, as we hinted about, precisely what elements are connected to what other elements, while the Function Matrix describes either the instantaneous or cumulative (as above) record of how often these structural connections fire. A whole nervous system which is an idealized version of that occurring in the human body can be described in such matrix terms, which in turn represent a description in terms of the Calculus of Relations. This example gives some indication of the widespread applications of mathematical and symbolic logic.   Let us though return to our outline of the Calculus of Relations.

Very much as in the case of Boolean Algebra (the Calculus of Classes) we find statements of the form:-

$$R \subset S$$

which means that whenever the relation R holds between two things so does S (but not necessarily vice-versa).   So if

$$R \subset S$$

$$\text{and} \quad S \subset R$$

$$\text{then} \quad R \neq S$$

Similarly we have:-

$$R \cup S$$

$$R \cap S$$

and if xRy
(which could be written Rxy and Sxy)

$$xSy$$

then we can write

$$x(R \cup S)y$$

which is equivalent to

$$(xRy) \cup (xSy)$$

and we have of course

$$\sim (xRy)$$

which is sometimes written

$$x \ R' \ y$$

We can now derive more complex relationships such as the relative product (R/R)..

$$R^2 = R/R = "... \text{ is an R of an R of } ---"$$

$$R/S = "... \text{ is an R of an S of } ---"$$

i.e. If R is "a son of" then

$$R^2 ab \to a \text{ is a son of a son of b}$$

$$= a \text{ is a grandson of b.}$$

We can have the inverse R^{-1} of R which is such that

$$RR^{-1} = I$$

So $$R/R^{-1} = R^0 = \text{identification} = I$$

We can, of course, generalize these notions, so we get

$$R^{-2} = R^{-1}/R^{-1} \equiv (R^{-1})^2 \equiv (R^2)^{-1} \quad \ldots \text{ (1)}$$

and in general

$$R^m = R^n/R^p \text{ where } m = n + p$$

The usual rules of symmetry, transitivity and reflexivity hold for some relations and not for others and so we can go on and describe our calculus in increasing detail, although we shall not attempt to do so here.

We are, of course, also concerned with general relationships, and so we have general symbolic forms such as the following:-

$$(AB, \ldots, N)(xy, \ldots, z) \qquad\qquad \ldots \text{ (2)}$$

$$(AB, \ldots, N) (ab, \ldots, n) \qquad\qquad \ldots \text{ (3)}$$

$$(AB, \ldots, N)(xy, \ldots, w, ab \ldots, m) \qquad\qquad \ldots \text{ (4)}$$

where the so-called <u>rank</u> of the strings (formulae) is always the number of operators minus the number of class names or individual names, and we can say that a wff always has the rank -1. The following examples make the point clear:

$$RSTxyzw \qquad\qquad \ldots \text{ (5)}$$

is a wff, but

$$MNxzwq \qquad\qquad \ldots \text{ (6)}$$

is not.

(5) can be written alternatively as

$$(((Rxy)Sz)Tw) \text{ or } (((xRy)Sz)Tw) \qquad\qquad \ldots \text{ (7)}$$

while

$$(Rx(yS(zTw)))$$

is written

$$RxSyTzw \qquad\qquad\qquad \cdots \ (8)$$

$$R = \text{"is the father of"}$$

$$S = \text{"is the brother of"}$$

$$T = \text{"is the sister of"}$$

Then (7) means

"x is the father of y who is the brother of z who is the sister of w" and (8) means

"z is the sister of w and y is the brother of z and x is the father of y"

So (7) = (8)

If, of course, R meant add, S subtract and T divide, then

$$(7) \quad \neq \quad (8)$$

For example, if x = 4, y = 5, z = 6 and w = 7

$$Rx \ SyTzw = - \ 1/7$$

and

$$RST \ xyzw = 3/7$$

We say the relationships in the first case are <u>commutative</u>, and in the second case <u>non-commutative</u>.

We now say that where the transitive relation holds between a pair of operators

e.g. $\qquad RSxyz$

then $\qquad ((Rxy)Rz)$

if $\qquad R = \text{"is in } \ldots \text{"}$

then $\qquad (Rxy) = \text{"x is in y"}$

and $\qquad ((Rxy)Rz) = \text{"x is in y" and "y is in z"}$

therefore "x is in z"

or $\qquad ((Rxy)Rz) = Rxz \qquad\qquad \cdots \ (9)$

and this implies a transitive relation R, since if R = "is the father of" then precisely because of its intransitive nature (9) will not hold.

We have here a powerful formal language which can clearly be mapped
onto the theory of probability, giving us an "empirical" calculus of
relations suitable for descriptive purposes in conditions of uncertainty,
provided we can sufficiently specify the meaning of the terms used.

EMPIRICAL LOGIC

So much of logic is concerned with analyzing forms and structures
that one is liable to forget that logistic systems can be constructed
for the purpose of making linguistic and scientific systems more precise.

We have just discussed briefly the predicate calculus (in chapter
six) and the calculus of relations which are clearly very closely
related to ordinary linguistic analysis and can clearly be used for
empirical descriptive purposes. Other such systems have been developed
which we can apply to specific branches of science and we supply one
brief sample of an application to biological systems.

Let us think of an organic system Y and with various components,
so if the members of Y are organic units with components x and y, we
can write:-

$$\left[Yxy \supset Org(x) \ . \ Org(y) \right]$$

If we now suppose Yxy and that u is the end slice of z and v is
the first slice of y, then u is either a part of v or v is a part of u.
i.e. $\left[Yxy \ . \ ES1i(u,x) \ . \ IS1i(v,y) \supset (u \neq v) \ . \ (Puv \ V \ Pvu) \right]$

Given next that Mom(x) means that spatio-temporal area is only
momentary, we have

$$Mom(x) \equiv (Au)(Av)(Pux \ . \ Pvx \supset \sim Tr(u,v))$$

where Tr is the asymmetric time relation

$$Tr(x,y) \supset \sim Tr(y,x)$$

and we can say that every individual has momentary parts:-

$$(Ax)(Ey)(Pyx \ . \ Mom(y))$$

and so on.

The versatility of logical descriptions is again demonstrated,
although it may be felt here that such precision and inevitable resulting
complexity is hardly worth the effort entailed.   This however raises
two major points for our whole thesis in this book.   The first is that
we must be capable of being as precise as is made necessary by the
situation in which we find ourselves and the second is that to be capable
of such precision of description (formalisation) in the world of computers
holds out the possibility of enormous progress in our understanding such
as the biological field, an example of which we have just given.   What
is being attempted ultimately is something akin to a detailed blueprint
for all organismic systems.

We now come to an example of the use of logic in a goal-seeking empirical situation.   This time we shall merely describe in general terms the nature of the application and not discuss the very detailed logistic system required to carry through the job.

GOAL ORIENTATED APPLIED LOGIC (GOAL)

GOAL is the name applied to our second example of an empirical logic.   GOAL has been developed for problem solving.   The purpose of a goal-oriented applied logic is to provide a logical (or logistic) system, which allows inference making in a goal-oriented situation of the type which we often call a problem solving situation.   GOAL is computerized and includes simulation, learning and inference making facilities.

The difference between learning and problem solving is mainly that problem solving is applied to a particular aspect of the environment at any particular time, in conditions where information necessary to achieving the goal is lacking..   Whereas, in general, learning applies to the collection of information regardless of whether a particular problem confronts the learner or not.

The main difficulty encountered in the use of logic in problem solving is that logic is in general a permissive discipline not a mandatory one.   This means that in the case of formal logic, whether or not in axiomatic form, you are told what inferences may be made or what entailments follow from the use of words, but you will not be told what inferences need to be made.   This is because no specific goal is there to be achieved, and there can as a result be no argument for a necessity.

GOAL applies logical methods to specific problem solving situations, where the solution to the problem is the goal, and sub-goals are points on the route to the goal.

The basic thinking is that when one is confronted with a novel situation, such as when one is playing a new game, there is a strong tendency in human beings to alternate between inference making, from the rules of the game, to actually trying to play the game in practice to see how the rules work, and then switch back to inference making again; the inference making being both of a deductive and an inductive kind.

If learning is not possible in practical situations, then a simulation of the situation is made which allows learning to take place with respect to the modelled situation, which is equivalent to actually learning from experience.

We can illustrate the use of GOAL in simple maze learning.   If we have to get to a goal box as a result of turning left, turning right or moving straight on at various choice points in a maze, we would simply record whether we turned left, right or went straight on and whether in fact this led to success in the maze.   In a sense it is the noting of non-success which is achieved by turning left, say, when straight on is the correct solution, which would be immediately remembered.   This false move is then eliminated in the next run through the maze.

It should be noticed in passing that a successful route through
the maze learned this way will not necessarily be an optimal route,
since what will be recorded is the first successful route with no mistakes
being made, and this is not necessarily an optimal route.   If now we
wanted the learner to _infer_ the correct (optimal) route through the maze
without actually running the maze, we could only do so provided he could
either "perceive" the maze as a whole or use (devise) a map of it, or have
some rule which would tell him, for instance, that you never turn left
twice running or every left turn is followed by a right turn.   It is the
use of _heuristics_ (sometimes algorithms) of this kind that provides the
basis for deducing what is the correct turning to make at each choice
point in the maze.

One's experience of the maze is the basis for setting up the
heuristics, and the actual inference making follows from the heuristics.
This inference making from heuristics in the actual maze running situation
is therefore a basis for verifying the correctness of the heuristics.

In the above circumstances we should turn our attention away from
the maze for the moment to consider a scheduling problem of the kind
that one might encounter in industry.   Suppose, for example, that you
had to schedule a throughput for a production line which manufactured
products, composed in turn of components, and the problem was to provide
a schedule of optimum value for the products and components.   The value
would be determined, say, by the cost, or by considerations of general
profitability to the organization.   The goal would clearly be one of
filling up a schedule and then running it off in practice.   It could be
filled up and you could run it off as a simulation or in an actual
application.   It could be filled up on a trial-and-error basis or it
could be filled up on the basis of inference.

We are assuming here a situation sufficiently complicated that no
algorithm is economic to use and therefore the schedule varies from
period to period and the only practical method of doing it is the
heuristic one.

The obvious thought is that we should supply an axiomatic system
and rules of inference which allow us to deduce from the axioms of the
system theorems which are applicable to the running of the maze or the
setting up of the schedule.   We would also want to say that there are
certain constraints which pertain to the system which give it its goal
orientation.

We already have examples of this in the psychological literature
in rats running mazes and one particularly thinks of a situation like
the following.

Consider the example below of a diamond-shaped maze which has the
bottom point (A) as the starting point, the left-hand point (B) as an
intermediate boz, the right-hand point (C) as another intermediate
box and the top point (D) of the diamond as the goal box.   Now if we
consider a group of rats which is allowed to run equally often from
the bottom point A to the left-hand point B, and to the right-hand
point C.   Then, in the second stage of the trial, the group of rats
is divided into two equal groups, half running from B and half running

from C to the goal box D, where all are rewarded by food when hungry.
Then finally at stage three all the rats are placed back in box A for
the third and final part of the trial.   They are now hungry again and
they are allowed to run either to B or to C.   If they have made the
correct inference they will run to B if they did so before, because
B has been associated in their experience with successful feeding at
D whereas other will run to C for the same reason if they did so before.

    In practical situations, a statistically significant number of the
rats in certain experiments have made this inference and made the correct
trip A=B=D, whereas others have not always made the correct trip and
sometimes have gone A=C=D or A=B=D in an apparently random fashion.

    From the above classical situation it would appear that inferences
can be made without complicated axiomatic foundations.   In other words,
it is merely a matter of keeping a check on simple associations and
behaving as if "A causes B" and if the causal connection, whether
justified or merely thought to exist, is used, then the solution correct
or otherwise may be achieved.

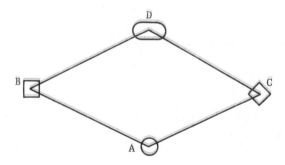

Figure 2

The diamond shaped maze with alternative routes ABD,
ACD to the goal box.   Stage 1 of the experiment is
that the group of subjects go equally often AB and
AC and stop at B and C respectively because of blocks
at B and C.   Then at Stage 2 half the group run BD
and half run CD, where all are "rewarded".   Finally in
Stage 3 all are placed in A and free to choose ABD or
ACD, so we would expect those who ran BD and were rewarded
to run ABD, and vice versa.   This is a paradigm of
simple inference-making (after J. P. Seward, 1956
Psychol. Rev. 105 = 113)

    The whole of this can be formalized as an axiomatic system if a
detailed description is given of the maze and the principles involved
in running the maze, the heuristics used and the constraints (very much
the same as heuristics) which exist to help determine an optimal solution.

A very clear example of this can be given in the scheduling problem,
when we think of manufacturing components to make a product.   If a
particular component completely fills a schedule and yet is never the
complete product (i.e. a product has always got more than one component),
then to manufacture only the one component in the period is clearly a
failure from the point of view of a maximum value schedule because it
ensures that no complete product can be manufactured.   The reason for
this, as a principle, is something which is immediately obvious to a
human being, so much so that often it is not clear why it is so.   We
are suggesting, therefore, that if we want to computerize, and this really
is the object of the exercise, the process of problem solving by a mixture
of trial-and-error learning and the use of inference making, we can do it
on the basis of a simple system of keeping a check on associations and
assuming the associations are causally valid.

From the set of tables which keep the records of the associations
we can formulate a complete description of the system and a description
in a meta-language, which describes in great detail, as much as we
could need in any particular set of circumstances, the way the system
operates.   We do not follow out in practice the providing of these sets of
descriptions but they do represent the sort of thing that has taken place
in learning theory and also taken place to some extent in logic.   One
could start with simple learning theory such as that of Tolman or Hull,
which can be formalized and re-formalized and ultimately reduced to a
most detailed and lengthy description in an axiomatic form.

GOAL can be thought of as a computer program for solving the problem
of a maze running or scheduling type.   It operates by having a costing
feature which determines the rate of success by trial-and-error or near
trial-and-error activity in the problem solving situation and when
progress falls below a certain arbitrary level the program switches
back to the inference making approach, and vice versa.

The program in the first mode uses a random scheduling, or one
determined by certain simple heuristics, such as "fill up the production
line with one of each of the needed components before you place in a
second of any one of them".   The schedule is then run off and evaluated.

In the course of experience, information will be accumulated as
to the likely value of schedules for different order types, so that a
reasonable guess can be made as to the adequacy of the evaluation of
any one schedule.   If it is not good enough, it will be re-run with
a new heuristic, or if a new heuristic is not available it will move
into the inferential mode and generate a new heuristic.

The generation of an heuristic can be achieved in more than one
way.   It can either be by a modification of an existing heuristic,
e.g. read "product" for "component" in the above example, or it can
operate directly from the tables of previous occurrences, which are
similar to Markov nets, in that they record order patterns, the equivalent
schedules and their values.   GOAL can then run through these tables
looking for any relevant causal patterns and see if they satisfy the
constraints as stated in GOAL'S meta-language.   This is an aspect of
inductive logic which we described in Chapters Eight and Nine.

This last point can be illustrated by an example.   If we see that
a particular order pattern, say where an equal number of 20 different
products is required, has always been evaluated and run at a low level
by a particular heuristic (or range of heuristics) we can re-schedule
previous examples using new heuristics, which can be manufactured
ab initio.

This manufacturing from scratch of an heuristic can take two forms.
One is derived by examining all the ways that a schedule can be compiled.
There are clearly only a finite number of ways for a finite number of
products in the order pattern, and we can continue this until we hit upon
a heuristic that provides higher evaluations than the existing heuristics
and also satisfies the constraints.   If we further ask that it fits in
with the "sensible entailments" of the schedule's needs, we see that we
can eliminate whole sets of schedules immediately or, to put the matter
rather differently, we now are making inferences of a goal-directed
character as to what are likely heuristic types.

The second method open to us is where the tables already show
likely numerical patterns which could supply the basis of a heuristic.
This process can be illustrated very simply.   If two events are related
by five different intermediate events, and we record the success of the
causal connections (these can be five choice points in a maze between a
starting box and a goal-box) then it should be immediately clear which
is the likely correct (or best) route.   We can always translate this
best route from its numerical table form into a verbal heuristic, e.g.
"turn left and right alternately" is a general heuristic, while a detailed
description might have to specify each turn separately;   another example
of an inductive process.

In the larger practical example of scheduling a very large production
line, we should expect to find the general heuristic rather than the
particular solution which details, in algorithmic fashion, what is to be
done.

The most important feature of GOAL lies in the fact that it is very
much a practical undertaking, and we shall certainly some day see it
being used to solve practical problems of a scientific and business kind.

This chapter represents a turning point in our monograph.   We are
moving or have moved over from the development of formal symbolic logics
to their descriptive use, or application.   This is very much like the
step between the development of pure mathematics and its application as
applied mathematics.   We now turn explicitly to the processes of
formalisation.

EXERCISES

1. What distinction would you make between formal logic and informal logic?
    Explain with examples.

2. How do you distinguish applied logic from formal logic?

3. Compare applied, inductive logic and probability theory.

REFERENCES

GEORGE, F.H.   Goal Data Processing. 13, 4, 260 - 262

KORZYBSKI, A.   Science and Society. Science Press, 1933

CHAPTER 14

FORMALISATION

In this chapter we shall be attempting to achieve two things.   The first is to provide a brief summary of the techniques implicit in formalisation, and the second is to carry through the first stage of a proposed formalisation for the pragmatic theory outlined in a semi-formal way in Part II of this book.

After we have provided this first stage formalisation, at least as far as the central core of the theory is concerned, we shall proceed in the last three chapters to a further stage of formalisation by suggesting suitable automata that might reasonably be regarded as being appropriate as an underlying structural model for the suggested pragmatic theory.

But before we start the formalisation of the theory, let us say a few general words about the process of formalisation.   Pap (1949) says of formalisation:-

"The process of making the logical structure of a language, or of sentences, explicit by replacing descriptive terms with variables. The formalisation of a language also involves the statement of formation rules, transformation rules and (in case the language is a semantic system) semantic rules for that language."

While Braithwaite (1953) has proposed what he called a "zip-fastener" approach where we can zip down from the theory to the model or up from the model to the theory.

The idea of using models in science is by no means new, and Braithwaite, among many others, has analysed, in some detail, the use of such models and their relation to theories in science.   There is a sense in which almost anything can be used as a model for almost anything else, but as in the use of analogies or metaphors, so models, to have predictive value, must bear some measure of similarity to the structure or process being modelled.

We can classify models in various ways into at least those which model structure, those which model function and those which model both. These are static (for structure) and dynamic models (for processes or functions).   We also have models which are obviously physical (e.g. a wind tunnel model) and those which are obviously symbolic (e.g. mathematical and statistical models for simulation), and so on and so forth.

Following Braithwaite's line of thought, we might regard scientific theories as capable of being formalised.   This process of formalisation is essentially one of stripping down theories in ordinary language and showing the underlying logic, it is almost indeed a matter of making the

original theory more precise, where we take some theory and rewrite in
greater detail and in more 'molecular' fashion;   this is the "zipping
down" process.

We can also argue that a scientific theory is made up of empirical
statements which use terms capable of operational definition, whereas
the model uses logical statements, which are not in themselves verifiable.
We can illustrate the intended meaning by a simple example.   This
example shows one sort of formalisation:

In Hull's theory of learning, we find a statement to the effect
that:-

"The greater the similarity between the conditioned stimulus and
the unconditioned stimulus, the greater the absolute value of the
increment of tendency to respond to the conditioned stimulus."   (1)

To formalise this needs a lot of detailed definitions, but if s is a
stimulus and r is a response, then the strength of association $_s H_r$ can
be defined:

$$_s H_r(t_2) = _s H_r(t_0) + \Sigma \delta \; _s H_r(t_2, s', r')$$ (2)

where (t_0, t_2) is a time interval, and $\Sigma \delta \; _s H_r$ is the change of strength
of association during the interval (t_0, t_2), s' and r' are sets of s's
and r's that occur in the interval (t_0, t_2).

We now define a function $F(x,y,z,w)$ such that:-

$$F(x,y,z,w) = \delta \; _s H_r(t_2, s', r')$$ (3)

and where $x = J(t_1, t_2)$, $t_1 = T(r')$, $y = S(s,s')$, $z = S(r,r')$ and
$w = T(r') - T(s')$

Suffice it for our purposes that the variables x,y,z and w can be
precisely defined, but roughly speaking x is concerned with drive reduction,
and y and z are concerned with stimulus and response similarity, and
finally w is a function of time delay between the occurrence of the
stimulus and the response.

This leads to a statement (or axiom):-

$$\frac{\delta F}{\delta y}(x,y,z,w) > o$$ (4)

and this total argument, given here in skeleton form, is a formalisation
of Hull's original statement (1).   This is formalised in (2), (3) and
(4), although even this is barely adequate as an approximation to the
much more precise statement still required.

Another kind of example we might mention is that of the Russell and
Whitehead's formalisation of number in Principia Mathematica.

By 'formalising' then, we mean 'making more precise', or 'reducing
statements' to their underlying logic, and clearly 'formalising' is
itself a vague word, which could well mean 'to expose the model underlying

the theory'.   Not only is formalising vague, but it is also a matter of
degree.

Similarly we can look at the matter the other way around, and
interpret models in many different ways to get many different theories.
Models and theories are connected by formalising and by interpretation,
and theories are linked directly with empirical descriptions.   Let us
now look at an example of interpretation e.g. the well-formed formula:-

$$p \supset \cdot p \supset q$$

or

$$p \supset (p \supset q)$$

is from an axiomatic system P and can be interpreted so that p, q are
propositions, and $\supset$ is the logical connective called 'material implication'.
The dot is a bracket as illustrated by our alternative rendering of the
formula.   This interpretation is a part of what is called the propositional
calculus.

But the identical statement $p \supset \cdot p \supset q$ could be interpreted as a
statement in a Boolean Algebra B.   When the second interpretation is
adopted, a conventionally different notation is used.   So we have:-

$$A \rightarrow (A \rightarrow B)$$

or since

$$A \rightarrow B = df. \quad A' \cup B$$

where $A' \equiv df.$ not $-A$
and $A \cup B = df.$ the sum of the two classes A and B, then

$$A \rightarrow (A \rightarrow B)$$

becomes

$$A' \cup (A' \cup B)$$

The fact is that the same model is being given two different
interpretations.

Here the process could be described as taking a model or structure,
which by itself has no meaning or reference, and supplying the model with
the meaning.   The word (name) 'Chicago' refers to the city Chicago,
only by the common agreement that 'Chicago' is the name for Chicago.
The process of naming is like tying labels on physical objects.

A FIRST STAGE FORMALISATION OF THE PRAGMATIC THEORY

We shall start this section by bringing together all the "glossary"
definitions we have previously developed.   They are at this stage of
definition already reasonably precise; our aim is to increase their
precision.   But let us go straight to our definitions.

1. BELIEF: A relatively permanent state of the organism which represents
    the association, through experience, of the activating stimulus
    state (S_1) with a means-outcome $(R_1 - S_2)$.

2. STIMULUS (S): Any change of energy which impinges upon the nervous
    system such that it brings about activity in that system.   The
    source of this energy change may be either external or internal
    to the organism.

3. STIMULUS COMPLEX (S*): A subclass of the class of stimuli, both
    internal and external to the organism, that has become associated
    with particular beliefs.   This does not include stimuli which are
    derived from motivational states (Sms).

4. MOTIVATIONAL STIMULI (Sm): A subclass of the class of stimuli,
    internal to the organism, which derive from motivational states and
    which have become associated with particular beliefs.

5. MODIFYING MOTIVATIONAL STIMULI (MMS): A subclass of the class of
    stimuli, both external and internal, which may either include,
    be included in, or be equivalent to the stimulus complex (S*), and
    which have the properties necessary to modify the motivational
    state of the organism.

6. ACTIVATING STIMULUS STATE (S_1): That state of the central nervous
    system which is capable of transforming specific beliefs into
    expectancies.

7. SIGNS (Sns): A subclass of the class of activating stimulus states
    $(S_1 s)$ which the organism through the acquisition of beliefs, has
    learned stand for other stimuli.

8. MOTIVATION (M): A state of the organism, compounded of drive and
    urgency, factors, which, through the medium of motivational stimuli
    (Sms), produces behaviour, in conjunction with stimulus complexes
    (S*s) through the elicitation rehearsal and selection of expectancies,
    and the elicitation of response.

9. DRIVE (D): Specific needs of the organism, both primary and
    secondary, which manifest themselves in the motivational stimuli (Sms).

10. URGENCY (U): A special state of the organism which manifests itself
    in the motivational stimuli (Sms).

11. EXPECTANCY $(E(R_1 - S_2))$: A relatively temporary state of the organism,
    elicited by S_1, which is derived from and has the same content as
    the correlative belief.

12. REHEARSAL: A process of scanning expectancies for selection.

13. SELECTION: A process by which the organism selects a particular
    expectancy $(E(R_1 - S_2))$ in terms of (1) maximum valence and (2)
    maximum strength of belief correlative with the expectancy.

14. VALENCE: A function of the anticipated effort and anticipated value contained as part of a belief and, hence, with an expected means-outcome.

15. ANTICIPATED EFFORT: The amount of effort believed to be, and hence expected to be, necessary in order to attain a certain goal.

16. ANTICIPATED VALUE: The amount of reward believed to be, and hence expected to be, forthcoming upon the attainment of a certain goal.

17. RESPONSE ELICITATION: A process, following automatically upon selection, in which the selected means is elicited as a response.

18. RESPONSE: The behaviour of the organism following immediately upon the selection process. The response ;may or may not be overt, and may itself act as a stimulus for further behaviour.

19. CONFIRMATION: The process of validation of an expectancy which, in turn, strengthens the evoking belief.

20. SURPRISE: The state of the organism resulting from the disconfirmation of a belief. Such a state may or may not be manifest in overt behaviour.

21. CUES: A subclass of the class of activating stimulus states (S_1s) which stems from objects or events, either internal or external, which are being apprehended directly by the organism through knowledge by acquaintance.

22. CLUES: A subclass of activating stimulus states (S_1s) which stems from the context, ground or surround in which the apprehended object or event, either external or internal, is imbedded. The apprehension of a clue by the organism is direct, i.e. through knowledge by acquaintance.

23. VALUE: The amount of reward intrinsic to an object or act involved in the attainment of a goal. It is that part of its total reward value which is invariant with respect to the context of its occurrence.

24. RISK: The amount of negative reward which may be involved in the attainment of a goal.

25. HEURISTIC: Ad hoc strategies or shortcuts used in the attempted solution of a problem; a heuristic entails both beliefs and expectancies, and is like a hypotheses-in-action.

26. PLAN: Synonymous with strategy which is virtually synonymous with heuristic or hypothesis.

27. THINKING: The process which we can regard initially as that of symbolising events and then the manipulation of the symbols themselves by various processes of logical (and illogical) inference, where the processing may be accompanied by imagery.

28. PROBLEM SOLVING: The process of acquiring an appropriate set of
     responses to a novel situation, the filling of an "information gap".

29. LEARNING: The process of adapting to changing circumstances and
     the recording of success and failure in the process which is usually
     goal-oriented.

30. IMAGERY: The private impression people claim to have which suggests
     a shadowy equivalent of actual perceived events.

31. SYMBOLS: A subclass of the class of signs which have specific
     reference to concepts (or beliefs) and may also have external
     referents in the form of physical objects.

     We now turn to consider a first stage formalisation of our theory.

A FIRST FORMALISATION OF THE THEORY

     A belief (B) is a part of what we mean by a heuristic, but it is
also capable of representing any empirical statement whatever.
We might write B as of the form:-

$$B = R_1 \supset S_2 \qquad \qquad \dots (1)$$

but to avoid confusion with <u>material implication</u> we should write:-

$$B = R_1 \rightarrow S_2 \qquad \qquad \dots (2)$$

where we mean the $\rightarrow$ to stand for "leads to", but even here the class
of beliefs is a small subclass of all possible beliefs which are more
generally of the form:-

$$B = BR_1 S_2 \qquad \qquad \dots (3)$$

where B provides some relationship between R_1 and S_2 and then we can
conjoin and disjoin B's so that we get:-

$$B = B_1 \cdot B_2 \cdot \quad \dots \cdot B_n \qquad \qquad \dots (4)$$

$$B = B_1 v B_2 v \quad \dots v B_n \qquad \qquad \dots (5)$$

which we could write:-

$$(R_1 S_2) \cdot (R_2 S_3) \cdot \dots v (R_1 S_2) \; v \; (R_2 S_3) \; v \; \dots \qquad \qquad \dots (6)$$

and so on.

     We may now say that a stimulus S_1 initiates a belief B, which is
initially perceptual and subsequently may initiate a series of conceptual
beliefs $\underset{i\,=\,1}{\overset{n}{\times}} B_i$, so we can write using $\rightarrow$ now for 'initiates'.

By $\xrightarrow{\times}$, we mean "the set ..." and by $\underset{i\,=\,1}{\overset{n}{\times}} B_i$ we mean the set

B_1, B_2, ..., B_n.   We now say:-

$$S_1 \to \prod_{i=1}^{n} B_i \qquad \qquad \text{... (7)}$$

and the next question is as to the motivation (M) which is composed of drive (D) and urgency (U), so we have:-

$$M = f\ (D,U) \qquad \qquad \text{... (8)}$$

where f is some function that is largely contextually determined. The condition (7) to occur will be that:-

$$M > k \qquad \qquad \text{... (9)}$$

where k is some constant which is a function of the individual's experience and present state, so it is that:-

$$M = g\ (sm,\ MMS) \qquad \qquad \text{... (10)}$$

and S_1 to be effective in (7) must be such that (3) is satisfied and also (5) where:-

$$S_1 > j \qquad \qquad \text{... (11)}$$

where j, like k, is a constant which is a function of experience.   k and j are, of course, variables, which at the moment of occurrence of S have a constant value.

Then transformation of B's into expectancies (E's) is made possible by the S, so that:-

$$S_j \to \prod_{p=1}^{m} E_m \qquad \qquad \text{... (12)}$$

where $E_1 = h(R_1 - S_2)$ and $(R_1 - S_2)$ is called a "means-outcome" and is a "look ahead" relationship. Given that the reward V is a function of both valence (v_1) and value (v_2), then the beliefs B's provide a partially ordered set.

$$\text{... (13)}$$
$$V_1 \geqslant V_2 \geqslant \cdots \geqslant V_k$$

where $B_1 \to E_1(V_1), B_2 \to E_2(V_2)$ etc.

and where V_{max} will be the basis of the selected E.

Weightings of the E's in terms of risk and urgency will be represented within the values and valencies so these are automatically included.

It is now clear that the above process may occur iteratively until the problem ends, and it is also clear that we have depicted here only the molar aspects of the theory, and thus a series of levels should be involved with each B eliciting a series of b's by the use of s's and r's

within the system.   These internal associations will allow of elicitation
of beliefs of various orders of abstraction.

The partially ordered set (13)

$$V_1 \geqslant V_2 \geqslant \cdots \geqslant V_k \qquad \qquad \cdots (13)$$

can refer to "choice" situations where options are involved, or it can
refer to "interpretative" situations where a PBU is needed, followed
by a CBU which confirms or otherwise the "interpretation".   We move
therefore along a series of categorisations:-

$$I_1, I_2, \cdots, I_m$$

where urgency will decide at what point the categorising process stops.

We can ourselves supply tests from beliefs about an interpretation
which may supply new cues (C_1) or clues (C_2) which are themselves the
interpretation of a PBU.   We are in a position of trying to acquire
evidence (e) to confirm (c) a hypothesis (h) and do so, in general, in
terms of a probability (p).   So we have:-

$$c(h,e) = p \qquad \qquad \cdots (14)$$

The sequence of events will be of the form:-

$$P_1, C_1, P_2, C_2, \cdots, P_n, C_n$$

where cue (or clue) is represented by P_i (i = 1, 2, ..., n) and tests
are represented by C_j (j = 1, 2, ..., n).

The degree of reward is exemplified by the values and valences,
$V_1, V_2, \cdots, V_k$ and the basis for selection of a belief and the speed of
selection varies as a function of the differential between reward values
and anticipated effort (F), i.e.

$$V_i - V_j \geqslant k_1$$

and

$$F_k - F_1 \geqslant k_2$$

for sufficiently large k_1 and k_2.   These are the criteria for the speed of
selection.   The same argument applies to S(B) which is the strength of
belief, measured as a function of previous experience.   So:-

$$S(B)_m - S(B)_n \geqslant k_3$$

for sufficiently large k_3 which also decides (or helps to decide) speed
of selection.

The Drive function (D) is made up of further variables such as whatever
is a primary motivator in the situation (s(m) will mean the strength of
that primary motivator) and whatever is acquired by association as the
secondary motivator which is the same as the strength of the associated

belief.   So:-

$$D = f_1(s(m), s(B)) \qquad \qquad \qquad \qquad \dots (15)$$

for some function f_1.

Urgency is the motivating strength of the interval between the interpretation and the anticipated outcome (O) which is a strong associated belief of high or low value.

$$U = f_2 (I(sB(O))) \qquad \qquad \qquad \qquad \dots (16)$$

for some function f_2.   So we can rewrite:-

$$M = f_3 (D, U)$$

as

$$M = f_4((s(m), s(B)), g(I, SB(O))) \qquad \qquad \dots (17)$$

for some functions f_3 and f_4, and since:-

$$M = g (s(m) \text{ MMS})$$

then

$$g(s(m), MMS) = f_5((S(m), S(B)), g(I, SB(O))) \qquad \qquad \dots (18)$$

for some function f_5.   This says simply that the motivational stimuli contain the experiential features of the individual.

If we introduce individual differences (or types) T_1, T_2, $\dots$, T_k then we can say:-

$$T_I > k_4$$

and

$$T_E > k_4$$

where k_4 is some measure of the range of beliefs scanned with respect to any particular situation.

I and E are intended to be interpreted as introvert and extravert respectively and are to be thought of as representative of psychological types.

A problem solving situation may thus involve a type of person (T_i) with a particular set of beliefs (B_j) which may or may not evoke cues and clues with respect to that situation.   The degree of similarity between the relevant cues and clues and their relation to previous situations and their success is a key to the belief which will be utilised and the success which occurs in solving the problem.

The first step in the solution of the problem may be provided by PBU with effect to a cue or clue.   Then the flexibility is the key to the appropriate selection of the sequence of events which follows. So if we let G stand for goal, we have some sequence:-

$$P_1, \ C_1, \ P_2, \ C_2, \ \ldots, \ P_n, \ C_n \rightarrow G$$

and the minimum number of steps are required in the sequence.

The essential feature of the sequential processing is that of establishing evidence by correct interpretation of cues and clues, and noticing where differences occur so that a particular test is infirming rather than confirming.

The problem is to choose an expectancy E* so that

$$E_o \leqslant E* \leqslant E_1$$

within "similarity bonds" with respect to E*.

This means that the whole interval (E_0, E_1) must contain expectancies sufficiently similar to E* and to test it, rejecting if necessary, and then providing the final categorisation.

E* should be chosen in terms of recent and frequent success and this is reflected in the appropriate belief strength S(B*).

We can complete this chapter at this point with the simple statement that we could proceed to formalise in similar manner all aspects of the theory.   Rather than attempt to do this we shall proceed to look at a further formalisation in terms of automata theory in the next three chapters.

EXERCISES

1. Distinguish models and theories in the Braithwaitean sense.

2. What would you choose as a "model" for the human brain? Give your reasons for your choice.

REFERENCES

HEMPEL, C.G. and OPPENHEIM, P.	The Logic of explanation. <u>Philos. Sci.</u>, <u>15</u>
GEORGE, F.H.	<u>Models of Thinking</u>. Allen and Unwin, 1970
NAGEL, E.	<u>The Structure of Science</u>. London, 1961

CHAPTER 15

AUTOMATA THEORY

In this chapter we are paving the way for the final stages of formalising the pragmatic theory which has been the subject of the whole book. In Chapter Fourteen we discussed formalisation in general and took the first steps towards formalising our theory. We are, for the remainder of Part III, intending to provide a further formalisation in terms of automata.

We will think of automata first of all as tape machines, and we can think of such automata as composed of a <u>reader</u> (or scanner) and a single <u>tape</u> ruled into squares and capable of having symbols printed on (or erased from) each square. The automaton scans the squares one at a time, and as a result of conventions used in the tape representation of formulae and the like, we say it proves theorems, performs computations or solves problems. The field of automata theory has now a long and important history. Such methods have been used to prove theorems about the foundations of mathematics and are basic to what is known to be <u>computable</u>.

In recent years we have come to consider automata with many different types of tape; some tapes go both left to right and right to left, while other tapes go one way only, and they may have many channels, which may move either independently or together. The upshot of much of this work has been of purely mathematical importance, but one kind of automaton is of special interest to us here. These automata which we are especially concerned with are called neural nets and their description will form the bulk of the rest of Part III, especially in their relationship to our pragmatic theory.

In this chapter we shall describe automata in general terms and subsequently we shall consider particular interpretations of some of these automata, especially neural nets. The situation is exactly the same as it is with formal calculi such as the propositional or lower functional calculus, and their interpretation of descriptive systems, by way of semantic rules.

We shall first discuss a version of finite-state machines; we are assuming the word " machine" sufficiently understood as an "artificial" system, and we will not attempt to define it further. We are concerned with a machine or a model or a black box that is interacting with an environment. A stimulus or input to the machine is a response or output from the environment and vice versa.

We first need to distinguish between a deterministic and a non-deterministic machine. A <u>deterministic</u> machine, and these are the ones

we are mainly concerned with, is defined so that its output R, at time
t + 1 (this is written R(t + 1) is determined by the input at t, and the
previous history of the machine.   We can write this:

$$R(t + 1) = F (H(t), S(t)) \qquad\qquad \dots (1)$$

where H is the previous history and S is the input.   F is some function
relating the two main features to the output of the system.

A non-deterministic machine which is of special interest is one where,
for example, the input and history determine the probability of some
response.   This last type of machine is called probabilistic, and is a
particular case of the class of non-deterministic machines.

The internal state (Q) of the machine is defined as being dependent
upon its previous internal state and on the previous input.   We write
this:-

$$Q(t + 1) = G (Q(t), S(t)) \qquad\qquad \dots (2)$$

when G is some function relating the previous state and the previous
input.   We can further distinguish between automata that are able to
grow (and are therefore potentially infinite) and those that are fixed.
It seems that automata that can grow, but cannot do so beyond some
specified size, can do no more than an automaton that is fixed.   We
shall call these last automata growth automata, and the potentially
infinite ones we shall call growing automata.   Turing machines can be
thought of as being either "growth" or "growing" automata according to
their precise definition.

In passing it should be noted that when we say that a growth
automaton can do no more than a fixed automaton we are thinking in terms
of the computations it can perform and not in terms of the methods it can
use.   This therefore does not mean that, from a cybernetician's viewpoint
for example, growth automata are of no interest.   There is some good
reason to suppose the human brain comes precisely into this group of
automata.   We can further classify automata as continuous or discrete
(McNaughton, 1961);   they can also be classified as synchronous or non-
synchronous according to whether or not their input and output history
can be described completely as occurring during certain discrete moments
of time.   They may, of course, have any combination of these various
properties so far described.

In general, we shall say that automata are devices of finite size at
any particular time such that the defined output is a function of what
has happened at the defined input.   Our equations (1) and (2) make this
concept more precise.

As far as finite automata in general are concerned, we would remind
the reader that our brief description of these systems is meant only as a
general summary for our own special purpose.   Much of the mathematical
foundation of the theory can be found in the following references
(Davis, 1958, 1965; Minsky, 1961, 1967; Arbib, 1965; Rogers, 1966) for
those who are especially interested.   Our aim here is merely to introduce
the neural net version of automata to formalise our pragmatic theory.

The basic notion of a finite automaton is that by its present and
future behaviour only some finite number of classes of possible histories
can be distinguished or recognized.   These histories are what we have
called the "internal states" $(q_1, q_2, \ldots, q_n)$ of the machine.

Let us try and be clear about the recognition of a machine's history.
Before doing so however let us follow Minsky (1967) and describe some
representations of such nets.   The first is a simple tabular form, where
we represent our two defining functions F and G.   A simple "memory
machine" has the following definition:-

		State	
G		q_0	q_1
input	s_0	q_0	q_0
	s_1	q_1	q_1

		State	
F		q_0	q_1
input	s_0	r_0	r_1
	s_1	r_0	r_1

and this same automaton can be represented by a state-transition diagram
as follows:-

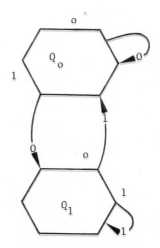

so that given input 1 (at base of arrow) in state q_o (or Q_o) the hexagon, the output is 0 (written on the arrow itself), and the new state is q_1 (or Q_1). We could write this same description in the form of a set of quadruples:

$$q_o \quad 1 \quad 0 \quad q_1$$

$$q_o \quad 0 \quad 0 \quad q_o$$

$$q_1 \quad 1 \quad 1 \quad q_1$$

$$q_1 \quad 0 \quad 1 \quad q_o$$

where the first q gives one state and the last q gives the next state, and in between the input and then the output occur and are depicted by 0's and 1's. We can also re-write our tabular description more simply as:

	G	State q_o q_1
input	0	q_o q_o
	1	q_1 q_1

	F	State q_o q_1
input	0	0 1
	1	0 1

Let us look at a slightly more complicated example. Here is the state-transition diagram:-

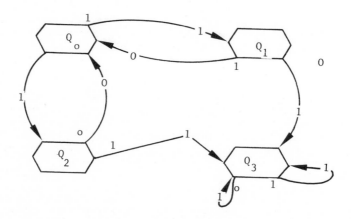

The quadruples are as follows:-

$$q_0 \quad 0 \quad 1 \quad q_2$$

$$q_0 \quad 1 \quad 1 \quad q_1$$

$$q_1 \quad 1 \quad 1 \quad q_0$$

$$q_1 \quad 0 \quad 1 \quad q_3$$

$$q_2 \quad 1 \quad 1 \quad q_3$$

$$q_2 \quad 0 \quad 0 \quad q_0$$

$$q_3 \quad 0 \quad 1 \quad q_3$$

$$q_3 \quad 1 \quad 1 \quad q_3$$

Now if this machine is to avoid the "deadend" of state q_3 from which it cannot escape then it must, if started at q_0, have an input tape that carried to q_1 or q_2 and then back to q_0.   So 1 at q_0 will send it to q_1 which must have a 1 to send it back to q_0.   Similarly, q_0 must have a 0 and q_2 a 0 immediately following to send it back to q_0.   Thus it is that for a 0 to appear on the output, the inputs must all be in pairs of 0's or 1's.   There is, of course, nothing to exclude the possibility of going to q_3 and this can be achieved (again presuming we start at q_0) if we started with inputs 10 or 01.   These would take us to q_3 via q_1 and q_2 alternatively.

From this automaton, it is easy to see that if at any time t we in fact get an output 0, which can only occur in states q_1 or q_2, then we can say that the history of the automaton is a sense of pairs of either 0's or 1's.   It is in this series that automata can distinguish or recognize certain features of its previous histories as [0000110011] and [1100001100], but it can carry some part of the recognition process.

The theory of automata, we must remember, is abstract and is concerned with the logical and mathematical consequences of precisely formed concepts.   In fact, while this is true, we can at the same time make the point that the full adder, very much part of an existing digital computer design, is a finite automaton, and its hardware realization is precisely the full adder used in digital computers.

We should, of course, distinguish between the structure and the behaviour of an automaton.   The structure is precisely what we would expect - the anatomy of the system, while its behaviour is the observable change of activity with respect to its input and output.   Clocks are typical of the sort of black box we have here in mind.   They may have many different mechanisms (structures or anatomies) but the behaviour of one clock is equivalent to that of another.   At least, to put it more carefully, there are whole sets of clocks with equivalent behaviour, however different their anatomy.

There are two further points which are next worthy of mention:
(1) An isolated finite automata.   (2) The question of initial states.
It can be shown that if an automaton is isolated from all external
stimuli it will fall into a perfectly periodic pattern of behaviour.
This may take some time but must sooner or later occur.   This is the sort
of result that is of interest when considering the experiments that have
been carried out in keeping people in strict isolation for periods of
time (Heron et al, 1965) when their behaviour seems to lose its usual
critical faculty and becomes increasingly unadaptive.

The second point seems to have no special consequences for behaviour.
It is the fact that some automata have not assumed initial states - in
other words it is assumed that they have an infinite past.   Such an
assumption is biologically unrealistic and must not (Kleene, 1951) be
used other than to simplify, as it might, problems of neural modelling;
it is a device comparable to the use of complex numbers in the
description of electrical circuits.   This means it is a sort of internal
computational "trick" which must not be part of the input or output.

In fact, we shall return to this problem when we consider that
class of automata called neural nets which is the main subject of Part III.
Moore (1956) considers automata with an infinite past in his discussion
of whether such automata are equivalent to each other.   Moore, in what
he describes as Gedanken experiments, selects inputs for machines which
are equivalent if in return they produce the same outputs.

The main point about Moore's work which is worthy of mention here
is that because his automata do not have an initial state his results
are distinctly more complicated.   So what might be a simplifying
condition for some purposes seems to be a complicating condition for
others, and perhaps this is especially so in the general theory of
automata.   We shall not though be concerned with either "isolated" or
"infinite past" automata.

We shall now give a different, in fact more precise, definition of
finite automata in terms of set-theory and provide a few results that
have been discovered by people working from this point of view.

McNaughton (1961) defines finite automata as follows:-

"It is an ordered quintuple $< S,I,U,f,g >$ where each of the five
items is itself an abstract mathematical entity.   S, I and U
are finite sets of abstract entities called elements; f is a
function that maps SxI into S, and g is a function that maps
SxI into U.   Thus, for every element s in S and i in I, f(s,i)
is an element of S and g(s,i) is an element of U."

In fact, of course, S is here the set of states, I is a set of input
values, U is a set of output values, f is a transition function that
defines the next state given the input value and present state (same as
G defined earlier) and g (same as F defined earlier) defines the output
value given the input value and present state.   It is of interest to
compare this definition with a slightly differently worded but
equivalent definition due to Arbib (1965):-

"A finite automaton is a quintuple A = (I,O,S,λ,δ) where
I is a finite set of inputs, O is a finite set of outputs,
S is a finite set of internal states, and where λ SxL→S is the
next-state function and λ SxI→O is the next output function."

Here λ is the same as f before (our G) and δ is the same as g before
(our F). Otherwise the word "ordered" is omitted now and indeed the
order of variables is different but they are directly given their
interpretation in automata terms. These definitions obviously amount
to the same thing, and there are many others, which differ slightly
in wording, but are also essentially the same. To all these definitions,
the usual point applies; they are abstract and we must not confuse the
abstract definitions and theorems with the interpretations we place
upon them.

Let us look now at some results for tape automata. We can think
of tapes as being two-way, as in the Turing machine, or one-way; we
can also think of them as being single-tape or multi-tape. Rabin
and Scott (1959) suggested and Shepherdson (1959) proved that for every
two-way automaton there exists an equivalent one-way automaton. The
equivalent one-way automaton is usually more complicated - needs more
internal states. The essential and perhaps fairly obvious condition
for the equivalence is that a one-way automaton must carry with it all
the information it will subsequently need, precisely because it cannot
go back.

If we think of human beings as one-way automata, where the
direction is through time, then it is saying, in effect, that the human
must have a memory store if it is to be capable of dealing with a
certain class of activity. Memoryless robots, so-called, have been
discussed (Culbertson, 1965), but although they can exhibit a degree of
apparent intelligence, there are serious and obvious limitations on
their abilities.

Rabin and Scott (1964) have shown that two-tape and multi-tape
automata which are one-way are equivalent to single-tape one-way
automata in the computations they can perform, although once again we
must remind ourselves that the methods used may be different. Two-way,
two-tape automata (Rabin and Scott, 1964) have no decision procedure
and we have no way of deciding whether the set of tapes (computations)
it can accept are empty or not.

Another comparison is between real-time and general (non real-time)
automata. This is a field which has been extensively researched by
Yamada (1961). Yamada defines a device which is capable of a limited
number of k operations at any time on a fixed number of tapes. But
again the general finding does not seem to be of great theoretical
importance since for every set of operations done by a real-time
automaton we can always devise an equivalent general automaton, and vice-
versa. Exactly the same argument applies, of course, to digital
computers. Everything that can be done on-line can be done off-line
and vice versa.

Yet another type of automaton is called a <u>linear-bounded</u> automaton
(Myhill, 1960). It is an automaton which is two-way and can do what a

Turing machine can do - it can write and erase symbols on the tape.
This type of automata is not strictly finite, but rather potentially
infinite, since the tape which is, in effect, an additional memory
store can be made as long as is necessary to compute the problem.   It
is because the amount of memory is a linear function of the length of the
problem that it was called a "linear-bounded automaton".   We will now
concentrate our attention on neural nets.

INTRODUCTION TO NEURAL NETS

    Neural or Logical Networks (or Nets) are a form of automaton
(McNaughton, 1961) and provide an alternative description of a finite
automaton to that of the tape variety of automaton.   They can also be
regarded as representing either fixed or growth processes, and could
therefore be regarded as offering an alternative description of either
a finite or an infinite (non-finite) automaton or, to quote the best
known example of this category of automaton, the Turing machine
(Turing, 1937).

    Our aim is to discuss various approaches to neural nets and various
notations and then, having decided on our notation, to develop nets as
models of cognitive processes.   These cognitive processes can be thought
of as representing either syntheses or simulations of systems, and may,
among other interpretations, by interpreted at the level of a simulation
of the nervous system.

    Neural nets are composed of elements combined into nets by
connecting fibres, according to specific rules, and these form what are
to be interpreted, at least in some cases, as idealized nervous systems.

    Warren McCulloch and Walter Pitts (1943) were the first people to
construct such neural net models, and they were the first people to call
such models 'neural nets'.   The name obviously stems from the intended
interpretation of the basic elements and their connections.   What they
had in mind was an artificial nervous system which could be constructed
theoretically in a well-defined way, and from which models could
actually be constructed.

    It is possible to construct neural nets in "hardware", and there
are various ways of doing so by the use of transistor or micro-
miniaturized methods.   McCulloch and Pitts designed neural nets as
blueprints for the special senses (the senses of sight, hearing, touch,
taste and smell) as well as the central processes of the human brain
which involves the ability to learn, think and solve problems.   We will
now describe briefly how neural nets are constructed.

    The points of resemblance to the human nervous system are obvious
in each case from the way the nets are drawn up.   It should be added
that there have been many other contributors to neural net theory, some
of which we shall be discussing (George, 1956, 1963; da Fonseca, 1966;
Culbertson, 1950, 1952, 1963; Blum, 1962; Verbeek, 1962; Cowan, 1962;
Lofgren, 1962).

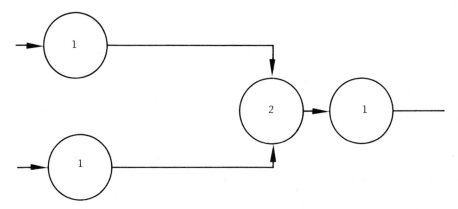

Figure 1

Figure 1 shows four neurons (or elements) represented by circles, connected in a simple net.   The reason for calling them elements rather than neurons is to avoid any misunderstandings as to their necessarily representing actual neurons, or being called literally the model of actual neurons.   A logical element is, in many ways, obviously different from a neuron.   The circles represent the neurons or elements;   and on the right we usually, by tradition, draw the output from the neuron, while the inputs to the neuron are on the left;   such a tradition is not however a rule.

This net is of the kind which we sometimes call a finite automaton and it is represented in this bit-by-bit form where we have several elements connected with lots of other elements.   These elements can be connected in quite a complicated manner, but they must be connected according to certain well-defined rules and the rules for the connection of neural nets are relatively simple;   we shall state them now.

The first rule is that an output (generally on the right) must either contain an impulse or not, at any instant in time.   In other words, the output may ramify and go to various other elements, but these other elements all either receive a single pulse at any instant or no impulse at all.   There is no possibility of mixing the outputs so that some carry pulses and some do not;   they must all be of one kind.

The second rule is that the inputs (generally on the left) can be pulse-carrying at any instant of time and one can have any pattern composed of 1's (which represents a pulse) and 0's (which represents the absence of a pulse) in a set of input fibres.   Neural nets can be thought of as geometrical rendering of Boolean algebra.   The only difference between the Pitts-McCulloch neural nets and the ordinary formulae of Boolean algebra lies in the fact that these nets have time co-ordinates attached to them, so that we have to think of this element firing at time t, and subsequent elements at t + 1, t + 2, ..., etc. Indeed we say that each element holds up the firing one instant at a time.

Now the instant of time can be any sort of unit one wishes. We should add though that we can make our nets sufficiently complicated to take us beyond Boolean algebra, although we still remain in the domain of mathematical logic.

All elements are assumed to take one instant of time to fire, so that if there is one obviously non-realistic feature in the system, it is that all neurons in the human system are not identical in this respect. Each neuron has a threshold represented by the letter which operates over the domain of all integers, both positive and negative. We say that the number of excitatory inputs firing at time t must at least equal the number of inhibitory inputs firing at time t plus the constant, i the threshold h. We assume, also contrary to neural fact, that the firing time for every neuron is the same.

We can represent pictorially excitatory inputs by little filled-in triangles and we usually use open circles for inhibitory inputs.

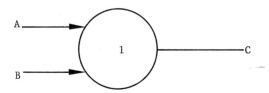

Figure 2

Let us label the inputs A and B in Figure 2 and a single output we will label C.   The threshold of this element is 1, and we can state the condition for this element to fire as follows.

We say that C fires at time t if and only if (represented by the three parallel lines ≡) A fires at t - 1, or B fires at t - 1, or both.   We write this

$$C_t \equiv A_{t-1} \vee B_{t-1}$$

where v means 'or' in inclusive sense of Boolean Algebra.   If we reproduce the same element with the threshold of 2 instead of 1 then our condition of firing changes so that we say that C fires at t if and only if A fires at t - 1 and B at t - 1.   Both inputs have to fire simultaneously to fire the neuron in the second case, whereas in the first case either of them alone would be sufficient to fire the neuron.   The threshold of elements are all real numbers and they may thus include negative numbers or zero.   The formula in the second case is

$$C_t \equiv A_{t-1} \cdot B_{t-1}$$

where . means 'and' as in Boolean algebra.   If, however, you have a

threshold of zero, an output C for an input A (we want an inhibitory
input this time), we say that C fires at t, if and only if A does <u>not</u>
fire at t - 1.   In other words, the element is "live" and fires <u>all</u>
the time unless there is an inhibitory input; and this represents the
logical operator 'not'.   We write this

$$B_t \equiv \; \sim A_{t-1}$$

where $\sim$ means 'not' as in Boolean Algebra.   The figure is shown by
Figure 3.

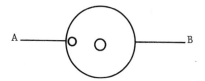

A ———   ——— B

Figure 3

    One of the things that is important about neural net models is
that hardware systems can be built from them, so that they are clearly
blueprints, and are therefore effective.   Neural nets can as we have
seen also be represented as diagrams with elements or neurons connected
by fibres, and they can be made as complicated as we like, but we can
always think of them as being represented solely by <u>not</u> and <u>and</u> or
<u>not</u> and <u>or</u>, even though in practice we will often use elements which
are far more complicated.   We can always, however, show that these
more complex nets can be reduced to combinations of those which we
know to be effective.

    To complete our initial picture, we want one other particular type
of element for storing information.   The element is a loop element
which fires back on itself.   This is shown in Figure 4.

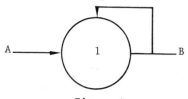

A ———   1   ——— B

Figure 4

Hence the output, B for example, fires at t + 1 if A fires at t, and
continues firing indefinitely, unless of course there is some inhibitory
input available.   If such an input is not available, then it will
never stop.   B will stop at some future time, if and only if some
further input C fires at t, and not—A(A').

    We can write this:

$$B_t \equiv A_{t-1} \; v \; (EA)_{t-n} \; F(A)_{n>1}$$

It should be said that there are many different renderings of
neural nets, some of which are designed to show how by duplicating or
triplicating information in the net we can ensure that the system is
error-free (Von Neumann, 1951; Cowan, 1962, and others).

EXERCISES

1. Draw up the set of quadruples for an automaton that starts with a
    series of thirty consecutive 1's on the tape and you wish to finish
    with five sets of five 1's with four gaps of single 0's in between
    each group of five.

2. Draw a neural net which stores 1's and erases them by 0's, when fed
    by a series 1010011001.

REFERENCES

ARBIB, M.A.   Brains, Machines and Mathematics. McGraw
                            Hill, 1965

CULBERTSON, J.T.   Consciousness and Behavior. Brown, Dubuque,
                            Iowa, 1950

CULBERTSON, J.T.   Hypothetical Robots. Rand Memo, P. 296

da FONSECA, J.S.   Neuronal Models. Faculty of Medicine, Lisbon,
                            1966

DAVIS, M.   Computability and Unsolvability. McGraw
                            Hill, 1958

GEORGE, F.H.   The Brain as a Computer. Pergamon Press,
                            1961, Ed. II, 1973

GEORGE, F.H.   Cognition. Methuen, 1962

McNAUGHTON, R.   The theory of automata: a survey. Advances
                            in Computers 2, 379 - 421. Academin Press, 1961

TURING, A.M.   On computable numbers, with an application to
                            the Entscheidungs-problem. Proc. Lond. Math.
                            Soc., Ser. 2, 42, 230 - 265

VERBEEK, L.   On error minimising neural nets. In:
                            H. Von Foerster and G.W. Zopf (Eds.)
                            Principles of Self-Organization. Pergammon
                            Press

CHAPTER 16

A NEURAL NET APPROACH TO
A PRAGMATIC THEORY

1   A BELIEF NET

We have argued before (George, 1961) that the primary problems of
cognition can be solved by a model which is sufficiently flexible and
sufficiently complex to allow of relatively free associations to operate
and to be adequately recorded.   We have suggested a B-net (to be
interpreted as "belief net") as a basic formalisation of the neutral
process of association, and the main task of this section is to show
what the consequences of this suggestion are.

A simple (6,2) B-net is defined in what follows by both net diagrams
and its equivalent formula.   The number 6 refers to the number of storage
elements and the number 2 refers to the number of inputs to be associated.
Therefore in general B(n,m) means a B-net with n memory elements and
associating m different inputs.   The B(6,2) net is defined in formulae
(1) – (8).

Having established the B(6,2) net as representative of the sort
of nets we shall be interested in, we must discuss further the development
of the organs which are of behavioural interest in the logical network
context.

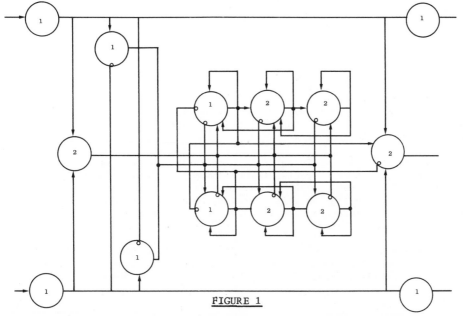

FIGURE 1

Our next task is to develop further the organs of the logical networks. Let us describe what we shall call a B-network. Figure 1 shows the simplest kind of such general network, where the relevant formula are:

$$K_t^1 \equiv S_{t-1}^1 \cdot S_{t-1}^2; \qquad \ldots (1)$$

$$L_2^1 \equiv S_{t-1}^1 \cdot \sim S_{t-1}^2; \qquad \ldots (2)$$

$$L_t^2 \equiv \sim S_{t-1}^1 \cdot S_{t-1}^2; \qquad \ldots (3)$$

$$M_t^1 \equiv \sim L_{t-1}^1 \cdot \sim L_{t-1}^2 (K_{t-1}^1 v(Et^*)M^1(t^*)); \quad (4)$$

$$R_t^1 \equiv S_{t-1}^1; \qquad \ldots (5)$$

$$R_t^2 \equiv S_{t-1}^2; \qquad \ldots (6)$$

$$R_t^{1.2} \equiv R_t^{2.1}(S_{t-1}^1 \cdot M_{t-1}^1)v(S_{t-1}^1 \cdot S_{t-1}^2 \cdot M_{t-1}^1) \quad \ldots (7)$$

By substitution of (1), (2) and (3) in (4) and by further substitution of (4), (5) and (6) in (7) we get:

$$R_t^{1.2} \equiv (S_{t-1}^1 \cdot \sim L_{t-2}^1 \cdot \sim L_{t-2}^2 \cdot$$

$$(K_{t-2}^1 v(Et^*)M^1(t^*))v(S_{t-1}^1 \cdot S_{t-1}^2)v(S_{t-1}^2 \cdot \sim L_{t-2}^1 \quad (8)$$

$$\sim L_{t-2}^2) \cdot (K_{t-2}^1 v(Et^*)M^1(t^*))),$$

where $t_o \leqslant t < t$, and t_o is the initial time for the machine's operation, t is the present. There will be no firing of L^1 and L^2 between t^* and t, where t^* represents the last time K^1 fired and a memory of this is retained in the loop of M^1.

The formulae (1) - (8) define a B-net which has an associated function B(m,n) where m denotes the number of counters available and n the number of inputs to be completely classified or associated. The simplest B-function is illustrated by figure 1 and is B(1,2), while figure 2 illustrates B(6,2). It is easy to see how the generaliz- ation of these systems could take place in terms of logical networks.

The number of elements required for the realization of B-nets capable of recording greater numbers of conjunctions and disjunctions is easily achieved. Thus:-

$$B(1,2) = 1 + 2 + 6 = 9$$

$$B(2,2) = 2 + 2 + 6 = 10$$

. . .

$$B(m,2) = m + 2 + 6$$

. . .

$$B(1,3) = (3C_2 + 3C_5)(6 + 1)$$

. . .

$$B(1,n) = (nC_2 + nC_3 + \ldots + nC_n)(6 + 1)$$

. . .

$$B(m,n) = (nC_2 + nC_3 + \ldots + nC_n)(6 + m)$$

i.e. $$B(m,n) = (2^n - (n + 1))(6 + m)$$

So we have a simple general formula for the number of elements
needed on this method of construction.   Thus it is easy to compute
the number of elements needed to realize a set of B-functions, provided
we know the values for n and m of each function.

The effectiveness of a B-net for any particular association is
given simply by a single number r where

$$r = x - y$$

and x = conjunction of the associated events and y the disjunctions
of those events.   Thus $B_t(r)$ is the single-valued function, having as
its possible domain all real integers, that describes the state of any
B-unit at any time t, with respect to any particular association.
There will be such a function for each possible association.

A special modification of the B-net should now be mentioned where
the original conditions are changed.   This can be shown by substituting
for (7) a new formula

$$R_t^{i \cdot j} \equiv (S_{t-1}^i . v(S_{t-1}^i . M_{t-1}^i - 1) v(S_{t-1}^i . S_{t-1}^j - 1) v(S_{t-1}^j . M_{t-1}^i - 1)) \quad \ldots \quad (9)$$

for i = 1, j = 2.

.This means that stimulation of S^i will always fire $R^{i \cdot j}$ as well
as R^1.   This particular B-net is therefore the analog of the conditional
response or any relation where a new stimulus has come "to stand for"
in some sense an existent permanent S-R connection.

We can, using the above B-nets, now develop a conditional probability machine of the kind suggested by A. M. Uttley (1954, 1955, 1967).
Thus consider the following tables for occurrences of the firing of the
inputs S^1 and S^2.

S^1	1	1	1	0	1	1	1	0	1	1
S^2	1	1	0	1	1	1	0	1	1	1

In the above table, in the 11th column for example, if S^2 fired, the probability of S^1 firing will be given by some number p, which may be calculated according to the particular nature of the B-net and for particular choice of x and y.   But in particular for the most general form of B-net, p will be 6/10 and S^2 will fire if x   2 and y need take no value other than zero.   If the above table had started:

S^1	0	0	0	1	1	1
S^2	1	1	1	0	1	1

then S^1, firing at 7th column will not cause S^2 to fire, since the non-contiguous firing of S^1 and S^2 up to the fifth occurrence did influence the state of the network, provided y took some value.   y = 4 would be sufficient to keep the full record of non-contiguous firing.

2   CLASSIFICATION AND CONTROL MACHINES

Let us define a classification and control machine of n-inputs as that collection of B-nets which connect each of the n-inputs in every possible combination 1, 2, ..., n at a time.   Thus a 2-input machine will be a simple B-net given by (9);   a 3-input machine will have

$$3^C_1 + 3^C_2 + 3^C_3 = 7 \text{ direct outputs,}$$

where three of these come straight from the inputs (i.e. R^1, R^2, R^3), and the other four come from the four B-nets connected to the three inputs S^1, S^2, S^3 in pairs and in a triad.

We can represent a 3-input machine by the diagram in Figure 3 where the squares are taken to represent the B-functions connecting inputs as stated in the relevant squares.

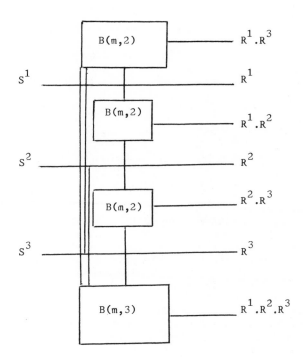

FIGURE 3

The blocks replace the detailed structure of all the counters and we are assuming m counters in each block.

The words 'direct output' refer to the immediate results of classification
on inputs.   Clearly the direct outputs can be mapped onto any number
of actual outputs, although this number will generally not be less than
the number of inputs.

In general an n-input classification and control machine will have

$$n^{C_1} + n^{C_2} + \ldots + n^{C_n}$$

direct ouputs and this will have

$$n^{C_1} + n^{C_2} + \ldots + n^{C_n} - n$$

B-nets, each represented by a closed square.

Although the B-nets so far discussed in detail relate to two inputs,
the generalization to 3, 4, ..., S inputs is quite simple.   The need
is for a new set of counters, 1-elements and k-elements for each
association as we have already mentioned.

One important thing to be noticed is that motivation is not
explicitly catered for by this "paper machine" (Turing, 1955) as yet.
We can, of course, easily introduce motivators and such would be
necessary to bring the model into line with the facts of behaviour.

The above point is important because it accounts for the fact that
all contiguous events are not retained by the organism.   The ones
retained are those that are reinforced in terms of the motivations of
the organism.   Thus motivational stimuli can, for example, be thought
of as S_m's firing into all the B-units and into the K-elements of the
general B-unit and changing the threshold of these elements by one
apiece;   we call such a motivational net an M-net.

The process of reinforcement will operate by firing more M-units
with each contiguous occurrence of S's together and diminishing by
some multiple all S's that are not fired contiguously with certain S's that
are fired.

This operation of inhibiting connections not reinforced is performed
automatically when B-units are connected as they are in our classifying-
and-control machine.   The point is that the mere occurrence of two
stimuli simultaneously would lead to the setting up of associations
as mirrored by B-nets.   This would be unrealistic from the behavioural
point of view and thus only those associations that stop the motivator
input lead to strong associations.   Indeed at this stage this means
that, in the machine, the response must inhibit the motivator and thus
stop the input, bring about a state of homeostasis in the machine.

The general formulae defining the B-function B(m,n) is given by:

$$K_t^1 \equiv S_{t-1}^1 \cdot S_{t-1}^2 ; \qquad\qquad \dots (10)$$

$$L_t^1 \equiv S_{t-1}^1 \cdot \sim S_{t-1}^2 ; \qquad\qquad \dots (11)$$

$$L_t^2 \equiv \sim S_{t-1}^1 \cdot S_{t-1}^2 ; \qquad\qquad \dots (12)$$

$$R_t^1 \equiv S_{t-1}^1 ; \qquad\qquad \dots (13)$$

$$R_t^2 \equiv S_{t-1}^2 ; \qquad\qquad \dots (14)$$

$$C_t^1 \equiv (K_{t-1}^1 v(Et^1)c^1(t^1)).(\sim L_{t-1}^1 \cdot \sim L_{t-1}^2 \cdot \sim D_{t-1}^n); \quad (15)$$

$$C_t^2 \equiv ((K_{t-1}^1 v(Et^1)c^1(t^1)(Et^2)c^2(t^2)(\sim L_{T-1}^1 \cdot \sim L_{t-1}^2); \quad (16)$$

$$C_t^n \equiv ((K_{t-1}^1 \cdot C_{t-1}^{n-1})v(Et^n)c^n(t^n))(\sim L_{t-1}^1 \cdot \sim L_{t-1}^2); \quad (17)$$

$$D_t^1 = \equiv ((L_{t-1}^1)vL_{t-1}^2)v(Et^{n+1})D^{n+1}$$

$$(t^{n+1})).(\sim K_{t-1}^1 \cdot \sim C_{t-1}^n);$$

$$\dots (18)$$

$$D_1^2 \equiv ((L_{t-1}^1 vL_{t-1}^2)v(Et^{n+2})D^{n 2}(t^{n+2})).(\sim K_{t-1}^1); \quad (19)$$

$$D_t^m \equiv ((L_{t-1}^1 vL_{t-1}^2)v(Et^{n+m})D^{n+m})).(\sim K_{t-1}^1); \qquad \dots (20)$$

$$R_t^{1\cdot2} (S_{t-1}^1 \cdot C_{t-1}^n)v(S_{t-1}^1 \cdot S_{t-1}^2).S_{t-1}^3)v(S_{t-1}^2 \cdot C_{t-1}^n);$$

$$\dots (21)$$

3   PROPERTIES OF NEURAL NETS .

We so far have merely introduced some of the basic ideas of neural nets.   We must now make this point once more that there are two different views of the use to which neural nets should be put;   one view is that these are merely ways of representing finite automata.

We can indeed study the properties of finite automata through neural nets as well as through tape automata.   It is also important to be aware that McCulloch and Pitts, while constructing neural nets, had the actual nervous system in mind, and felt they were supplying - or helping to supply - a method for its modelling.   It is obvious indeed from the choice of elements and their connections that an idealized nervous system was envisaged.   At the same time, it can be made explicit that no one believes for one moment that such networks are identical with the actual nervous nets.   Perhaps we should list just a few of the differences:

1.   Actual neurons differ from each other both in size and firing time, and perhaps in other respects.

2.   The actual nervous systems of organisms when they fire are accompanied by chemical changes which may directly affect the overall properties of the system.

3.   Neurons in the human being are thought to fire "across" the cells which are contiguous to each other, as well as along the traditional pathways of synapses and dendrites.

4.   Some theorists have also thought there were (electrical) field effects operating in the nervous system, though there is little evidence to support such a point of view.

So far, we have introduced Neural Nets with the equivalent logical formula (in various forms), and although we shall include some of the formulae for the sake of those who are interested, we shall generally assume that the system is a simple network whose behaviour can generally be followed quite easily.

It will be remembered also that neural net automata can be synthesised as digital computers and to bring this point home clearly let us look at a gating network with a simple memory.

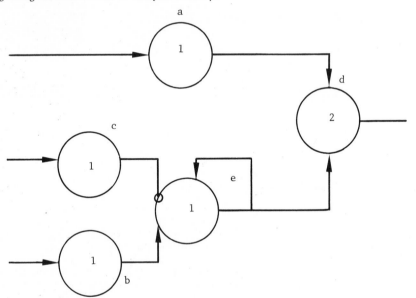

FIGURE 4

The formula for Figure 4 is:

$$d_t \equiv a_{t-1} \cdot e_{t-1} \qquad \cdots (1)$$

and since

$$e_{t-1} \equiv (e_{t-2} \cdot \cdot \sim c_{t-2}) v (b_{t-2} \cdot \sim c_{t-2}) v (e_{t-2} \cdot b_{t-2}) \qquad \cdots (2)$$

we can substitute (2) in (1) which gives

$$d_t \equiv a_{t-1} \cdot ((e_{t-2} \cdot \cdot \sim c_{t-2}) v (b_{t-2} \cdot \sim c_{t-2}) v (e_{t-2} \cdot b_{t-2})) \quad (3)$$

The logical formulae defining the firing conditions of even simple nets soon become extremely complicated so we shall omit this part of the description after the next figure (Figure 5). We shall show the logical formulae for that if only to show the alternative logical description in Polish notation. Figure 5 is a serial binary adder.

$$h_t \equiv f_{t-1} vg_{t-1} \qquad \dots (4)$$

$$f_{t-1} \equiv d_{t-2} \cdot c_{t-2} \qquad \dots (5)$$

$$g_{t-1} \equiv e_{t-2} \qquad \dots (6)$$

$$d_{t-2} \equiv a_{t-3} vb_{t-3} vc_{t-3} \qquad \dots (7)$$

$$c_{t-2} \equiv (a_{t-3} \cdot b_{t-3})v(a_{t-3} vc_{t-3})v(a_{t-3} \cdot c_{t-3}) \qquad \dots (8)$$

$$e_{t-2} \equiv a_{t-3} \cdot b_{t-3} \cdot c_{t-3} \qquad \dots (9)$$

so

$$h_t \equiv (a_{t-3} vb_{t-3} vc_{t-3}) \cdot \sim((a_{t-3} \cdot b_{t-3})v(a_{t-3} \cdot c_{t-3})$$
$$v(a_{t-3} \cdot c_{t-3}))v(a_{t-3} \cdot b_{t-3} \cdot c_{t-3}) \qquad \dots (10)$$

(4) – (10) rewritten in Polish notation are as follows as (4p) – (10p)

$$hEfog \qquad EhOfg \qquad \dots (4p)$$

Note here that the following ruling can be applied

$$p \supset \cdot q \supset p = p \supset (q \supset p) = IpIqp$$

and

$$p \supset q \supset p = (p \supset q) \supset p) = IIpqp$$

so we accept

$$EhOfg \qquad \dots (4p)$$

as the correct form of (4) in Polish notation.

$$EfAdNc \qquad \dots (5p)$$

$$Ege \qquad \dots (6p)$$

$$Ed00abc \qquad \dots (7p)$$

$$Ec00AabAacAbc \qquad \dots (8p)$$

$$EeAAabc \qquad \dots (9p)$$

so we get

$$EhSOOOOOsbcNAabAacAbcAAabc \qquad \dots (10p)$$

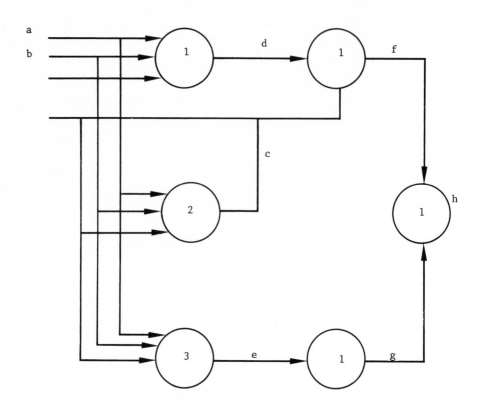

FIGURE 5

Or if we wish to make the timing explicit, we could write the equations as follows:

$$EhOf1g1 \qquad \ldots (4p^1)$$

$$Ef1Ad2Nc2 \qquad \ldots (5p^1)$$

$$Ef1e2 \qquad \ldots (6p^1)$$

$$Ed200a3b3c3 \qquad \ldots (7p^1)$$

$$Ec200Aa3b3Aa3c3Ab3c3 \qquad \ldots (8p^1)$$

$$Ee2AAa3b3c3 \qquad \ldots (9p^1)$$

$$EhA00000a3b3c3NAa3b3Aa3c3Ab3c3AAa3b3c3 \qquad ,\ldots (10p^1)$$

One important aspect of the use of neural nets is that of supplying another way of representing finite automata, and therefore a way which is capable of dealing with all the metamathematical problems such as those involving recursive function theory and set theory, which are dealt with by ordinary tape automata whether of a one-way or two-way or single channelled or many channelled type.

The second aspect, and this is the part we have been concerned with, has lain in the need to provide automata which have a function much more nearly in keeping with the function of the central nervous system.   We are fully aware all the time of the ways in which our neural net automata differ from the structure, and also therefore the function, of the actual human nervous system, but believe there is a great deal of merit to be derived from working on a system which is somewhat like it, so that the eventual gap to be bridged is nothing like as great as it would be if we were working directly from tape automata.

We should add that whereas we are claiming that simulation is one of the main aims, and the reason for using neural nets as our formalised model is that it bears a closer resemblance to actual nervous systems, we have to accept the fact that it is also quite convenient as a way of representing theories about cognition and is also indeed a perfectly legitimate way of dealing with activities which are both heuristic and algorithmic.   Two particular problems are going to beset us; one is that it is difficult to represent the full complexity demanded of an artificially intelligent system in neural net form and this can be circumvented in some measure by using computer representations, probably of the matrix form of neural nets.   The other difficulty, of course, is that we have very little detailed information of the structure and function of the actual human nervous system and therefore in a sense neurological textbooks and neurological research papers are almost as much representative of their conceptual nervous systems as the neural network representation itself.

The main aim though is to get certain precision into our argument before making it more realistic, rather than looking for a realistic model which we ultimately can make precise.   There are two different philosophies involved and there is no reason to suppose that they are not complementary to each other and at least it seems that they should be.

What this chapter has attempted to achieve is to specify more precisely - in neural net terms - what is required of a formalisation of our pragmatic theory and also what is required to bring such a formalization into line - at least ultimately - with what we know of the workings of human brains and human nervous systems.

EXERCISES

1. Draw a B-net with just two looped elements for associating two inputs only.

2. Explain, with examples, Polish notation as opposed to "classical" ("Principia Mathematica") notation.

3. Devize a third notation (as opposed to the two in 2. above) for logic. Give some simple examples.

REFERENCES

UTTLEY, A.M.   The classification of signals in the nervous system. Electroenceph. Clin. Neurophysiol. 6, 479, 1954

UTTLEY, A.M.   The conditional probability of signals in the nervous system. RRE Memo. No. 1109 - 1955

CHAPTER 17

HIERARCHICAL NETS

NEURAL NETS IN ACTION

We shall start by giving an illustration of the use of neural nets
in action.   Here we are using the neural nets to construct models for
intelligent behaviour with respect to the environment.

If the environment is a simple maze, then our neural net represents
an automaton capable of running a maze.   This is not itself very complic‑
ated but raises certain questions of interest and leads cumulatively to
neural nets of greater behavioural interest, while raising further
problems of modelling.

It will be realised clearly that the <u>neural</u> nets – perhaps better
now thought of as <u>logical</u> nets – are an abstract version of the sort of
hardware models which run mazes or solve equivalent problems of learning.
Consider a simple maze such as the following:

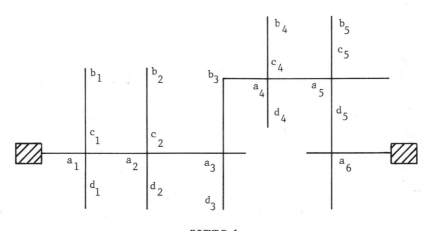

FIGURE 1

For convenience we now label the choice points a_1, a_2, a_3, a_4, a_5
and a_6.   We shall also label the routes at each of the choice points
(they are all "three-choice" points) b_1, c_1, d_1, b_2, c_2, d_2, ... etc.
The problem now is what sort of neural net can solve this maze.

If we assume that the discriminations needed between a's and b's, c's and d's is given and that the net incorporates the principle of getting from start to finish as quickly as possible, then our net must simply establish the connections

$$a_1 c_1 a_2 c_2 a_3 b_3 a_4 c_4 a_5 d_5 a_6$$

which gives the correct solution.

The sort of association net which we have used before (George, 1961) could be the basis for such a model.   Here we show the net in abstract form:

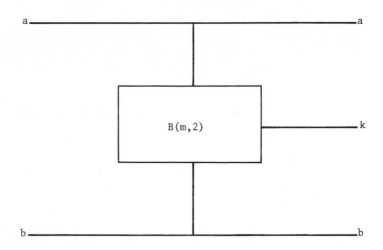

FIGURE 2

We assume m counters connecting a and b.

a activates a', b activates b', and if a and b have occurred together more often than not in the <u>recorded</u> past, then a alone or b alone will fire k' as well as a' or b'.

The counters are made up of looped elements which are wired to do whatever job we need, and using C for the positively firing looped counter (d would be used to depict it if its score was negative), we can write the logical formula as follows:

$$k_t = (a.b)_{t-1} \ v \ (a.c)_{t-1} \ v \ (b.c)_{t-1} \qquad \ldots \ (4)$$

Now we can use a notation which is more "molar" than (4) to represent the same state of affairs, i.e.

Aab or A(avb)k

since aa' and bb' are given connections as in our example what may be
learned is that a and b are positively associated, or what amounts to
much the same thing a or b is associated with k.   In other words, the
firing of k tells us that a and b are positively associated.   If k does
not fire when either a or b fire alone, then we know that a and b have
been negatively associated.

From the behavioural point of view we must now ask a few basic
questions.   Suppose we have a large scale systems with inputs.

$$s_1, s_2, \ldots, s_n$$

and outputs

$$r_1, r_2, \ldots, r_m$$

and we allow positive or negative association for all combinations of
s's and r's.   We have then a completely classified association system,
wherein a subset of s's, s_1, s_2, s_3, say.   Similarly, we may have
$s_1 s_2 \sim s_6 \sim s_7$ associated with $r_7 r_8 \sim r_{10}$.   So overlooking the behavioural
implausibility of complete classification, we still have to consider the
question of whether the inputs and outputs must always stand for the same
organic activities.   The most plausible answer to this question is "yes"
at the sensory and motor level of activity, but "no" at the central level.

If we have a centrally organised 'brain' which asserts that a will
be "interpreted as ..." or "stand for ...", some particular event and b
will "stand for ..." some other event, and so on, we need to be able to
clear such sets of neurons from time to time and reassign them to new
duties.   This clearly implies the need for a sort of hierarchical
organisation, so that a meta-system exists whose duty is to name the
variables so used;   this in turn suggests the need for hierarchical nets
which we shall discuss next.

In neural net terms, we now need a set of layers of elements making
up a three-dimensional array if we are to simulate the more intelligent
types of human behaviour.   Let us illustrate the point with a simple
example of "concept formation".   If in our lower net level, we find
such states as:

$$A(a_7 a_8 a_9)(b_1 b_2) \qquad \ldots (5)$$

$$A(a_9 a_{10} a_{11})(b_1 b_2) \qquad \ldots (6)$$

or in general

$$A(a_n a_{n+1} a_{n+2})(b_1 b_2) \qquad \ldots (7)$$

then some recoding is possible by clearing all the particular associations
(5), (6), etc. and retaining at the higher level only the association
(7).   (7) represents a statement (or concept) about the state of the
lower level of elements.

MANY LEVELLED NETS

Having considered neural nets and the way they represent associations
between different stimuli (inputs) and different responses (outputs) in all
the various possible ways in which this can be done, it is natural that
we should think about the way in which neural nets can be used to
represent cognitive processes of higher order than are involved in simple
learning or conditioning processes.

It is natural to feel that the hierarchical net should be able to
supply one of the answers to this problem, since we know that there are
various degrees of abstraction involved in any sort of intelligent
activity which means that one level of description has an abstraction
developed from it to another level which is more general but more
"dilute", and there is another level beyond that differing in the same
way from the level below it, and so on more or less indefinitely.

There is also a hierarchy involved with language which refers to
language which sooner or later refers to things which are not language,
i.e. to events, to things, to relationships which are not themselves
symbolic.   To some extent the degrees of abstraction referred to are
similar in both cases but there are also differences and this serves as
a reminder that we may in a variety of different contexts have a variety
of different ways of abstracting from a description of the immediately
given.   All the time one should be reminded of the fact that the
knowledge we acquire is as much by description, if not more so, than by
direct acquaintance with the environment in which we live.

This involves us in a discussion of linguistic signs and symbols,
or lansigns as we have called them.   We have now got to face the fact
that all the paraphenalia of language, concepts, logic, etc. have somehow
to be mirrored in neural net terms.   The basic notion must be that of a
hierarchical set of nets and we could assume a B-net at one level is a
process which is associative in that events become associated with each
other by contiguity.   Level 2 nets can be another series of B-nets which
picks up information from level 1 and represents some generalisation of
the features of level 1;   therefore if one type of input a_1 and another
type of input a_2 are sufficiently similar to each other and obviously
different from b_1, say, then A could be the name of the set which
contains a_1 and a_2 and this representation at the higher level will
therefore tend to suggest that the level 2 net is more dilute than the
level 1 net and includes lots of different level 1's as particular
cases.   Figure 3 shows level 1 and level 2 nets and their interconnections.
They are shown in the same abstract form as was used in the last chapter.

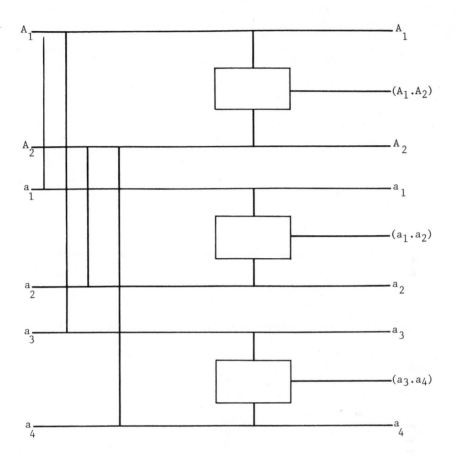

FIGURE 3

If we consider the C-level to contain A_1, A_2 and the B-level to contain a_1, a_2, a_3, a_4 then their relationships are such that:

$$A_t^1 = a_{t-1}^1 \cdot a_{t-1}^3$$

$$A_t^2 = a_{t-1}^2 \cdot a_{t-1}^4$$

or any other such combination which is appropriate.

The same principle can now be applied to higher levels, level 3, level 4, etc., where some of the higher levels can be the words that are used to represent the categories of lower levels and indeed the words are used to refer to themselves, since, of course, it is the self-referential nature of language which is the cause of a certain amount of difficulty. If we take level 3 to be words, we may take level 4 to be a total language which involves the syntax in the manipulating of the

words on the lower level which in turn refer either to the particular
items of level 1 or the generalities of level 2.   Figure 4 shows again
in skeleton form the kind of interconnections that exist between these
four levels.   In fact, in Figure 4, we have drawn it as a three-
dimensional neural net since it is easier to see in that way.

The logical side of this emerges, of course, in abstracted form by
simply creating rules, like the rules of syntax, surrounding the selected
use of a certain subset of all the symbols that are available in the
system, of which there are potentially an infinite number.   But the
concepts of logic are widely agreed to be pre-linguistic and therefore
one may assume that the logic that we formalise at the higher levels of
level 4 and beyond, really refers to certain relationships which occur
at level 1.   These are the relationships of association.   Thus it is,
to put it very simply, that the implication relation between two items or
two classes at level 2, represent their contiguous occurrence.   From
this simple notion of contiguity or simultaneity, we can build up a
notion of implications, of course, within the linguistic structure
itself which usually refers to some relationship such as a causal
relationship existing between the events which are counted and sensed
in the first place.

In talking in this way about hierarchical nets, we have to expect
to consider the questions of growth.   We have already said that as far
as the human nervous system is concerned, the same argument applies to
any other conceivable workable system, then there must be the possibility
of making and breaking connections.   This could be produced by a growth
process although it could, as in our B-nets, be produced by a process
literally changing the connections as a function of frequency of occurrence.
We can show a kind of growth relationship between elements which is
perhaps more physiologically plausible than as represented so far in our
B-nets, but yet still refers to a functional state.   It may be that we
need to go further into this particular matter and consider a relationship
between "having learned" and learning.

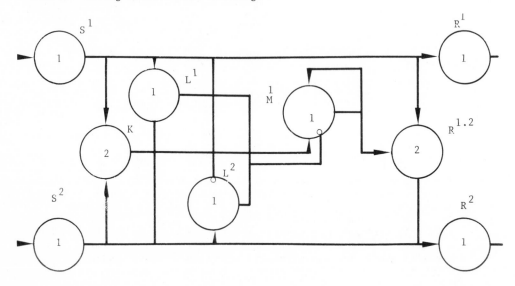

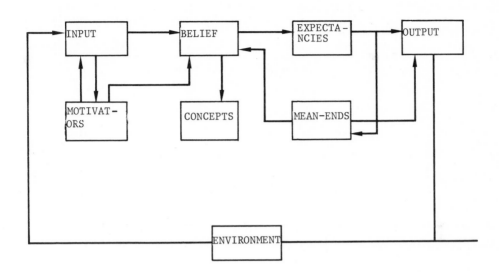

FIGURE 5

We are not really concerned too much at this stage with the methods
by which the nets can be constructed in detail, we are concerned still
with the possible representation of these things in principle, or
referring to them as a mathematical operation and to be put on the
computer; we are not at this stage considering the actual construction
of such complicated hierarchical neural nets. When we come to the point
of thinking about them in detail, the chances are that for the degree
of complexity required, we should need to provide a growth pattern for
wiring the system in the first place. Since the kind of complexity
envisaged is far greater than in any existing computer and that itself
already takes a great deal of very careful representing. It may well
be that what we need to design is a machine which does the wiring - a
sort of genetic process.

Another way of considering the question of B-nets is to consider
replacing the looped elements by binary counters or even decimal counters,
but we shall not pursue this line of argument here.

ARTIFICIAL INTELLIGENCE AND NEURAL NETS

The main object behind the development of neural nets, as far as
we are concerned, is to use them as a method of modelling. By such a
use, we can distinguish between various different theories either at a
cognitive or at a neural level of organisation.

In this chapter, the intention is to develop neural nets as a descriptive model of an artificially intelligent system.   So we should now look at the block diagram of an artificially intelligent system;   this block diagram (Figure 5) must be thought of at a very general level but nevertheless sufficiently indicates the basic procedures involved. Immediately below (Figure 6) we show a new block diagram where we replace the ordinary cognitive terms such as motivation, beliefs, etc. by their equivalent in neural net terms such as M-net, B-net, etc.

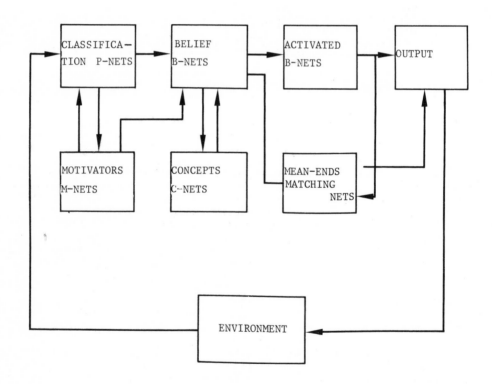

FIGURE 6

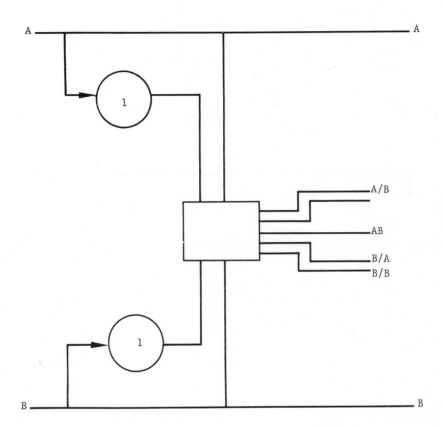

<u>F IGURE 7</u>

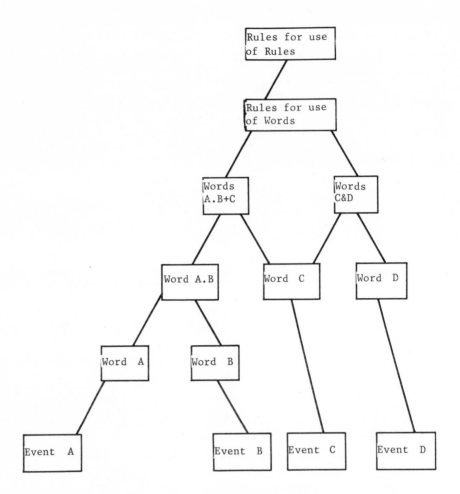

FIGURE 8

A symbolic representation of a hierarchical net leading up from
events to words to syntax and meta-syntax, where each box is
composed of sets of B(m,n) nets.

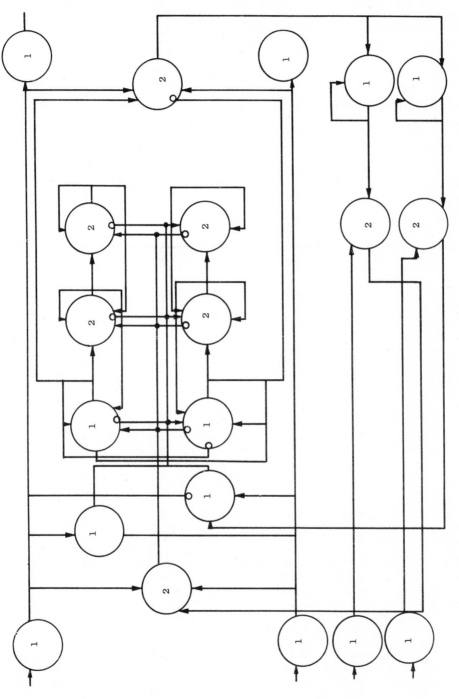

FIGURE 9

The idea is to be quite explicit, and it is that we should be
able now to draw up artificially intelligent system composed solely
of neural nets.   The difficulty lies in the tremendous size of the
system needed and the fact that it is essentially hierarchical, in the
manner that we have discussed.   We therefore have to say that the B-net
(already described earlier) is still the basic unit and underneath the
B-net, as it were, is the M -net (Figure 9 shows a fairly characteristic
M-net; there are various alternative versions of an M-net), bringing out
the point that the M-net, which may be thought of as the forcing function
that encourages the operation of the B-net, can be independent of the
B-net, and be the necessary condition for a satisfactory association
being set up by the B-net.

We can now extend the ordinary B-nets that were described earlier
in the following manner.   We can ensure that by virtue of a P-net,
subserving a perceptual system, there is a total classification for
all the required input.   This total classification for any finite number
of any inputs is then fed into the B-net where associations can be made
along the lines already described, but now extended to events which can
succeed each other.   The B-net has become a <u>sequential processor</u> and
performs the same sort of function as a Markov Net.   Figure 7 shows
an extended B-net acting as a sequential processor.

We now think of a number of levels of the hierarchy with what we
have called C-nets and L-nets above the level of the B-nets.   By the
C-net we mean a conceptual net which includes a whole set of B-nets,
and by an L-net we mean a linguistic net which again includes a whole
set of B-nets.   The point to be clear about is the fact that the way
the C-nets and L-nets are constructed is in general identical with the
way B-nets are constructed.   In other words, the processes are simply
associational.

The critical issue that we have to discuss now is how the vertical
connections are made between the different levels of the nets.   Figure 5
illustrated one sort of connection which exists between a B-net at the
ordinary B-level and an upper B-net at what we have called the C-level.
It should be noticed that the question of whether an automaton should
be a growth automaton, a growing automaton or a pre-wired (i.e. fixed)
automaton here becomes of some considerable interest.

Figure 1 (chap. 16) showed the sort of net that you need if you want the
equivalent of the growth net in a pre-wired net;   this allows the
making and breaking of contacts and yet also allows the retention of a
completely pre-wired system.   This sort of net would be necessary if
we think of a neural net automaton as being like a digital computer and
being able to carry information in different addresses, dumping that
information,   then importing more information and so on;   it seems
likely that this is the situation at the cerebral-cortical level of the
human being and therefore this is the situation we would like to depict
when pursuing the goal of brain simulation.

By these means we gradually build up a very large automaton
structured in some ways like a human brain, with its connections in
the human body and capable of performing control processes in rather a
humanlike way.   The difficulty of course, is one we have already

noticed and is that of representing a very large net in terms which
allow us to discover what its properties are, and it does seem here that
we are going to have to write computer programs to simulate the net,
either in its full anatomical detail through the use of structure and
status matrices (Landahl and Runge,1946), or functional in terms of the
actual sequential operations performed.

If either of the above methods are followed up, then it is
possible to construct a large scale neural net automaton with humanlike
qualities and then discover how it in fact processes its environment.
The object here would be presumably to bring it into line more and more
completely with the behaviour observed in human beings so that we could
then examine the structure or function of the equivalent neural net.

To summarise, the type of neural net assumed, for both simulative
and synthetic purposes, is one that has the characteristic of being
capable of interpreting a variety of different inputs in the same B-net.
Thus we can use information in B-nets in the same way as general purpose
registers use information in a computer.   Figure 6 illustrates the
principle in the simplest possible way where events A and B are both
computing to fire the outputs.   We have already made clear that the
other characteristics the system must have are that of being <u>partitioned</u>,
<u>partial</u>, <u>adaptive</u> and <u>hierarchical</u>.   Figure 8 illustrates the sort of
relationships envisaged which allows us to go from the simple association
nets right up to complicated self-referencing nets involving language,
syntax and all the requirements of a formal axiomatic system.

This really brings our story to an end since the object behind
the monograph is to discuss automata and in particular, neural net
automata and discuss them in the pragmatic context which was entirely
concerned with brain modelling and behaviour modelling.   We now see
how this process can be carried through, we see the form which it will
inevitably take and we see that the scene is set for the construction
of a suitable computer program, granted a sufficiently large computer
store, or granted the possible partitioning of the system.   This
provides a considerable technical problem but at least one sees, in
principle, how the whole operation might successfully be carried through.

The next stage is clearly to provide a neurological interpretation
of the model and this requires a great deal of further work in terms
of what is actually known about the central nervous system.

EXERCISES

1. Draw two alternative block diagrams to Figures 5 and 6 which you
    believe are just as good for "their purpose", or even better.

2. What would be your next investigation in trying to develop Hierarchical
    Nets for either brain studies or behaviour studies?

3. Summarise, in a few pages, the contents of the whole book.

REFERENCES

ARBIB, M.A.   Brains, Machines and Mathematics. McGraw Hill, 1965

BLUM, M.   Properties of a neuron with many inputs. Bionics Symposium (Wright-Patterson Air Force Base). Off. Tech. Serv. US Dept. of Comm. Washington, 1960

CULBERTSON, J.T.   Consciousness and Behaviour. Brown, Dubuque, Iowa, 1950

CULBERTSON, J.T.   Hypothetical Robots. Rand Memo. P. 296, 1952

CULBERTSON, J.T.   Some economical robots. Jour. Automata Studies. Shannon, C.E. & McCarthy, J. (Eds.) Princeton University Press, 1956

da FONSECA, J.S.   Neuronal Models. Faculty of Medicine, Lisbon, 1966

DAVIS, M.   Computability and Unsolvability. McGraw Hill, 1958

DAVIS, M.   The Undecidable. Raven Press, Hewlett, New York, 1965

GEORGE, F.H.   Logical Networks and Behaviour. Bull. Math. Biophys. 18, 337 - 348, 1956

GEORGE, F.H.   Nerve, Brain and Memory Models. Wiener, N. & Schade, J.P. (Eds.) 37 - 52, 1963

KLEENE, S.C.   Representation of Events in Nerve Nets and Finite Automata. Rand Memo. RM - 704

McCULLOCH, W.S. and PITTS, W.   A logical calculus of the ideas of immanent in nervous activity. Bulletin of Math. Biophys. 5, 115 - 133, 1943.

McNAUGHTON, R.   The theory of automata, a survey. Advances in Computers. 2, 379 - 421, 1961

MYHILL, J.   Linear bounded automata. WADD Technical Note 60 - 165. Wright-Patterson. AFB. Ohio. 1960

RABIN, M.O. and SCOTT, D.   Finite automata and their decision problems. IBM Journal of Research and Development 3, No.2, 114 - 125, 1959

ROGERS, J.R.H.   Theory of Recursive Functions and Effective Computability. McGraw Hill, 1966

SHEPERDSON, J.C.   The reduction of two-way automata to one-way
                         automata. IBM Journal of Research and
                         Development. 3, No. 2, 198 - 200, 1959

VON NEUMANN, J.   Probabilistic logics and the synthesis of
                         reliable organisms from unreliable components.
                         California Tech. Monograph.

YAMADA, H.   Real-time computation and recursive functions
                         no real-time computable. IRE Trans. on
                         Electronic Computers EC - 11, 753 - 760, 1962

ADDITIONAL REFERENCES

BRUNER, J.S., GOODNOW, J.J.   A Study of Thinking.   John Wiley,
and AUSTIN, G.A.   New York, 1956

BLACK, M.   Language and Philosophy.   Cornell
                                   University Press, 1949

CARNAP, R.   Testability and Meaning.
                                   Phil. Sci. 3, 419 - 471; 4, 1 - 40, 1937

CARNAP, R.   Foundations of Logic and Mathematics.
                                   Encyclopedia of Unified Science.
                                   1, 3. Chicago, 1939

CARNAP, R.   Meaning and Necessity.   Chicago
                                   University Press, 1947

CHISHOLM, R.   Intentionality and the theory of signs.
                                   Philos Studies. III, 56 - 63, 1952

CRAWSHAY-WILLIAMS, R.   Methods and Criteria of Reasoning.
                                   Routledge and Kegan Paul, 1957

GEORGE, F.H. and   Towards a general theory of behavior.
HANDLON, J.H.   Methodos. 1, 25 - 44, 1955

GEORGE, F.H. and   A language for perceptual analysis.
HANDLON, J.H.   Psychol. Rev., 64, 14 - 25, 1957

GEORGE, F.H.   Cognition, Methuen. 1963

GEORGE, F.H.   Belief statements and their logic.
                                   Analysis., 31, 3, 104 - 105, 1971

HULL, C.L.   Principles of Behavior. Appleton-
                                   Century-Crofts. N.Y. 1943

HULL, C.L.   A Behavior System: An Introduction to
                                   Behavior Theory Concerning the
                                   Individual Organism.   Yale University
                                   Press, 1952

KORZYBSKI, A.   Science and Sanity.   Science Press, 1933

MORRIS, C.W.   *Signs, Language and Behavior*.
                         Prentice Hall. N.Y., 1946

NAESS, A.   Towards a theory of interpretation and
                         preciseness. In *Semantics and the
                         Philosophy of Language* (Ed. L. Linsky).
                         University of Illinois Press, 1951

OGDEN, G.K. and   *The Meaning of Meaning*. Harcourt-
RICHARDS, I.A.   Brace, 1923

PAP, A.   *Elements of Analytic Philosophy*.
                         Macmillan, N.Y., 1949

PEIRCE, C.S.   *The Collected Papers of Charles Sanders
                         Peirce*. Harvard University Press,
                         1931 - 35

PRICE, H.H.   *Thinking and Experience*. Hutchinson,
                         1953

SELLARS, W.   Epistemology and the new way of words.
                         J. Philosophy, 44, 24, 1947a

SELLARS, W.   Pure pragmatics and epistemology.
                         Philos. Sci., 14, 3, 1947b

AUTHOR INDEX